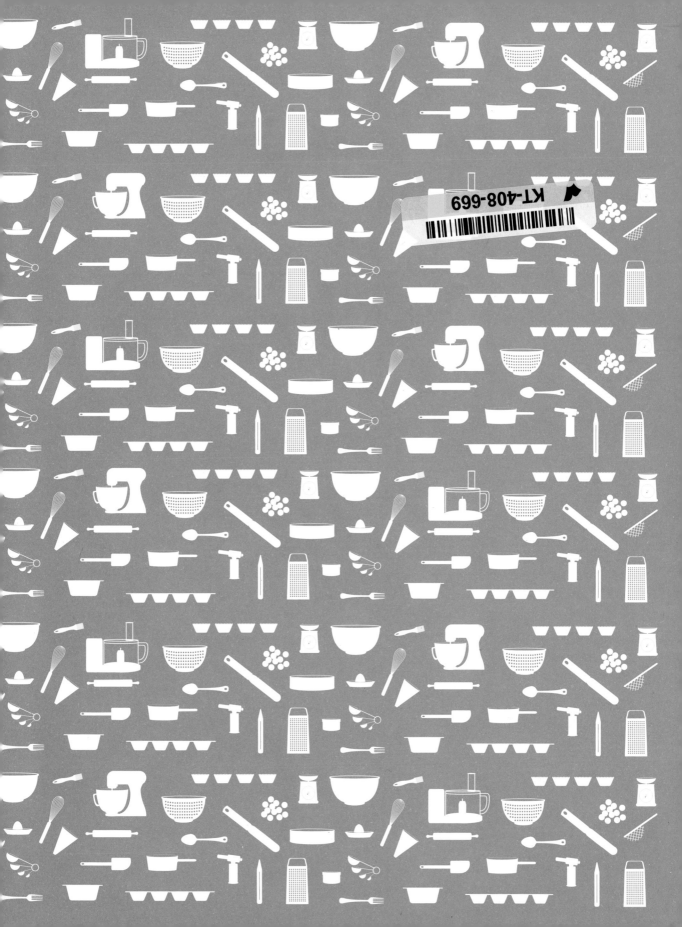

THE GREAT BRITISH
BAKE OFF
EVERYDAY

THE GREAT BRITISH
BAKE OFF
EVERYDAY

100 FOOLPROOF RECIPES

BY LINDA COLLISTER

FOREWORDS BY

MARY BERRY & PAUL HOLLYWOOD

BBC
BOOKS

CONTENTS

FOREWORD BY MARY BERRY

The fourth series of *Bake Off* is here with more amazing recipes for Paul and me to sample and, hopefully, savour! Year on year, we meet a whole host of bakers ready to impress us with even more skill, imagination and enthusiasm, dreaming up the most fantastic bakes to wow us with (and you watching at home too).

And for our part, we've set the bakers some really special challenges! Our Technical Challenges draw on classic recipes for bakes such as Tuiles, Angel Food Cake, English Muffins and Egg Custard Tarts – all essential recipes for a baker's repertoire. And as we were selecting the Signature and Showstopper Challenges for each episode, it seemed only fair that, this year, we reveal our recipes for those challenges too. So you can try my Signature Ginger and Treacle Spiced Traybake and Tipsy Trifle, and my Showstopper, Charlotte Royale, as well as Paul's Signature recipes for Olive Breadsticks and Tea Loaf and his filo pastry Showstopper, Spanakopita, to name just a few.

While many of these recipes are not very 'every day' (I would not advise trying my Opera Cake on a Monday evening after a long day at work!), if you fancy developing your skills, do try them when you have time to spend – a rainy Saturday perhaps? We've tried to make these recipes as thorough as possible so that anyone can have a go at recreating a bake from the show.

To complement our challenges and the bakers' elaborate concoctions, Linda Collister has done another sterling job creating delicious, reliable recipes that you can whip up every day. I firmly believe that baking at home should be about recipes that taste

wonderful, that you can make simply and easily and that delight the people you are baking for. Recipes that are popular with all the family, and that use ingredients you have in the store cupboard or are not too expensive to buy – looking through the book, Sticky Mousse Cake, Roquefort Loaf and Filo Venison Rendang have caught my eye!

And if your bake doesn't turn out first time, please don't be disheartened – such is the nature of baking! Oven temperature, the weather, your kitchen scales and many more variables might cause your bake to turn out rather differently to how you imagined. It's happened to all of us, even with our most trusted recipes – as you will have seen in previous series and this series. Just learn from the experience, take notes on what you might do differently – and try again!

Good luck with your baking!

FOREWORD BY PAUL HOLLYWOOD

One of the best things about the *Bake Off* is that it has got millions of people baking, and I'm dead chuffed to be a part of that. I know that many of you are already good bakers and, hopefully for you lot, the show offers new ideas and inspires you to invent your own bakes – or adapt old recipes with fresh twists. I hope Mary and I have also thrown you a few good challenges to get your teeth into!

For me, baking is an essential, daily part of life. If you haven't already realised, be warned that, when you know what you're doing, baking is addictive! As soon as you've made and mastered your own breads, cakes and pastry, there is no going back to shop-bought – it just won't compare with what you can make yourself, at home. Once you get into the habit of baking, you'll soon find it becomes second nature.

For those of you who do bake regularly, you'll find lots of easy, everyday ideas here. If you're a beginner, these recipes should give you the confidence to get started. Mary and I always try to test the skills and techniques of our bakers as much as possible. I know we look for different things (Bezza and I don't always agree!), but ultimately we both want to encourage our bakers and help them to perfect their techniques. We want their baking to be as spot on as it can be, and to guide them, and you, to avoid any future baking disasters!

You'll find our recipes from the series at the end of each chapter. I'm not going to say that these are easy – we designed them to challenge our bakers – but they are well worth a go, especially if you watch our Masterclasses too. And though I might not show it, our bakers always have brilliant ideas, even if their execution can be a bit off on the day…

INTRODUCTION

A HOME-BAKED CAKE IS ALWAYS SPECIAL, NO MATTER HOW SIMPLE OR EASY IT IS. THIS BOOK IS ABOUT THESE GOOD BAKES WE ALL LOVE TO MAKE – AND TO EAT.

'EVERY DAY' means home bakes to us – bakes that you can make with confidence. We have done everything we can to make the recipes as foolproof as possible, with straightforward techniques, easy-to-follow instructions and optional extras (depending on whether you have the time or skill to go further). Our aim is to help you to understand what you're doing so that you can get it right, whether you're learning from scratch or are a seasoned cook wanting to improve or pick up new skills. You probably know the answer to the soggy bottom problem by now, but we've got other tips to offer, from how to get a good crust to the best way to shape a tuile. We've also kept an eye on the ingredients – in the main, these recipes won't cost the earth to make (or need a trip to buy specialist ingredients or equipment).

Don't worry – all your favourite parts of *The Great British Bake Off* are here too, so you can reproduce the best of the Bakers' recipes, as well as the Judges' Challenges. Because good baking relies on learning good basic techniques, there are full, foolproof details and helpful step photos to guide you. From an Angel Cake and English Muffins to perfect Egg Custard Tarts and Trifle, the recipes cover a wide array of classic Signature and Technical bakes. And, because no *Bake Off* is complete without a few jaw-dropping Showstoppers, Mary and Paul have come up with their amazing Chocolate Creation, a 3-tier, stacked chocolate cake, covered in white chocolate ganache and finished with a lacy collar and curls – not 'everyday' perhaps, but definitely something to try if you're up for a challenge.

We hope that this book will encourage you to pick up your whisk and bake for any and every occasion and that you will return to these recipes over and over again. Make baking a way of life, an everyday event. Don't get stressed about it, just enjoy it!

Linda Collister

HERE ARE SOME GOOD REASONS TO BAKE

• FOR A WEEKNIGHT SUPPER: a chocolate cake made in a saucepan (just melt, mix and bake)

• FRESH FRUIT AND VEG FOR LUNCH: a spiced apple and rum sponge, a blackberry cake or a honey and courgette cake after supper

• FOR CHRISTMAS: a simple fruit cake studded with cubes of marzipan, or a lighter sponge version flavoured with fresh cranberries

• FOR A BIRTHDAY: a 3-layer creamed sponge with a light, fluffy filling

• FOR SNACKING: savoury crackers, easy to customise and great for dipping

• THE PERFECT END TO A DINNER MENU: a plain cake turned into an impressive dessert with a delicious sauce or topping, or pretty petits fours

• FOR TEATIME: Scottish shortbread or the French take – sablés, and fresh berry scones

• FOR BAKE SALES: blondies or an Italian chocolate traybake

• TIME AT THE WEEKEND: yeast breads – from fougasses and baguettes to Simnel buns – and mouthwatering pastries

• FOR SUNDAY LUNCH: a savoury meat pie – venison topped with filo or a party-sized hot-water-crust turkey and cranberry pie

ALL OF THESE AND MORE ARE HERE FOR YOU TO TRY. LET'S CELEBRATE THE HOME-MADE BAKE!

WHAT DOES IT MEAN?

FOLD: This is a way to delicately combine two (or more) ingredients so you don't knock out all the air you've carefully beaten or whisked in. Examples of folding are adding sifted flour to creamed butter, eggs and sugar for a cake mixture, or adding ingredients to whisked egg whites for a pavlova or meringue. Use a large metal spoon or plastic spatula to fold: cut down through the mixture with the side of the spoon until you touch the bottom of the bowl, then turn the spoon right way up and bring it up through the mixture to the top. Turn the spoon over so the mixture in it flops on to the rest in the bowl. Give the bowl a quarter turn (so you start from a different place) and cut down through the mixture, lift it and flop it over again. Continue this folding action, using the least number of movements possible, until you can't see any unmixed streaks.

KNOCK BACK: After proving (see below), the dough has to be punched or knocked down with your knuckles to return it to its original size. This process bursts the large bubbles of carbon dioxide gas in the dough that were created during proving and avoids over stretching and tearing the gluten strands that were developed during kneading. The result is a more even texture once your bread is baked.

PROVE: After kneading bread dough, you need to leave it to rise or prove. This is when the yeast gets to work producing millions of bubbles of carbon dioxide gas and the dough swells to double its original size. The yeast works best in warm, moist conditions so cover the top of the bowl with clingfilm or a damp tea towel, leaving plenty of room for the dough to expand. The best place to leave the dough to prove is on the work top – if the temperature is too warm the dough can expand too quickly causing it to collapse. If the temperature is really hot then the yeast will be killed.

RUB IN: This is how you combine butter and flour when making pastry and simple cake mixtures. Using both hands, pick up a little of the butter and flour between your fingertips and thumbs (try to keep your palms clean – your fingertips will be cooler). Lift your hands up to the top of the bowl, then gently rub your fingers together so the mixture falls back down into the bowl. Continue doing this until the mixture has a crumb-like consistency. The rubbing-in will add air, which will make the pastry or cake mixture lighter.

SIFT: This means putting dry ingredients such as flour, raising agents, cocoa powder, icing sugar and spices through a sieve to remove any lumps. Sifting also adds air and helps combine dry ingredients (this is important for raising agents added to flour, to be sure they are evenly dispersed to work well).

WORK: This is a way of saying to mix, stir, blend or combine ingredients using a spoon, plastic spatula or your hands until they have come together (or look smooth, or soft or thickened, depending on the recipe instruction).

HOW DO I DO THIS?

PREPARING TINS

GREASE AND BASE-LINE A SPRINGCLIP TIN, DEEP ROUND OR SQUARE TIN OR SANDWICH TIN: Lightly and thoroughly brush the base and sides of the tin (including the rim) with melted butter. Set the tin on a sheet of baking paper and draw around it, then cut out the circle (or square) of paper and press it on to the base of the tin.

GREASE AND LINE A SPRINGCLIP TIN OR ROUND DEEP CAKE TIN: Brush the base and sides with melted butter. Cut out 2 rounds of baking paper very slightly smaller than the base of the tin (see above). Also cut out a double-thickness strip of baking paper long enough to go around the tin and wide enough to stand about 5cm above it. Make a 2.5cm fold along one edge of this strip, then snip diagonally up to the fold at 1cm intervals (so it looks like a thick fringe). Press one paper round into the base of the tin, then place the strip around the inside of the tin so the snipped edge lies flat on the base and the rest of the paper strip is pressed neatly to the sides of the tin (no creases). Brush the round on the base and the snipped edge of the side strip with a little more melted butter, then press the second round of paper on top. Lightly brush this and the strip on the sides with melted butter to hold it all in place.

GREASE AND LINE A LOAF TIN: Lightly brush the base, sides and rim of the tin with melted butter. Cut a strip of baking paper the width of the tin and long enough to cover the base and 2 short sides, then press it into the greased tin to line it – the paper will help you lift out the loaf after baking.

CHECKING IF CAKES/BAKES ARE DONE

FINGERTIP TEST: For delicate sponge cakes the most reliable way to test is to gently press the top of the sponge, in the centre, with your fingertip – the sponge is ready if it springs back into place, and has started to shrink from the sides of the tin. If a slight dent remains in the sponge after you press it, it needs to be baked for a few more minutes.

SKEWER TEST: Use this for richer, heavier cakes, fruit cakes and dense chocolate cakes. Stick a fine skewer or wooden cocktail stick into the centre of the cake. If the skewer comes out clean, rather than damp with cake mixture, the cake is ready. Note, though, that for some recipes – such as Brownies – the skewer should come out slightly sticky to avoid overcooking.

COOKING WITH CHOCOLATE

MELT CHOCOLATE: Chop or break up the chocolate into even-sized pieces so it will melt at the same rate. Put it into a heatproof bowl and set over a pan of steaming hot but not boiling water – don't let the base of the bowl touch the water. As the chocolate starts to melt stir it gently so it melts evenly. It is ready to use as melted chocolate as soon as it is liquid and smooth, around 30°C. If the chocolate overheats and reaches 50°C it will seize up – become grainy and hard – and be unusable.

TEMPER CHOCOLATE: Melting and cooling chocolate (tempering) makes it shiny and very smooth, and will give a professional finish when you are covering or coating a cake or dessert, or when you are making decorations such as chocolate curls. First melt the chocolate (see above), then slightly increase the heat under the pan of water so the temperature of the chocolate rises to about 45°C. Keep stirring so the chocolate heats evenly. Remove the bowl from the pan and set it in a larger bowl of cold but not icy water to quickly cool the chocolate (take care not to let any water get into the chocolate bowl). Gently stir until the temperature falls to 27°C. Set the bowl over the pan of steaming hot water again and reheat the chocolate, stirring, until it reaches 29–30°C. As soon as the chocolate gets up to temperature, remove the bowl from the pan. The tempered chocolate is now ready to use.

WHISKING EGGS AND CREAM

WHISK EGG WHITES: Put the egg whites, which should be at room temperature for the best results, into a large, spotlessly clean and grease-free bowl (any trace of fat and specks of yolk stuck to the bowl or whisk will stop the whites from being beaten to their full volume). Whisk on low speed for about 30 seconds so they become frothy and the structure starts to develop. If you add a pinch of cream of tartar or vinegar or lemon juice at this point the slight acidity will help the structure to stiffen. Increase the speed and continue whisking until the mixture is a mass of tiny bubbles, with a very smooth and fine texture. The whites have reached soft peak stage when you lift the whisk and the peak of egg whites on it slightly droops down. The next stage, after more whisking, is stiff peak when the peak stands upright and you can turn the bowl upside down (without the whites falling out).

WHISK EGGS AND SUGAR: When whisking egg whites for meringues start adding the sugar when the whites reach soft peak stage. If you add the sugar too early on, it will dissolve quickly and make the mixture too wet. But don't wait until the whites have reached stiff peak stage because their structure then won't be elastic enough to hold the sugar and you'll get a lumpy, blobby meringue instead of a sleek, glossy result.

WHISK TO THE RIBBON STAGE: For whisked sponges, eggs and sugar must be whisked to build up a thick mass of tiny air bubbles and thus form the structure of the cake. Use a large bowl as the initial volume of eggs and sugar will increase 5-fold. Whisk on high speed for 4–5 minutes until the mixture becomes so thick that when the whisk is lifted out of the bowl the mixture on it falls back on to the mix in the bowl to make a thick, ribbon-like trail on the surface.

WHIP CREAM: Make sure the cream is thoroughly chilled before you start (in warm weather chill the bowl and whisk too), to prevent the butterfat from separating and the mixture curdling. If you are going to fold the cream into another mixture, whip to a soft peak (see egg whites left). Whip to a slightly firmer peak for piping.

MAKING A PASTRY CASE

LINE A FLAN TIN: Roll out the pastry dough on a lightly floured worktop to a circle about 8cm larger than your tin. Roll up the pastry around the rolling pin and lift it over the flan tin, then unroll the pastry gently so it drapes over the tin. Flour your fingers and gently press the pastry on to the base and up the side of the tin, pressing out any pockets of air. Roll the pin over the top of the tin to cut off the excess pastry (if there are any holes in the pastry case, use this leftover dough to patch them). With your thumbs, ease the pastry up the side of the tin, just slightly higher than the rim, to allow for shrinkage during baking. Curve your forefinger inside this new rim and gently press the pastry over your finger so it curves slightly inwards – this will make it easier to unmould after baking. Prick the base of the pastry case well with a fork, then chill for 20 minutes. If you need to keep the pastry case in the fridge for any longer, loosely cover it with clingfilm to prevent the pastry from drying out.

BAKE A PASTRY CASE BLIND: Crumple up a sheet of greaseproof or baking paper, then flatten it out (this makes the paper easier to fit). Line the pastry case with the paper and fill with ceramic baking beans or dried beans. Place in the heated oven and bake for 12–15 minutes until the pastry is firm. Carefully remove the paper and beans, then return the tin to the oven and bake for a further 5–7 minutes until the pastry is thoroughly cooked and starting to colour. Pastry containing sugar needs to be watched carefully as it can burn on the edges before the base is cooked through. If this happens reduce the oven temperature slightly, or cover the rim with a long strip of foil.

MAKING CHOUX

When you're making a choux dough it can be hard to tell exactly how much egg to beat in to achieve the correct consistency – if you add too little egg the pastry will be hard and dry; if you add too much the dough will be too floppy to rise and puff in the oven. An easy test is to take a small ball of the dough and stretch it between your forefinger and thumb: if the dough stretches out to 5cm then you can stop adding egg.

MAKING BREAD

KNEAD A YEASTED DOUGH: Working a dough develops the gluten (in the flour's protein) and turns it from a messy ball into neat bundles of strands that are capable of stretching around the bubbles of carbon dioxide gas (produced by the growing yeast). The dough will then rise slowly, thanks to the yeast and gluten, and set in the oven. You can knead by hand or in a free-standing electric mixer fitted with a dough hook.

To knead by hand, first lightly dust the worktop with flour or grease with a teaspoon of oil, to prevent the dough from sticking. Turn the dough on to the surface. Stretch the ball of dough away from you by holding down one end with your hand and using the other hand to pull and stretch out the dough as if it were an elastic band. Gather the dough back into a ball again and give it a quarter turn (so you start from a different section of the dough), then repeat the stretching and gathering-back movements. As you knead you'll notice the dough gradually changes in the way it looks and feels – it will start to feel pliable then stretchy and very elastic, and silky smooth. Most doughs need 10 minutes of thorough kneading by hand. In a mixer (set on the lowest possible speed) knead for about 5 minutes.

WINDOW-PANE TEST: You may wonder how to tell when a yeast dough has been 'thoroughly kneaded'. Use this foolproof test (known as the 'windowpane test'): pull off a small ball of dough and stretch it out between your fingers. If you can stretch it out so thin and fine you can just about read the recipe instructions through it, then it's ready. But if it snaps, tears or splits give it another couple of minutes kneading and test again.

PROVE DOUGH: If you leave a yeast dough to rise in a warm place – around 28°C – the yeast will be encouraged to grow quickly. Left in a cooler spot – around 20°C – the dough will take between 30 and 50 per cent longer to rise but the flavour of the dough will be more nuanced.

BAKE A LOAF WITH A GOOD CRUST: Make sure the oven is thoroughly heated so the dough quickly puffs (called 'oven-spring') and then sets, bakes evenly and forms a good crust.

BAKE A LOAF WITH A CRISP CRUST: Creating a burst of steam in the oven at the start of baking will help give your loaf a crisp crust – the steam keeps the surface moist, helping the bread rise easily; once the surface has set the moisture evaporates, leaving a crisp finish. To do this, put an empty roasting tin on the floor of the oven when you turn it on to heat it. Then, immediately after you've put the loaf in to bake, pour cold water, or throw a handful of ice cubes, into the hot tin and quickly close the oven door to trap the resulting steam inside.

BAKE A LOAF WITH A CRISP BOTTOM CRUST: When you turn on the oven, put a baking sheet or baking stone in to heat up. Then carefully transfer your loaf (in a tin or on a sheet of baking paper) on to the hot baking sheet or stone for baking.

TEST BREAD TO SEE IF IT IS COOKED: Carefully remove the bread from the oven and turn out, upside down (thick oven gloves needed here), then tap the underside with your knuckles. If the bread sounds hollow then the loaf is cooked through; if you just get a dull 'thud', put the bread back into the oven, without the tin, and bake for a few more minutes, then test again. Cool on a wire rack so the steam from the loaf doesn't condense during cooling and turn the crust soggy.

Hand-held mixer

Large metal spoon

Deep sandwich tin

Springclip tin

Juicer

Palette knife

Fork

Spatula

Citrus zester

Loaf tin

Bowls of varying size

Small saucepan

Balloon/wire whisk

Measuring spoons

Wire rack

CAKES

Cakes are as much about texture as they are about rich sweetness, and the secret behind any good cake is creating and trapping tiny bubbles of air in the mixture.

The butter needs to be soft and at room temperature (19–20°C) so that it is pliable enough to hold the increasing number of air bubbles. Butter straight from the fridge will be too hard, while very soft or oily butter will be too liquid to hold the air. So take the butter out of the fridge about 30 minutes before starting (don't leave it in the sun though).

Use caster sugar as it dissolves faster than the coarser granulated sugar, and helps create those precious air bubbles. Be sure your eggs are at room temperature too – if you add cold eggs to a creamed mixture it will seize up and make the cake's texture dense and heavy.

BLACKBERRY BUTTERMILK SPONGE

It is thanks to buttermilk that this sponge cake has such a lovely light and moist crumb, with berries adding small bursts of flavour. Sprinkle with crunchy demerara sugar before baking. For dessert, serve warm cut into wedges, with a Hot Berry Sauce (see page 20).

MAKES 1 MEDIUM CAKE
YOU WILL NEED: 1 X 20.5CM ROUND SPRINGCLIP TIN, GREASED AND BASE-LINED

150g fresh blackberries
125g unsalted butter, softened
175g caster sugar
½ teaspoon vanilla extract
2 medium free-range eggs,
    at room temperature

100ml buttermilk, at room
    temperature
200g self-raising flour
1 ½ tablespoons demerara sugar,
    for sprinkling

1 Heat your oven to 180°C/350°F/gas 4. Gently wipe the blackberries clean with kitchen paper – only rinse them if they look very dirty, then thoroughly drain and pat dry.

2 Put the soft butter into a mixing bowl and beat with an electric mixer until creamy. Gradually beat in the caster sugar. Once all the sugar has been added, scrape down the sides of the bowl, then add the vanilla and beat for a couple of minutes longer until the mixture looks paler and fluffy. Scrape down the sides of the bowl again.

3 Beat the eggs in a small bowl with a fork, just to mix, then gradually add to the butter mixture, beating well after each addition and scraping down the sides of the bowl from time to time as before. Add about a third of the buttermilk and gently fold in with a plastic spatula or large metal spoon, then fold in about a third of the flour. Fold in the rest of the buttermilk and flour in the same way, in 2 batches each.

4 Scrape the mixture into the prepared tin and spread evenly. Scatter the berries over the top and gently press them into the mixture so they are about half-submerged. Sprinkle evenly with the demerara sugar. Place in the heated oven and bake for 35–40 minutes until golden and a skewer inserted into the centre of the sponge comes out clean.

5 Set the tin on a wire rack. Run a round-bladed knife around the sponge to loosen it from the tin, then gently unclip the tin side and remove the cake. Leave it to cool a bit. Eat the cake warm or at room temperature the same or the next day (store in an airtight container).

HOT BERRY SAUCE

A quick sauce you can make with fresh or frozen fruit, this is great with the Blackberry Buttermilk Sponge Cake on page 18 as well as with ice cream, meringues and pancakes. For a bit of a kick, add a dash or two of kirsch before serving.

SERVES 6

150g fresh blackberries
150g fresh raspberries
2 teaspoons cornflour
2 tablespoons caster sugar

1 Put all the ingredients into a medium-sized pan and mix gently with a wooden spoon so the berries become thoroughly coated with sugar and cornflour.

2 Set the pan on low heat and stir frequently until the juices start to run, then increase the heat slightly and simmer gently until the fruit has softened and the juices have thickened to make a sauce. Keep stirring often as the fruit cooks.

3 Taste the sauce and add more sugar if you want it a bit sweeter. Serve hot, warm or cold.

FUDGY RASPBERRY CAKE

A very dark and rich cake with a dense, fudgy texture, this is easy to make – you just need a saucepan and a wooden spoon – but you'll need to wait a day before trying it, and it just keeps getting better! A fresh raspberry topping will really make the cake look glamorous.

MAKES 1 MEDIUM CAKE
YOU WILL NEED: 1 X 20.5CM ROUND SPRINGCLIP TIN, GREASED AND BASE-LINED

240g unsalted butter, diced
5 tablespoons raspberry conserve
75g cocoa powder
300g caster sugar
3 medium free-range eggs, at room
  temperature
1 teaspoon raspberry liqueur, kirsch
  or vanilla extract

100g plain flour
good pinch of salt

To finish
icing sugar and cocoa powder
  OR 2 tablespoons raspberry conserve
  and 150g fresh raspberries

1 Heat your oven to 180°C/350°F/gas 4. Put the pieces of butter and the jam into a heavy-based pan large enough to hold all the ingredients. Set over the lowest possible heat and melt gently, stirring frequently with a wooden spoon.

2 Once the butter has melted, remove the pan from the heat. Sift the cocoa into the pan, then add the sugar. Set the pan on a damp cloth (to prevent it from wobbling), then stir and beat the ingredients together with the spoon until thoroughly combined.

3 Put the eggs and liqueur in a small bowl and beat with a fork, just to combine. Gradually add to the cocoa mixture, beating well after each addition. Sift the flour and salt into the pan and stir in to make a very thick, smooth mixture with flecks of raspberry.

4 Scrape the mixture into the prepared tin and spread evenly. Place in the heated oven and bake for 15 minutes, then lower the heat to 160°C/325°F/gas 3. Continue baking for about 40 minutes until a skewer inserted into the centre of the cake comes out just slightly sticky.

5 Remove the tin from the oven and set on a wire rack. Run a round-bladed knife around the cake to loosen it from the tin, then leave until completely cold. Unclip the tin and remove the cake, wrap in greaseproof paper or foil and keep in an airtight container overnight.

6 The next day, set the cake on a serving platter. Dust generously with icing sugar, sifted through a tea strainer, and then more lightly with cocoa. Alternatively, cover the cake with fresh raspberries: gently warm the conserve and brush it liberally over the cake, then decorate with the berries. The cake can be kept in an airtight tin for up to 5 days (with the raspberry topping, the cake is best eaten the same or next day).

STICKY MOUSSE CAKE

More like a baked chocolate mousse than a cake, this gluten-free bake is a very rich and sticky affair! Coffee cuts the sweetness of the chocolate, giving the cake a bittersweet flavour; if you want it to be sweeter reduce the instant coffee to 1 tablespoon. For the best results make sure all the elements – the melted chocolate mixture, whipped cream and whisked egg mixture – are at the same temperature before you combine them. The cake is baked fairly slowly, in a bain-marie.

MAKES 1 MEDIUM CAKE
YOU WILL NEED: 1 X 20.5CM ROUND SPRINGCLIP TIN, GREASED AND BASE-LINED

1 Heat your oven to 160°C/325°F/gas 3. Set the prepared tin in the centre of a sheet of foil and wrap the foil tightly around the base and sides of the tin to make it completely watertight.

2 Stir the coffee with the boiling water in a cup until dissolved. Leave to cool. Meanwhile, chop or break up the chocolate and put it in a heatproof bowl. Pour over the cooled coffee and set the bowl over a pan of hot water. Melt gently, stirring occasionally. When the mixture is just smooth, remove the bowl from the pan and set aside to cool.

3 Whip the cream until it stands in soft peaks when the whisk is lifted out. Set aside at room temperature until needed.

4 Put the eggs into a large mixing bowl and whisk with an electric mixer until frothy. Add the sugar and whisk for 4–5 minutes until the mixture is very pale and mousse-like (this mixture won't quite form a ribbon when the whisk is lifted out of the bowl).

5 Using a large metal spoon carefully fold the coffee and chocolate mixture into the whisked egg mix in 3 batches. Sift the cocoa powder on top and fold in. Scrape down the sides of the bowl, then fold in the whipped cream in 3 batches.

6 Transfer the mixture to the prepared tin and spread evenly. Set the tin in a roasting tin and pour lukewarm water into the roasting tin to come halfway up the sides of the cake tin. Place in the heated oven and bake for 75–80 minutes until a skewer inserted into the centre of the cake comes out slightly sticky.

7 Remove the roasting tin from the oven but leave the cake tin in it. Run a round-bladed knife around the cake to loosen it from the tin, then leave to cool. When the cake is cold, remove from the roasting tin and carefully unclip the side of the cake tin. The cake will be quite soft, fragile and crumbly so wrap it in foil and keep overnight before cutting.

8 Serve dusted with icing sugar. Store in an airtight container in a cool place and eat within 4 days. Alternatively, if you want to add a crème fraîche topping, stir the crème fraîche until smooth, then spread it on top of the cold cake. Scatter over the chocolate beans and serve immediately. Store any leftover cake in an airtight container in the fridge and eat within 2 days.

1½ tablespoons instant coffee
powder or granules
150ml boiling water
300g dark chocolate
(about 70% cocoa solids)
225ml double cream
4 medium free-range eggs,
at room temperature

150g caster sugar
30g cocoa powder
icing sugar, for dusting

For the topping (optional)
200g crème fraîche, well chilled
50g chocolate coffee beans

CRUNCHY COFFEE CAKE

A crumbly streusel mix containing oats and nuts gives this well-flavoured and not too rich cake a good crunchy interior and topping. It's best freshly baked.

MAKES 1 MEDIUM CAKE
YOU WILL NEED: 1 X 20.5CM ROUND SPRINGCLIP TIN, GREASED AND BASE-LINED

For the streusel
100g light brown muscovado sugar
50g plain flour
25g porridge oats
1 teaspoon ground cinnamon
50g unsalted butter, softened
50g walnut or pecan pieces

For the coffee cake
2 tablespoons instant coffee
   granules or powder
2 tablespoons boiling water

120g unsalted butter, softened
200g caster sugar
2 medium free-range eggs,
   at room temperature
200ml buttermilk, at room
   temperature
250g plain flour
good pinch of salt
½ teaspoon baking powder
½ teaspoon bicarbonate of soda
icing sugar, for dusting

1 Heat your oven to 180°C/350°F/gas 4. To make the streusel put the sugar, flour, oats and cinnamon in a mixing bowl and mix with your fingers. Add the soft butter and work into the dry ingredients, rubbing and squeezing the mixture together, until it looks like very coarse crumbs. Stir in the nuts and set aside.

2 For the cake mixture, stir the coffee with the boiling water in a cup until dissolved. Leave to cool. Put the soft butter into a large mixing bowl and beat with an electric mixer until creamy. Add the sugar and beat for a couple of minutes until fluffy, scraping down the sides of the bowl from time to time.

3 Put the eggs in a small bowl and beat with a fork, just to combine. Gradually add to the butter mixture, beating well after each addition and scraping down the bowl as before. Gradually stir in the buttermilk using a plastic spatula or large metal spoon, then stir in the coffee. Sift the flour, salt, baking powder and bicarbonate of soda into the bowl and fold in with the spatula or spoon until thoroughly combined.

4 Spoon half of the mixture into the prepared tin and spread evenly. Scatter half of the streusel mixture on top in an even layer, and carefully and gently press it down on to the cake mixture. Spoon the rest of the cake mixture on to this and spread out evenly. Scatter the remaining streusel over the cake to cover completely and evenly.

5 Place in the heated oven and bake for about 1 hour until a skewer inserted into the centre of the cake comes out clean. After the cake has been in the oven for about 50 minutes, keep a close eye on the cake and be ready to cover the top with a sheet of greaseproof paper or foil if it starts to turn from golden to dark brown.

6 Set the tin on a wire rack. Run a round-bladed knife around the cake to loosen it from the tin, then carefully unclip the tin side. Wait until the cake is completely cold before removing it from the tin. Dust with icing sugar and eat the same or next day (store in an airtight container).

POPPYSEED AND LEMON CAKE

This light creamed sponge is so good it only needs a simple dusting of icing sugar before serving, and it gets better the longer it is kept. For the best results the butter should be soft – not oily or runny – so remove from the fridge a couple of hours before starting. If you forget you can soften the butter in the microwave for 8–10 seconds, but don't let it start to melt.

MAKES 1 MEDIUM CAKE
YOU WILL NEED: 1 X 20.5CM SPRINGCLIP TIN, GREASED AND BASE-LINED

225g unsalted butter, softened
finely grated zest of 1 medium
  unwaxed lemon
225g caster sugar
4 medium free-range eggs,
  at room temperature

100g ground almonds
100g self-raising flour
2 tablespoons poppyseeds
icing sugar, for dusting

1 Heat your oven to 180°C/350°F/gas 4. Put the soft butter into a large mixing bowl, add the lemon zest and beat with an electric mixer for a minute until creamy. (If you are using a hand-held mixer, set the bowl on a damp cloth so it doesn't wobble.)

2 Gradually beat in the sugar, a couple of tablespoonfuls at a time. Once all the sugar has been added, scrape down the sides of the bowl, then beat for a further 2–3 minutes until the mixture looks paler in colour and lighter in texture.

3 Put the eggs in a small bowl and beat with a fork, just to mix. Gradually add to the sugar mixture (roughly a tablespoonful at a time), beating well after each addition and scraping down the sides of the bowl from time to time. To prevent the mixture from curdling add a tablespoon of ground almonds with each of the last 2 additions of beaten egg.

4 Scrape down the sides of the bowl once again, then sift the rest of the ground almonds and the flour over the egg mixture. Carefully and thoroughly fold them in using a large metal spoon. When you can no longer see any streaks of flour add the poppyseeds and gently fold in.

5 Scrape the mixture into the prepared tin and spread evenly. Place in the heated oven and bake for 45–50 minutes until golden brown and the top springs back when gently pressed in the centre.

6 Set the tin on a wire rack. Carefully run a round-bladed knife around the sponge to loosen it from the tin, then unclip the side and leave to cool. Once cold remove the sponge from the tin and dust with icing sugar. Store in an airtight container and eat within 5 days.

APPLE CAKE WITH RUM BUTTERCREAM

Filled and topped with a fluffy rum buttercream, this creamed sponge cake is flavoured with chopped apples, raisins and pecans plus a touch of mixed spices. Buttermilk gives the sponge a delicate light texture.

MAKES 1 MEDIUM CAKE
YOU WILL NEED: 2 X 20.5CM DEEP SANDWICH TINS, GREASED AND BASE-LINED

1 Heat your oven to 180°C/350°F/gas 4. Put the soft butter and sugar into a large mixing bowl and beat for about 2 minutes with an electric mixer until thoroughly combined. Scrape down the sides of the bowl from time to time.

2 Beat the eggs with the vanilla in a small bowl with a fork, just until mixed. Gradually add to the butter mixture, beating well after each addition and scraping down the sides of the bowl as before.

3 Sift the flour, baking powder, bicarbonate of soda, cinnamon, ginger and nutmeg into another bowl. Add about a third of the flour mix to the egg mix and use a large metal spoon or plastic spatula to stir in gently. Then add about a third of the buttermilk and gently mix it in. Add the remaining flour and buttermilk in the same way, in 2 batches each. Add the apple, raisins and nuts to the bowl and gently stir in until everything is thoroughly combined.

4 Divide the mixture equally between the prepared tins and spread evenly. Place in the heated oven and bake for about 30 minutes until risen and golden brown and the top springs back when gently pressed in the centre.

5 Set the tins on a wire rack and run a rounded-bladed knife around each sponge to loosen it from its tin. Turn out the sponges on to the rack and leave to cool completely.

6 To make the buttercream, put the sugar and water into a small heavy-based pan and heat gently, without boiling, until the sugar dissolves. Then bring the syrup to the boil and boil until the temperature reaches 110°C on a sugar thermometer (this will take about 5 minutes). Don't let the syrup start to caramelise.

7 While the syrup is boiling, put the egg yolks into a heatproof bowl (set on a damp cloth to prevent wobbling) and whisk for a few seconds with an electric mixer until frothy. As soon as the syrup reaches the right temperature, slowly pour it into the bowl in a steady stream, whisking constantly. Then keep whisking until the mixture becomes very thick and mousse-like, pale in colour and completely cold.

8 Cut the butter into small pieces and gradually whisk into the egg mix, then whisk in the vanilla and rum to taste. The buttercream needs to be easy to spread but firm enough to hold its shape, so if necessary cover the bowl and chill briefly.

9 Set one sponge layer (crust-side down) on a serving plate. Spread half of the buttercream over the surface, then place the second sponge (crust-side up) on this. Cover the top of the sponge with the rest of the buttercream, swirling it with a palette knife or round-bladed knife. Leave, uncovered, at cool room temperature to firm up for a couple of hours before serving. Store in an airtight container in a cool spot (not the fridge) and eat within 4 days.

For the cake
150g unsalted butter, softened
300g caster sugar
3 medium free-range eggs,
  at room temperature
½ teaspoon vanilla extract
300g plain flour
1 teaspoon baking powder
½ teaspoon bicarbonate of soda
½ teaspoon ground cinnamon
¼ teaspoon ground ginger
¼ teaspoon freshly grated nutmeg
225ml buttermilk

1 medium eating apple (about 115g),
  peeled, cored and finely chopped
40g raisins
40g pecan pieces

For the buttercream
85g caster sugar
4 tablespoons water
2 medium free-range egg yolks,
  at room temperature
150g unsalted butter, softened
1 teaspoon vanilla extract
2-3 tablespoons dark rum, to taste

WHIPPED CHOCOLATE LAYER CAKE

Three layers of dark, soft-textured chocolate sponge are sandwiched with a rich chocolate buttercream. Chocolate flakes add a bit of crunch. The cake will slice more easily if you make it a day or so ahead.

MAKES 1 LARGE CAKE
YOU WILL NEED: 3 X 20.5CM DEEP SANDWICH TINS, GREASED AND BASE-LINED

For the sponge mixture
60g cocoa powder
250ml boiling water
30g dark chocolate (about 70% cocoa solids), finely chopped or grated
225g unsalted butter, softened
325g light brown muscovado sugar
2 medium free-range eggs plus 2 yolks, at room temperature
½ teaspoon vanilla extract
4 tablespoons crème fraîche
225g self-raising flour
good pinch of salt

For the filling and frosting
200g dark chocolate (about 70% cocoa solids), finely chopped
125ml double cream
2 medium free-range egg whites, at room temperature
200g caster sugar
450g unsalted butter, softened and diced
4 flaked milk chocolate bars (about 100g)

1 Heat your oven to 180°C/350°F/gas 4. Sift the cocoa into a heatproof bowl. Pour in the boiling water, whisking constantly. When the mixture is smooth and lump-free, whisk in the chocolate until melted and silky smooth. Set aside until needed.

2 Put the butter into a large mixing bowl and beat with an electric mixer until creamy. Press any lumps out of the sugar, then add to the butter and beat on low speed. Once all the sugar has been worked in, increase the speed and beat until the mixture looks fluffy and paler in colour. Stop the mixer and scrape down the sides of the bowl from time to time.

3 Place the whole eggs, yolks and vanilla in another bowl and beat with a fork, just to mix. Gradually add to the butter mixture, beating well after each addition. Scrape down the bowl as before. Fold in the cooled cocoa and chocolate mixture, then add the crème fraîche to the bowl and sift the flour and salt on top. Fold in using a large metal spoon until thoroughly combined.

4 Divide the mixture equally among the 3 prepared tins and spread evenly. Place in the heated oven and bake for 20–25 minutes until the centre of each sponge springs back when gently pressed in the centre with a fingertip.

5 Remove from the oven. Run a round-bladed knife around each sponge to loosen it from its tin, then turn out on to a wire rack. Leave to cool.

6 To make the ganache for the filling and frosting, put the chopped chocolate in a heatproof bowl. Heat the cream in a small pan until just boiling, then pour over the chocolate and stir until melted and smooth. Leave this ganache to cool to room temperature, stirring occasionally.

7 While the ganache is cooling, put the egg whites and sugar in a large heatproof bowl and whisk with a hand-held electric mixer until slightly frothy. Set the bowl over a pan of simmering water (don't let the base of the bowl touch the water) and whisk for 4–5 minutes until the mixture turns into a thick, white, stiff and glossy meringue. Remove the bowl from the pan and set it on a cloth to prevent any wobbling, then carry on whisking until the meringue is cold (don't skip this bit or the filling will split when the butter is added).

8 Gradually whisk the butter into the meringue, then whisk in the ganache to make a mousse-like buttercream. It needs to be firm enough to spread easily and to hold its shape so it doesn't slide off the cake, so if necessary cover and chill for a few minutes (don't chill it too long or it will become too firm to spread). Spoon half of the buttercream into another bowl and reserve for the frosting.

9 When you're ready to assemble the cake, set one layer of sponge, crust-side down, on a serving platter or cake board. Spread half of the buttercream filling over the sponge. Break up one of flaked chocolate bars into shards and scatter over the filling. Set a second sponge on top, cover with the rest of the filling and add shards of another flaked chocolate bar. Place the last sponge on top, crust-side up.

10 Using half of the reserved buttercream frosting, cover the side of the cake, spreading the frosting with a round-bladed knife or palette knife. Pile the rest of the frosting on top of the cake and spread out evenly. Decorate with the rest of the flaked chocolate bars, broken into large chunks. Leave the cake in a cool place to set and firm up.

11 For the best results, once the cake is firm store it overnight in an airtight container in a cool place (or the fridge in hot weather) before slicing. Eat within 4 days.

LIME CREAM CHEESE CAKE

In this loaf cake, some of the butter is replaced with cream cheese, which really improves the texture of the cake, making it less likely to be dry and crumbly. When it comes out of the oven the cake is soaked in a lime syrup – like a drizzle cake – then finished with a simple lime glacé icing.

MAKES 1 LARGE LOAF CAKE
YOU WILL NEED: 1 X 900G LOAF TIN (ABOUT 26 X 12.5 X 7.5CM), GREASED AND LINED WITH A LONG STRIP OF BAKING PAPER TO COVER THE BASE AND 2 SHORT SIDES

175g unsalted butter, softened
150g full-fat cream cheese, at room temperature
finely grated zest of 2 medium limes
250g caster sugar
3 medium free-range eggs, at room temperature
½ teaspoon vanilla extract
225g self-raising flour

For the syrup
4 tablespoons lime juice
50g caster sugar

For the glaze
150g icing sugar
finely grated zest of 1 medium lime
about 1 tablespoon lime juice

1 Heat your oven to 180°C/350°F/gas 4. Put the soft butter and cream cheese in a large mixing bowl. Add the lime zest and beat with an electric mixer until soft and creamy. Scrape down the sides of the bowl, then gradually beat in the caster sugar. Once all the sugar has been added, scrape down the sides of the bowl again and carry on beating until the mixture is light and fluffy.

2 Break the eggs into a small bowl, add the vanilla and beat with a fork until just mixed. Gradually add to the butter mixture, beating well after each addition and scraping down the sides of the bowl from time to time. Sift the flour into the bowl and gently fold in with a large metal spoon.

3 Transfer the mixture to the prepared tin and spread evenly. Place in the heated oven and bake for 50–55 minutes until risen and golden brown and a skewer inserted into the centre of the cake comes out clean.

4 While the cake is baking make the lime syrup. Put the juice and sugar in a small pan and heat gently, stirring, until the sugar dissolves. Bring to the boil, then remove from the heat. Keep hot.

5 When the cake is ready, remove from the oven and set it on a wire rack (do not turn it out). Prick the surface of the cake all over with a wooden cocktail stick. Spoon the hot syrup over the top of the cake and leave to soak in and cool.

6 When the cake is cold run a round-bladed knife around the cake to loosen it from the tin, then gently lift the cake out of the tin using the long strip of paper to help you. Set the cake on the wire rack.

7 Now make the glaze. Sift the icing sugar into a mixing bowl and add the zest, then stir in enough lime juice to make a thick but runny icing. Spoon the icing over the cake and allow to drip down the sides. Leave to set before slicing. Store the cake in an airtight container and eat within 5 days.

STICKY CHOCOLATE GINGERBREAD

Like all good ginger cakes, this is made by melting butter in a pan with sugar and syrups before whisking in flour, spices, eggs and milk (the melting method). But this round cake also has dark chocolate added to the sticky dark gingerbread mix – a great combination. You can leave it at that or, for even more richness, top with Ginger and Chocolate Icing (opposite).

MAKES 1 MEDIUM CAKE
YOU WILL NEED: 1 X 20.5CM ROUND SPRINGCLIP TIN, GREASED AND BASE-LINED

125g unsalted butter
125g dark brown muscovado sugar
2 lumps (about 40g) stem ginger in syrup, drained and chopped
2 tablespoons ginger syrup from the jar
200g golden syrup
250g self-raising flour
good pinch of salt
4 teaspoons ground ginger

1 teaspoon ground mixed spice
1 teaspoon ground cinnamon
1 teaspoon bicarbonate of soda
2 medium free-range eggs, at room temperature
250ml milk, at room temperature
100g dark chocolate or chocolate chips (about 70% cocoa solids) OR 1 x 100g bar dark chocolate with crystallised ginger

1 Heat your oven to 180°C/350°F/gas 4. Cut the butter into chunks and put into a medium-sized pan with the sugar, chopped stem ginger, ginger syrup and golden syrup. Stir gently over low heat until melted. Remove from the heat and leave to cool for a few minutes until barely warm.

2 While the mix is cooling, sift the flour, salt, ground ginger, mixed spice, cinnamon and bicarbonate of soda into a large mixing bowl. Put the eggs and milk in a small bowl and beat with a fork until just mixed. Finely chop the chocolate (unless using chips).

3 Pour the syrup mixture into the flour mix in the big bowl, add the milk mixture and gently beat everything together with a wire whisk or wooden spoon to make a thick smooth batter (with small pieces of ginger). Stir in the chopped chocolate.

4 Pour into the prepared tin. Place in the heated oven and bake for 40–50 minutes until a skewer inserted in the centre comes out clean (take care

not to undercook this cake or the centre will sink as it comes out of the oven).

5 Set the tin on a wire rack. Run a round-bladed knife around the cake to loosen it from the tin, then leave to cool – the cake will shrink a little. When it is cold unclip the tin side and remove the cake. Wrap in greaseproof paper or foil and keep overnight in an airtight container before cutting. This is best eaten within 6 days.

GINGER AND CHOCOLATE ICING

Here's a quick, optional finish for the Sticky Chocolate Gingerbread (opposite). It also makes a good topping for chocolate cupcakes or can be used to sandwich meringues and sablés (see pages 78–80).

MAKES ENOUGH TO ICE A 20.5CM ROUND CAKE

100g dark chocolate (about 70% cocoa
   solids), chopped or broken up
100g unsalted butter, diced
1 teaspoon ginger syrup from the jar
2 lumps (about 40g) stem ginger
   in syrup, drained

1 Put the chocolate, butter and ginger syrup into a heatproof bowl. Set the bowl over a pan of hot water and melt gently, stirring frequently, until smooth. Remove the bowl from the pan.

2 Dry the lumps of ginger on kitchen paper, then cut into thin slices. Dip into the melted chocolate mixture so they are half-covered. Lay them on a small piece of baking paper and set aside. Leave the rest of the chocolate mix to cool, stirring occasionally, until it has thickened but is still fluid.

3 Turn the cold cake over so the flat underside is facing up and set on a serving platter. Spoon the chocolate mixture over the top of the cake and allow it to drip a little down the sides. Leave to set, then decorate with the slices of ginger.

LEMON MERINGUE CAKE

This has an ultra-lemony filling and fluffy white meringue, plus a light lemon-soaked whisked sponge. There's a fair amount of work here, but everything can be assembled a day before serving. The lemon curd needs to be thoroughly chilled so weigh it out, then cover and return to the fridge.

MAKES I LARGE CAKE
YOU WILL NEED: 2 X 20.5CM DEEP ROUND CAKE TINS, GREASED AND BASE-LINED, THEN DUSTED WITH PLAIN FLOUR

I Heat your oven to 180°C/350°F/gas 4. To make the sponges put the eggs into a mixing bowl and whisk until frothy. Add the sugar and whisk for about 5 minutes until the mixture has greatly expanded and is very light and mousse-like – stop whisking when the mix will make a ribbon trail on itself.

2 Sift a third of the flour plus the salt into the bowl and very gently fold into the mousse using a large metal spoon. Repeat to add the rest of the flour in 2 batches, and stop folding as soon as you can no longer see any specks of flour.

3 Divide the mixture equally between the prepared tins and gently spread evenly. Place in the heated oven and bake for 17–20 minutes until a light golden brown and the top of each sponge springs back when gently pressed in the centre.

4 While the sponges are baking cover a large wire rack with a sheet of baking paper and sprinkle this with caster sugar. As soon as the sponges are ready, remove them from the oven. Run a round-bladed knife around each sponge to loosen it from its tin, then turn out on to the sugared paper so the sponge is browned crust-side down. Carefully remove the lining paper and leave until the cakes are cold.

5 While the sponges are cooling, make the lemon syrup. Put the sugar and lemon zest and juice into a small, heavy-based pan and heat gently, stirring frequently, until the sugar has completely dissolved. Bring to the boil and simmer for a couple of minutes to make a light syrup. Keep hot.

6 Place one sponge, still upside down, on a cake board or serving platter and brush with half of the hot syrup. Brush the second sponge – still upside down on the wire rack – with the rest of the syrup. Leave to soak in for an hour.

7 Spread the chilled lemon curd over the sponge on the cake board. Set the second sponge, browned crust-side up, on top. Very lightly cover the cake (or put it into a large container) and chill for a couple of hours.

8 For the meringue frosting, put all the ingredients into a large heatproof bowl and beat with a hand-held electric mixer on low speed for a minute. Set the bowl over a pan of simmering water (don't let the base of the bowl touch the water) and whisk on high speed for about 7 minutes to make a very thick, stiff, white and glossy meringue. Remove the bowl from the pan, set it on a heatproof surface and whisk for a further 5 minutes until the meringue is cold.

9 Now you need to work quickly, while the meringue is still pliable. Remove the cake from the fridge and rapidly cover the sides, and then the top, with the meringue, swirling and peaking it with a round-bladed knife or palette knife – rather like adding the topping to a lemon meringue pie. Once the meringue looks good, lightly brown it with a kitchen blowtorch. Leave uncovered at cool room temperature (not the fridge) to firm up – overnight if possible – before cutting. Store in an airtight container and eat within a couple of days.

250g Lemon Curd (see page 38), well chilled

For the whisked sponges
4 medium free-range eggs, at room temperature
120g caster sugar, plus extra for sprinkling
120g plain flour
pinch of salt

For the lemon syrup
75g caster sugar
finely grated zest and juice of 1 medium unwaxed lemon

For the meringue frosting
2 medium free-range egg whites, at room temperature
¼ teaspoon cream of tartar
good pinch of salt
4 tablespoons water
300g caster sugar

LEMON CURD

This is a stiffer and less sweet version than the usual curd, making it perfect for filling sponge cakes as well as to use in a bread and butter pudding (see recipe on page 269).

MAKES ABOUT 400G
YOU WILL NEED: 2 X STERILISED 200G SCREW-TOP JARS

70g unsalted butter, diced
125g caster sugar
finely grated zest of 3 medium unwaxed
    lemons
100ml lemon juice
2 medium free-range eggs plus 2 yolks, at
    room temperature

1 Put the butter, sugar, and lemon zest and juice into a heatproof bowl. Set the bowl over a pan of simmering water (don't let the base of the bowl touch the water) and stir with a wooden spoon until the sugar has completely dissolved – you should no longer feel or see any gritty crystals in the base of the bowl.

2 Remove the bowl from the pan and set it on a heatproof surface. Beat the whole eggs with the yolks in a small bowl with a fork until well mixed, then strain into the lemon mixture and mix well. Set the bowl over the pan of simmering water again and stir the mixture until it becomes very thick and opaque. Don't be tempted to hurry things by turning the heat up: the eggs will scramble if the mixture gets anywhere near boiling. The lemon curd is ready when you can draw a finger through the mixture on the wooden spoon and make a clear path.

3 Immediately lift the bowl from the pan and spoon the lemon curd into 2 screw-topped jars or other containers. Cover with wax discs if using, then leave until cold. Seal tightly with lids or clingfilm and store in the fridge. Use within 2 weeks.

HONEY AND COURGETTE LOAF

Grated courgette adds moistness to this unusual wholemeal loaf cake, while honey provides sweetness, and hazelnuts and chocolate chips make sure there is plenty of texture. The recipe is easy – just mix and bake.

MAKES 1 LOAF CAKE
YOU WILL NEED: 1 X 900G LOAF TIN (ABOUT 26 X 12.5 X 7.5CM), GREASED AND LINED WITH A LONG STRIP OF BAKING PAPER TO COVER THE BASE AND 2 SHORT SIDES

2 medium free-range eggs,
   at room temperature
100g clear honey
100ml sunflower oil
70g light brown muscovado sugar
1 medium courgette (about 200g)

225g plain wholemeal flour
2 teaspoons baking powder
1 teaspoon ground mixed spice
50g chopped toasted hazelnuts
100g dark or milk chocolate chips
1 tablespoon honey, warmed, to finish

1 Heat your oven to 180°C/350°F/gas 4. Break the eggs into a large mixing bowl. Add the honey, sunflower oil and sugar and beat with a wooden spoon until thoroughly combined.

2 Rinse and dry the courgette, then trim off the ends. Coarsely grate the courgette and weigh 175g (you won't need the rest). Stir into the egg mixture.

3 Sift the flour, baking powder and mixed spice into the bowl; add any pieces of bran left in the sieve too. Mix in with the wooden spoon, then stir in the nuts and chocolate chips until thoroughly combined.

4 Transfer the mixture to the prepared tin and spread evenly. Place in the heated oven and bake for about 45 minutes until a good golden brown and a skewer inserted into the centre of the cake comes out clean.

5 Set the tin on a wire rack and immediately brush the top of the cake with the warmed honey. Run a round-bladed knife around the cake to loosen it from the tin, then leave to cool for 15 minutes. Carefully lift the cake out of the tin and on to the rack, using the strip of lining paper to help you. Leave until the cake is cold before slicing. Store in an airtight container and eat within 4 days.

ORANGE AND OLIVE OIL LOAF

Made with white spelt flour, which has a 'nuttier' taste than regular plain flour, this unusual cake is quick to put together. Olive oil adds a gentle fruity flavour and moist texture. There's no need to use an expensive olive oil, but for the best results pick one that's fairly light and just mildly peppery.

MAKES 1 LARGE LOAF CAKE
YOU WILL NEED: 1 X 900G LOAF TIN (ABOUT 26 X 12.5 X 7.5CM), GREASED AND LINED WITH A LONG STRIP OF BAKING PAPER TO COVER THE BASE AND 2 SHORT SIDES

2 medium free-range eggs, at room
    temperature
125ml mild, fruity, extra virgin olive oil
finely grated zest of 1 large orange
175ml semi-skimmed or full-fat milk
200g caster sugar

200g white spelt flour
½ teaspoon baking powder
½ bicarbonate of soda
good pinch of salt
1 tablespoon marmalade, warmed, to finish

1 Heat your oven to 160°C/325°F/gas 3. Break the eggs into a large mixing bowl. Add the oil, orange zest and milk and whisk with a balloon whisk until thoroughly combined. Whisk in the sugar. Sift the flour, baking powder, bicarbonate of soda and salt into the bowl and mix in well with a wooden spoon to make a smooth but runny batter-like mixture.

2 Transfer the mixture to the prepared tin and spread evenly. Place in the heated oven and bake for 55–60 minutes until risen and golden brown and a skewer inserted into the centre of the cake comes out clean.

3 Set the tin on a wire rack. Immediately brush the top of the cake with the warmed marmalade. Run a round-bladed knife around the cake to loosen it from the tin, then leave to cool completely before removing it from the tin. Store in an airtight container and eat within 5 days.

VANILLA MACAROON CAKE

A decoration of macaroons transforms a vanilla sponge cake – those here, flavoured with coconut and almonds, are attached to the cake with jam or chocolate. The topping is a giant crunchy macaroon, added to the cake halfway through baking.

MAKES I LARGE CAKE
YOU WILL NEED: I–2 BAKING SHEETS, LINED WITH BAKING PAPER; I X 20.5CM ROUND SPRINGCLIP TIN, GREASED AND BASED-LINED

For the macaroons
100g desiccated coconut
100g ground almonds
100g flaked almonds
250g caster sugar
2 tablespoons cornflour
2 medium free-range egg whites,
   at room temperature
½ teaspoon vanilla extract

For the cake mixture
225g unsalted butter, softened
225g caster sugar
4 medium free-range eggs,
   at room temperature
I teaspoon vanilla extract
200g self-raising flour
25g desiccated coconut
25g ground almonds
2–3 tablespoons apricot jam or melted
   chocolate, to finish

I Heat your oven to 160°C/325°F/gas 3. Make the macaroons first. Put the coconut, ground and flaked almonds, sugar and cornflour in a mixing bowl. In another bowl whisk the egg whites and vanilla together with a fork for a minute or so until frothy, then add to the dry ingredients. Mix well with a wooden spoon to make a stiff mixture. Leave to firm up for 10 minutes.

2 Set aside half of the mixture to top the cake. Carefully spoon the rest of the mixture on to the lined baking sheets to make about 15 macaroons 4cm across and about 1.5cm high. Space them well apart to allow for spreading. Place in the heated oven and bake for 15–20 minutes until a light golden brown. Remove from the oven and leave the macaroons on the baking sheets until completely cold before peeling them off the baking paper.

3 While the macaroons are cooling, turn up the oven to 180°C/350°F/gas 4, and make the cake. Put the soft butter into a mixing bowl and beat with an electric mixer until creamy. Gradually whisk in the sugar, scraping down the sides of the bowl from time to time. Once all the sugar has been incorporated, beat for a couple of minutes until the mixture is light and fluffy, scraping down the bowl as before.

4 Beat the eggs with the vanilla in another bowl until just mixed, then gradually add to the butter mixture, beating well after each addition and scraping down the bowl as before. To prevent the mixture from curdling add a tablespoon of the flour with each of the last 2 additions of egg. Sift the rest of the flour into the bowl. Add the coconut and ground almonds and carefully fold in with a large metal spoon until thoroughly combined.

5 Transfer the mixture to the prepared tin and spread evenly. Place in the heated oven and bake for 45 minutes. At this point the mixture will only be half cooked and barely set. Carefully remove from the oven and gently spoon the rest of the macaroon mixture on top of the cake to make an even layer.

6 Return the cake to the oven, reduce the heat to 160°C/325°F/gas 3 and bake for a further 30–35 minutes until the macaroon topping is golden brown and a skewer inserted into the centre of the cake comes out clean (make sure you find the middle of the cake mixture below the macaroon). Keep an eye on the cake towards the end of the baking time – you may have to cover the top with a sheet of foil to prevent the macaroon from getting too brown.

7 Set the tin on a wire rack. Gently run a round-bladed knife around the cake to loosen it from the tin, then unclip the tin side. Once the cake is cold, remove it from the tin.

8 To finish, set the cake on a serving platter. Cover the side of the cake with the macaroons, using a dab of jam or melted chocolate as glue. If the macaroons are slightly too tall then trim them to the height of the cake (place them so the trimmed edge is at the base of the cake). Store in an airtight container and eat within 3 days. The cake and macaroons can also be stored separately for 4 days before assembling.

CHEDDAR, APPLE AND WALNUT LOAF

Richer than a scone or soda bread, here is a robust savoury cake that is good thickly sliced for a snack or to go with soup or a salad. The cake is packed with flavour and texture, and even better a day after baking.

MAKES 1 MEDIUM LOAF CAKE
YOU WILL NEED: 1 X 450G LOAF TIN (ABOUT 19 X 12.5 X 7.5CM), GREASED AND LINED WITH A LONG STRIP OF BAKING PAPER TO COVER THE BASE AND 2 SHORT SIDES

50g walnut pieces
175g self-raising flour
¼ teaspoon salt
125g unsalted butter, chilled and diced
50g bran flake cereal
125g extra mature Cheddar cheese, grated
1 medium eating apple, cored and cut into small pieces

3 medium free-range eggs, at room temperature

To finish
25g extra-mature Cheddar cheese, grated

1 Heat your oven to 180°C/350°F/gas 4. Spread the walnut pieces in a small baking dish or tin and toast in the heated oven for 8–10 minutes until they turn a light golden brown. Set aside to cool, leaving the oven on.

2 Sift the flour and salt into a big mixing bowl. Add the diced butter and rub into the flour with your fingertips until the mixture looks like coarse crumbs. Gently crush the bran flakes in your hands, just to make them slightly smaller (they shouldn't be like crumbs), and add to the bowl with the cooled walnuts, grated cheese and apple.

3 Lightly beat the eggs in a small bowl with a fork, just to mix. Add to the big bowl and stir in with a wooden spoon to make a stiff mixture (similar to a rock cake mixture).

4 Spoon the mixture into the prepared tin and spread evenly. Scatter the 25g Cheddar cheese on top. Place in the heated oven and bake for 45–50 minutes until a good golden brown and a skewer inserted into the centre of the loaf comes out clean.

5 Set the tin on a wire rack. Run a round-bladed knife around the loaf to loosen it from the tin, then leave it to cool for 20 minutes before turning out. Once cold wrap in foil and eat within 2 days.

SIMPLE FRUIT CAKE

For a traditional, festive touch you can replace the lemon juice with a tablespoon of brandy, sherry or dark rum. Finish the cake with a marzipan topping covered with white icing and your favourite Christmas decorations or leave the cake plain, simply tied with a pretty ribbon.

MAKES 1 LARGE CAKE
YOU WILL NEED: 1 X 20.5CM SPRINGCLIP TIN OR ROUND DEEP CAKE TIN, GREASED AND LINED (WITH BAKING PAPER OR A READY-MADE CAKE LINER)

For the cake
175g unsalted butter, softened
175g dark brown muscovado sugar
finely grated zest of 1 unwaxed lemon plus 1 tablespoon juice
4 medium free-range eggs, at room temperature
250g plain flour
1 teaspoon ground mixed spice

500g luxury mixed dried fruit (with glacé cherries and apricots)
200g marzipan

To finish
2 tablespoons apricot jam or apricot glaze
300g marzipan
icing sugar, for dusting
½ quantity Royal Icing (opposite)
Christmas ribbon or decorations

1 Heat your oven to 150°C/300°F/gas 2. Put the soft butter, sugar and lemon zest into a large mixing bowl (set the bowl on a damp cloth so it doesn't wobble). Beat with an electric mixer for about 3 minutes until the mixture looks very smooth (no lumps of sugar) and it has turned much paler in colour. Scrape down the sides of the bowl every minute or so.

2 Lightly beat the eggs in a small bowl, just to mix. Gradually add the eggs to the butter mixture, a tablespoonful at a time, beating well after each addition and scraping down the sides of the large bowl from time to time. To prevent the mixture from curdling, add a tablespoonful of the flour with the last 2 additions of egg.

3 Sift the rest of the flour and the mixed spice into the bowl. Add the lemon juice and gently fold into the butter mixture with a large metal spoon. Add the mixed fruit and fold in until thoroughly combined with the cake mixture. Cut the marzipan into cubes about 1.5cm and gently fold into the cake mixture.

4 Spoon the mixture into the prepared tin and smooth the surface so it is even. Place in the heated oven and bake for 2–2½ hours until the cake is a good golden brown and a skewer inserted into the centre comes out clean. It's a good idea to test the cake in several places to make sure you haven't just hit a molten lump of marzipan.

5 Set the tin on a wire rack and leave to cool. When the cake is completely cold remove it from the tin and peel off the lining paper. Wrap the cake in greaseproof paper or foil and store it in an airtight container for at least a day before you add the finishing touches.

6 When you're ready to finish the cake, place it upside down on a cake board or serving platter (the flat underside is smoother for icing). Gently warm the apricot jam in a small bowl in the microwave for 10 seconds (or in a small pan over very low heat), then brush it over the top of the cake to make a sticky surface for the marzipan.

7 Gently mould the marzipan in your hands to make a ball. Sprinkle your worktop with a little icing sugar, then roll out the marzipan to a circle about the same size as the top of the cake and as thick as two stacked one pound coins. Set the (empty) cake tin on the marzipan and cut around it with a small sharp knife to make the circle very neat. Lift the marzipan circle on to the cake and press it down firmly with your palm. Cover the cake loosely with a sheet of clingfilm or an upturned cake tin and leave it to firm up overnight.

8 Spoon the royal icing on to the marzipan on top of the cake and spread it out with a round-bladed knife to cover the marzipan completely. You can make a smooth surface or swirl the icing into peaks or even a ski-slope, ready for your decorations. If you're adding edible sprinkles or sparkles, you can do this while the icing is still soft and sticky, then leave overnight to set firm. Add non-edible decorations or a ribbon the next day. Store in an airtight container and eat within 3 weeks.

ROYAL ICING

This snow-white icing can be spread smooth or swirled into peaks. It is also suitable for piping and for 'flooding' and run-outs. If you are covering a cake, add a few drops of glycerine to the icing so it sets firm but not inedibly rock-hard.

Royal icing can be tinted using food colouring pastes, which are available in many colours and even shimmery tones. Add a tiny amount of colouring using a cocktail stick and mix in well before adding more – some colours darken as they set.

MAKES ENOUGH TO COVER A 20.5CM ROUND DEEP CAKE

**2 large free-range egg whites (very fresh),
  at room temperature
few drops of lemon juice**

**½ teaspoon glycerine (optional – use
  if covering a formal celebration cake)
500–600g icing sugar, sifted**

1 Using a wooden spoon, beat the egg whites with the lemon juice, and glycerine if using, in a large bowl until thoroughly combined. Gradually beat in the icing sugar – the icing must be very smooth with no air bubbles, which could ruin the final appearance. (If your icing does have a lot of bubbles simply press a piece of clingfilm on to the surface and leave at room temperature overnight.)

2 Icing for coating and piping should be fairly thick and leave a solid trail on its surface when the spoon is lifted out. Icing for run-outs and flooding should be slightly softer and almost runny, so add a few more drops of lemon juice. Once made the icing can be kept – with clingfilm pressed on to the surface, and the bowl also tightly covered – for up to a week. Don't attempt to freeze royal icing.

3 To make piped and run-out shapes to attach to cookies and cakes, spoon the icing into a piping bag fitted with a small plain tube and pipe the outline of the shape on a tray lined with baking paper (if necessary draw the shape first on the underside of the paper to guide you). Fill in the shape with slightly softer icing, spreading it right up to the piped lines. Leave to set overnight. You can also pipe on top of the icing shapes in a contrasting colour.

Variation: Quick Royal Icing

Put 5 tablespoons water into a large mixing bowl and gradually add 500g Royal Icing sugar (about a tablespoonful at a time), beating with a wooden spoon or hand-held electric mixer on low speed until the icing is very thick. To check if the icing is the right consistency, lift out the spoon or whisk: the tips of the icing peaks should just flop over. If the icing is runny or too floppy, beat in more sugar a teaspoon at a time; if the icing feels too stiff or seems hard to spread, stir in more water a few drops at a time. Use immediately, while the icing is spreadable, then leave to set firm.

CRANBERRY AND MARZIPAN CAKE

A pretty red-flecked golden sponge, rich with seasonal flavours – cranberries, nuts and marzipan – this makes a lighter alternative to a traditional fruit cake or, served warm with ice cream or custard (see recipe on page 255), for Christmas pudding. Like most cakes made with nuts it tastes even better a day or so after baking.

MAKES 1 MEDIUM CAKE
YOU WILL NEED: 1 X 20.5CM ROUND SPRINGCLIP TIN, GREASED AND BASE-LINED

115g cranberries (thawed if frozen)
100g unsalted butter, softened
65g caster sugar
200g marzipan
3 medium free-range eggs, at room
    temperature
120g ground almonds
120g plain flour
2 teaspoons baking powder
25g flaked almonds
icing sugar, for dusting

1 Heat your oven to 180°C/350°F/gas 4. Chop the cranberries fairly coarsely in a food processor or by hand. Set aside until needed.

2 Put the soft butter and sugar into a mixing bowl and beat with a hand-held electric mixer until light and creamy. Scrape down the sides of the bowl. Crumble or break up the marzipan into small pieces and add to the bowl. Beat thoroughly until very smooth and creamy, scraping down the sides from time to time.

3 Beat the eggs in a small bowl with a fork until broken up, then gradually add to the butter mixture, beating well after each addition and scraping down the bowl as before. Gently stir in the ground almonds with a large metal spoon.

4 Sift the flour and baking powder into the bowl and fold in with the metal spoon. As soon as all the flour has been incorporated, carefully fold in the cranberries. Avoid over-mixing at this point – stop as soon as the cranberries look evenly distributed in the cake mixture.

5 Scrape the mixture into the prepared tin and spread evenly. Scatter the flaked almonds over the top. Place in the heated oven and bake for 40–45 minutes until risen and golden brown and a skewer inserted into the centre comes out clean.

6 Set the tin on a wire rack. Run a round-bladed knife around the cake to loosen it from the tin, then carefully unclip the tin side and leave the cake to cool completely. Once cold, wrap in greaseproof paper or foil and store in an airtight container overnight. Dust with icing sugar before serving.

WEEKEND BAKING

Recipes from Mary, Paul and the bakers

- Spiced and Iced Carrot Cake

- Mary's Angel Food Cake with Lemon Curd

- Mary's Spiced Whole Orange Cake

- Mary's Opera Cake

- Mary and Paul's Chocolate Creation

- Carrot and Pistachio Cake

SPICED AND ICED CARROT CAKE

A richly flavoured, very moist cake with plenty of spice, sandwiched and topped with a vibrant orange cream cheese icing.

MAKES 1 LARGE CAKE
YOU WILL NEED: 2 X 20.5CM DEEP SANDWICH TINS, GREASED WITH BUTTER AND BASE-LINED

For the cake
4 large free-range eggs, at room
  temperature
175ml light olive oil
115g light muscovado sugar
115g dark muscovado sugar
225g plain flour
2½ teaspoons baking powder
½ teaspoon freshly grated nutmeg
1 teaspoon ground cinnamon
¼ teaspoon ground cloves
375g carrots (6–7 medium), coarsely grated
75g walnut pieces
75g desiccated coconut
100g raisins
finely grated zest of 1 large navel orange

For the candied peel
1 large navel orange
20g caster sugar
3 tablespoons water

For the drizzle syrup
juice of 1 large navel orange
juice of 1 medium lemon
50g caster sugar

For the icing
135g unsalted butter, at room temperature
200g full-fat cream cheese, at room
  temperature
115g icing sugar
4 tablespoons Orange Curd (see page 55),
  well chilled
50g walnut halves, to decorate

1 Heat your oven to 180°C/350°F/gas 4. Start by making the cake. Put the eggs, olive oil and both muscovado sugars into a large mixing bowl. Whisk with an electric mixer for 4–5 minutes until very frothy. Sift the flour, baking powder and spices into the bowl and gently fold in with a large metal spoon. Add the carrots, walnut pieces, coconut, raisins and grated zest to the bowl and fold in until thoroughly combined.

2 Spoon the mixture into the prepared tins and spread evenly. Place in the heated oven and bake for 30–35 minutes until a skewer inserted into the centre of each cake comes out clean.

3 While the cake layers are baking, make the candied peel and the drizzle syrup. Using a vegetable peeler, carefully shave strips of coloured peel off the orange, leaving all the white pith on the fruit. Cut the strips into very thin shreds and put them into a small pan. Add water to cover. Bring to the boil, then simmer gently for 10–12 minutes until soft. Drain the shreds, then return them to the pan and add the sugar and 3 tablespoons water. Heat gently until the sugar has dissolved, then simmer for a few minutes until the mixture becomes thick and syrupy. Pour the candied peel on to a heatproof plate and leave until cold.

4 For the drizzle syrup, put the orange and lemon juices in the rinsed-out pan that you used for the candied peel. Add the sugar and heat gently until it has dissolved, then bring to the boil and boil for 1 minute. Remove from the heat and keep warm.

5 When the cake layers are ready, remove from the oven and set the tins on a wire rack. Prick the cakes all over with a cocktail stick, then quickly spoon 3 tablespoons of the hot drizzle syrup over each cake. Leave to soak in and cool completely in the tins.

6 To make the icing, put the butter into a large bowl and beat thoroughly with an electric mixer or wooden spoon. Beat in the cream cheese until smooth and evenly combined. Sift in the icing sugar and mix in, on low speed if using an electric mixer. Stir in the chilled orange curd. Cover and chill the icing until it is firm enough to spread.

7 When ready to assemble the cake, turn out the cake layers on to a large board. Spread half of the icing over the top of each sponge, then set one on top of the other. Transfer the cake to a serving platter. Swirl the icing on the top of the cake using the handle of a teaspoon. Decorate with the strips of candied peel and walnut halves. Store in an airtight container in a cool spot. Best eaten within 4 days.

Decorate with strips of candied peel

ORANGE CURD

Use this to flavour butter icing as well as the cream cheese frosting and filling on page 52. Or spread on buttered scones for tea.

MAKES ABOUT 100G

3 large navel oranges
2 large free-range eggs, at room
 temperature
juice of ½ medium lemon
75g caster sugar
75g unsalted butter, diced

1 Finely grate the zest from the oranges into a medium heatproof mixing bowl. Cut 1 or 2 of the oranges in half and squeeze out the juice into a measuring jug – you need about 100ml. Pour the juice into a small pan and boil rapidly until reduced to about 2 tablespoons. Add this reduced juice to the bowl containing the zest and leave to cool a bit until lukewarm.

2 Lightly beat the eggs in a small bowl with a fork, just to mix. Add to the heatproof bowl with the lemon juice, sugar and butter and set the bowl over a pan of simmering water. Stir constantly with a wooden spoon until the butter has melted and the sugar dissolved. Keep stirring until the mixture thickens, but don't let it get near to boiling.

3 Quickly pour the curd into another heatproof bowl. Leave to cool, then cover with clingfilm and chill thoroughly. The curd can be kept in the fridge for up to 2 days.

MARY'S ANGEL FOOD CAKE WITH LEMON CURD

A pure white, light-as-air sponge mixture made with a great many egg whites – the yolks are used to make lemon curd. The cake is covered with whipped cream and finished with a bright topping of lemon curd and passionfruit.

MAKES I LARGE CAKE (TO SERVE 12–15) PLUS 2 X 350G JARS LEMON CURD
YOU WILL NEED: I X 25CM ANGEL FOOD CAKE PAN WITH LEGS, 2 X 350G STERILISED JAM JARS

For the cake
125g plain flour
300g caster sugar
10 large egg whites, at room
   temperature
finely grated zest of 2 large
   unwaxed lemons
I tablespoon lemon juice
I teaspoon cream of tartar
½ teaspoon salt

For the lemon curd
10 large egg yolks
400g caster sugar
finely grated zest of 2 large unwaxed lemons
juice of 4 large lemons – about 200ml
175g unsalted butter, cubed

For the topping
300ml whipping cream, well chilled
½ teaspoon vanilla extract
2 passionfruits

1 Heat your oven to 170°C/325°F/gas 3. Place the oven shelf in the bottom third of the oven.

2 Sift the flour and 100g of the caster sugar into a bowl and set aside. Put the egg whites into a very large bowl and whisk with an electric mixer on high speed for 1 minute until frothy. Add the lemon zest and juice, cream of tartar and salt and continue whisking for 2–3 minutes until soft peaks will form when the whisk is lifted. Whisking on high speed, add the remaining 200g sugar a tablespoon at a time, then whisk until the whites form firm but not stiff peaks.

3 Sprinkle a third of the flour mixture over the egg whites and gently fold in with a large metal spoon or plastic spatula until combined. Repeat with the remaining flour mixture, in 2 batches, folding gently to keep as much air in the mixture as possible.

Whisk until firm peaks form

Mary's tip: To make a home-made angel food pan, use a 25cm loose-bottomed cake tin and set an empty, clean fizzy drink can in the centre.

4 Transfer the mixture to the ungreased pan, then gently run a knife through the centre of the mix to dislodge any large pockets of air. Place in the heated oven and bake for 45–50 minutes until a skewer inserted into the centre of the cake comes out clean.

5 Remove the pan from the oven and immediately turn it upside down on its cooling legs. (If your pan doesn't have legs, turn the pan upside down and support the centre hole on a jam jar or can of food so that the surface of the cake is exposed to the air as it cools.) Leave to cool for at least 1 hour. Run a palette knife around the inner and outer edges of the cake to loosen it from the pan, then invert the pan on to a plate and use a palette knife to loosen the cake from the base of the pan, if necessary. Leave to cool completely on a wire rack.

6 Meanwhile make the lemon curd. Mix together the egg yolks, sugar and lemon zest and juice in a large pan. Cook gently over low heat, stirring with a wooden spoon (make sure to stir the sides and base of the pan thoroughly) for 5–7 minutes until the mixture thickens enough to coat the back of the spoon. Remove from the heat and stir in the butter until melted and smooth.

7 Strain the lemon curd through a sieve into a large jug. Fill two 350g sterilised glass jars with curd and seal each with a lid. When the curd is completely cold, store the jars in the fridge for up to 2 months. Put the remaining lemon curd in a bowl, cover with clingfilm and leave to cool – this will be used for topping the cake.

8 When ready to assemble the cake, whip the cream with the vanilla extract until it will form soft peaks when the whisk is lifted. Spoon the cream over the cold cake and, using a palette knife, coat the top and sides, smoothing as you go.

9 Cut the passionfruits in half and scoop out the seeds and pulp. Stir into the reserved, cooled lemon curd and drizzle over the angel food cake before serving.

Run a knife through the centre of the mix in the tin

Mary's tip: You could reserve some lemon curd and serve it in a small jug with the cake, if you prefer.

MARY'S SPICED WHOLE ORANGE CAKE

This cake has a wonderful citrus flavour. Add a little more spice if you want it to be very spicy. You'll need a food processor to make it.

MAKES 1 MEDIUM CAKE
YOU WILL NEED: 2 X 20CM DEEP SANDWICH TINS, GREASED AND BASE-LINED

For the cake
1 small, thin-skinned orange
275g self-raising flour
2 teaspoons baking powder
275g caster sugar
275g baking spread, taken straight from the fridge
4 medium eggs, at room temperature
1 teaspoon ground cinnamon
1 teaspoon ground mixed spice

For the orange icing
50g unsalted butter, softened
175g icing sugar, sifted
250g full-fat mascarpone cheese

To decorate
1 large, thin-skinned orange
50g caster sugar

1 To make the cake put the whole orange in a small pan. Cover it with boiling water from the kettle, then boil for 30 minutes until soft when prodded with the tip of a small knife (top up with more boiling water as needed). Drain the orange and leave to cool.

2 Heat your oven to 180°C/350°F/gas 4. When the orange is cold, cut it in half and remove any pips. Put the whole orange, including the skin, into a food processor and blitz until you have a medium chunky texture. Remove 2 tablespoons of the mixture and save for the icing. Scoop out the remaining pulp into a bowl and set aside.

3 Add the remaining cake ingredients to the processor (no need to rinse out the bowl) and blitz until just smooth – be careful not to overbeat the mixture. Remove the blade, then carefully stir in the orange pulp using a plastic spatula.

Carefully stir in the orange pulp

4 Divide the cake mixture equally between the prepared tins and spread it out evenly. Place in the heated oven and bake for 30–35 minutes until the sponges are well risen, lightly golden brown and shrinking away from the sides of the tins. Allow to cool in the tins for a few minutes, then turn out the sponges on to a wire rack. Peel off the paper and leave to cool completely.

5 To make the icing, put the soft butter into a mixing bowl and gradually beat in the icing sugar using a hand-held electric mixer. When the mixture is very smooth add the mascarpone and beat together until thoroughly combined. Add the reserved 2 tablespoons of orange pulp and mix in evenly with a wooden spoon.

6 Carefully slice each sponge in half horizontally to make 2 layers. Divide the icing into 4 portions, then use to sandwich the 4 layers, finishing with icing on the top.

7 For the decoration, use a rinder or canelle peeler to take long, thick strips of coloured peel from the large orange. Alternatively, thinly peel the orange using a vegetable peeler, then cut the peel into fine pencil-thin strips. (Use the leftover orange for juice or a fruit salad.) Put the orange peel strips into a small pan. Cover with boiling water from the kettle and add half the sugar, then boil for 1 minute.

8 Drain the strips and place them on a small sheet of baking paper. Sprinkle over the remaining sugar and toss the strips gently to coat (they will curl). Leave in a warm place to dry out for as long as possible – overnight is best. Decorate the cake with the orange curls. This cake is best eaten on the day it is made, but can be kept for up to 3 days in a cool place.

Sandwich the 4 layers

MARY'S OPERA CAKE

A richly flavoured cake made from 4 layers of almond sponge, soaked in a kirsch syrup and sandwiched with a French vanilla buttercream and dark chocolate ganache. The perfect decoration is simple and very elegant – tiny glazed raspberries. The cake is made in an everyday swiss roll tin so that anyone can have a go at making this showstopper cake at home – if they are feeling adventurous!

SERVES 8

YOU WILL NEED: I SWISS ROLL TIN, 23 X 33CM, BUTTERED AND LINED WITH BAKING PAPER

For the kirsch soaking syrup
100g caster sugar
200ml water
3 tablespoons kirsch

For the joconde sponge
3 medium egg whites, at room
    temperature
15g caster sugar
100g ground almonds
100g icing sugar, sifted
3 medium eggs, at room temperature
30g plain flour, sifted
30g unsalted butter, melted

For the ganache
100ml double cream
100g dark chocolate (about 36% cocoa
    solids), broken into small pieces

For the crème au beurre
3 medium egg yolks
75g caster sugar
3 tablespoons water
225g unsalted butter, cubed and softened
2 teaspoons vanilla paste

To decorate
70–80 small raspberries
200g seedless raspberry jam, melted

I To make the soaking syrup, put the sugar and water into a small pan. Heat gently, stirring frequently, until the sugar has dissolved, then bring to the boil. Simmer for 4–5 minutes until the syrup has reduced by half. Remove the pan from the heat, add the kirsch and set aside to cool completely.

2 Meanwhile, make the sponge. Heat your oven to 220°C/425°F/gas 7. Put the egg whites into a spotlessly clean mixing bowl (note: the yolks will be used later on for the crème au beurre) and whisk with an electric mixer until they will stand in stiff peaks. Whisk in the caster sugar a teaspoon at a time, whisking between each addition, to make a glossy meringue. Cover the bowl with clingfilm and put on one side.

3 Tip the ground almonds and icing sugar into the bowl of a large free-standing electric mixer (or a

large mixing bowl if using a hand-held electric mixer) and add the whole eggs. Whisk together at high speed for 3–5 minutes until doubled in volume. Gently fold in the flour using a large metal spoon or plastic spatula, then gently fold in the meringue in 3 batches. Pour the melted butter down the side of the bowl and fold in until it is evenly incorporated.

4 Turn the mixture into the prepared tin and level the surface with a palette knife; make sure the mixture goes right into the corners of the tin. Place in the heated oven and bake for 5–7 minutes until a pale golden colour and springy to the touch in the centre. While the cake is baking, lay a sheet of baking paper over a wire rack. Turn out the cooked sponge on to the paper-lined rack, peel off the lining paper and leave to cool completely.

5 To make the ganache, gently heat the cream in a small pan until just bubbling. Remove the pan from the heat and add the pieces of chocolate. Stir until melted, smooth and glossy. Pour into a bowl and leave to set until firm but spreadable.

6 For the crème au beurre, put the egg yolks into the washed and dried bowl of your large electric mixer fitted with the whisk attachment. Put the sugar into a small pan with the water and dissolve over gentle heat, then boil steadily until the syrup reaches 110°C on a sugar thermometer. With the electric mixer running at high speed, slowly pour the syrup over the egg yolks, then continue whisking until the mixture is very thick and mousse-like. Gradually whisk in the butter, then whisk in the vanilla paste.

7 To assemble the cake, slice the sponge in half horizontally, so you have 2 thin 23 x 33cm sponges. Now cut each sponge in half lengthways, so you have 4 sponges each 11.5 x 33cm.

8 Place one of the sponges on a cake board and brush with a quarter of the kirsch syrup. Spread over a third of the crème au beurre. Top with another sponge and brush with another quarter of the syrup, then spread the chocolate ganache over the surface. Set a third sponge on top, brush with half of the remaining syrup and spread over half of the remaining crème au beurre. Add the final sponge, brush with the remaining syrup and spread the rest of the crème au beurre evenly on top.

9 Arrange the raspberries on top of the cake in 14–16 rows of 5, then carefully brush the berries and the top of the cake with the warm melted jam to glaze. Refrigerate the cake for 2 hours to firm up the layers – this makes it easier to trim. Before serving, neatly trim the sides of the cake with a sharp knife to reveal the layers.

Spread ganache on the second sponge layer

MARY AND PAUL'S CHOCOLATE CREATION

A truly impressive 'wow' creation for a special occasion, here is a stack of rich chocolate sponge cakes, filled and covered with a creamy white chocolate ganache and decorated with chocolate lace collars and curls.

MAKES A 3-TIER CAKE
YOU WILL NEED: 2 X 20CM DEEP SANDWICH TINS, I X I5CM CAKE TIN AND I X I0CM CAKE TIN, ALL GREASED AND THE BASE AND SIDES LINED WITH BAKING PAPER, A SUGAR THERMOMETER

For the cakes
125g cocoa powder, sifted
200ml boiling water
6 large eggs, at room temperature
100ml milk, at room temperature
350g self-raising flour
I tablespoon baking powder
200g unsalted butter, softened
550g caster sugar

For the white chocolate ganache
400g white chocolate
300ml double pouring cream (not thick spooning cream)

300g full-fat cream cheese, at room temperature
6 tablespoons apricot jam, to glaze

For the chocolate lace collars
200g dark chocolate (about 70% cocoa solids

For the chocolate curls
100g plain cooking chocolate (also called chocolate cake covering)
100g plain chocolate (about 36% cocoa solids)

I Heat your oven to 180°C/350°F/gas 4. Put the cocoa powder into a large heatproof bowl and stir in the boiling water until smooth. Lightly beat the eggs with a fork in a small bowl, just to mix, then add to the cocoa mix together with the milk, flour, baking powder, butter and sugar. Beat with a wooden spoon or electric mixer until the mixture has become a smooth, thickish batter.

2 Divide the cake mixture among the prepared tins so the 2 sandwich tins are each half full, and the 2 smaller cake tins are each two-thirds full. Spread the mixture evenly. Place all 4 tins in the heated oven. Bake until well risen and the tops spring back when lightly pressed: 25–30 minutes for the sandwich cakes, 35–40 minutes for the 10cm cake and 45–50 minutes for the 15cm cake. Check halfway through the baking time and rotate the tins if the cakes are cooking unevenly.

3 Allow the cakes to cool in their tins for a few minutes, then turn them out on to a wire rack. Peel off the lining paper, then leave them to cool completely. (The cakes can be made up to a day in advance and kept well wrapped or in an airtight container until needed.)

4 While the cakes are cooling make the white chocolate ganache. Break or chop up the chocolate into even-sized pieces. Heat the double cream in a medium-sized pan until just hot enough to melt the chocolate – small bubbles will have appeared around the edge of the pan. Drop the chocolate into the cream and stir gently until melted and smooth. Remove from the heat and leave to cool until stone cold.

5 Beat the cream cheese in a bowl to soften it, using a wooden spoon. Gradually beat in the cold chocolate cream. Keep covered, at room temperature, until ready to use.

6 To assemble the creation, cut the 10cm and 15cm cakes in half horizontally, then sandwich the cut cakes back together with some of the ganache. Sandwich the two 20cm sponges together with more of the ganache. Now stack up the cakes on a cake board or platter: put the 20cm sponge cake sandwich on the board first, then set the 15cm cake in the centre of the sponge and top with the 10cm cake, sticking each tier to the one underneath with a little ganache.

7 Warm the apricot jam in a small pan to melt it, then brush all over the stacked cakes. Using a palette knife spread the remaining chocolate ganache over the layered cakes to cover completely.

8 To make the chocolate lace collars, break or chop up the dark chocolate into even-sized pieces. Put 150g of the chocolate into a heatproof bowl, set over a pan of hot water and stir until the chocolate melts and reaches a temperature of 47°C. Remove the bowl from the heat, add the remaining chocolate and stir until smooth and the chocolate has cooled to 31°C.

Assemble the tiers of the cake

Create a lace effect on the strips of paper

9 Cut 2 strips of baking paper or acetate, one measuring 10 x 45cm (for the middle tier) and the other 10 x 60cm (for the bottom tier). Lay the strips on the worktop. Pour the chocolate into a piping bag fitted with a fine writing tube. Holding the bag vertically over the paper, let the chocolate fall out while moving the bag up and down, to create a lace effect on the strips of paper. Don't worry if the chocolate falls outside the paper strips – just gently move the chocolate on to the paper before it sets and sticks to the worktop (see photo on previous page).

10 Leave the chocolate lace to cool for about 15 minutes until just set and firm enough to wrap around the sides of the cake tiers. The ganache on the cake should not have set completely and will be sticky, helping you fix the collar around the cake. Once you have done this, leave the chocolate collars to set completely – about an hour – before carefully peeling off the paper or acetate. (Don't be tempted to set the chocolate collars in the fridge as this could dull the chocolate so it doesn't shine when the paper is removed.)

11 To make the chocolate curls, break or chop up both chocolates, put into a heatproof bowl and melt as before, stirring gently. As soon as the chocolate is smooth pour it over a cold marble or granite surface (or a similarly cold, solid surface) to create a sheet of chocolate about 5mm thick. Leave to cool until just set. Using a cheese plane or a potato peeler, gently shave off very thin slices, starting at the top of the chocolate sheet and continuing down to the bottom in one movement. As you shave off the slices they will curl up.

12 Sprinkle the curls over the top tier of the cake. Store the finished cake in a cool place, but not in the fridge, until ready to serve. This cake is best eaten on the day you assemble and ice it.

Assemble the lace collars

Shave off chocolate curls

CARROT AND PISTACHIO CAKE

Both the carrot cake, flavoured with spices, nuts and raisins, and the buttercreams are dairy-free. Chocolate 'planks' are used to clad the shed and make the fencing surrounding the plot and the veg garden. You can fill the veg patch with shapes of dried apricot and sliced pistachios for carrots, seedlings made from shreds of lime peel, tomato vines made from lime peel and goji berries and so on.

MAKES 1 LARGE CAKE
YOU WILL NEED: 1 TRAYBAKE TIN OR ROASTING TIN 23 X 30 X 5CM, GREASED AND BASE-LINED; A 20.5CM SQUARE CAKE TIN, GREASED AND BASE-LINED

For the carrot cake
800g self-raising flour
½ teaspoon salt
1 tablespoon baking powder
1 tablespoon ground cinnamon
1 tablespoon ground mixed spice
½ teaspoon ground ginger
finely grated zest of 4 limes
750g carrots, grated
200g shelled, unsalted pistachios, chopped
100g pecan nuts, chopped
300g raisins
9 large eggs, at room temperature
500g light brown muscovado sugar
360ml corn or sunflower oil
250ml coconut milk

For the pistachio buttercream
200g dairy-free spread (or unsalted butter), softened
500g icing sugar, sifted
200g shelled, unsalted pistachios, coarsely ground
1 tablespoon lime juice, or to taste

For the plain buttercream
100g dairy-free spread (or unsalted butter), softened
350g icing sugar, sifted
juice of 1½ limes

For the wooden planks
600g dark chocolate (about 70% cocoa solids), tempered (see page 11)

For the decoration
70g poppy seeds (for the soil)
100g shelled unsalted pistachios, ground (for the grass)
2 tablespoons freeze-dried mango pieces (for the path)

plus your choice of 'fruit' and 'veg' for the plot (see page 73)

For the shed roof
225g caster sugar
80ml water
100g flaked almonds

1 To make the cake, heat your oven to 180°C/350°F/gas 4. Sift the flour, salt, baking powder and spices into a very large bowl. Add the lime zest, grated carrots, all the chopped nuts and raisins and mix thoroughly, breaking up any clumps of carrots. Break the eggs into another bowl, add the sugar, oil and coconut milk and mix well with a wire hand whisk. Add this mixture to the flour mixture and mix everything together well with a wooden spoon.

2 Transfer the mixture to the 2 prepared tins, filling them both to the same height. Place in the heated oven and bake for 40–45 minutes until a skewer inserted into the centre of each cake comes out clean. Leave to cool in the tins set on a wire rack.

3 While the cakes are cooling, make the pistachio buttercream. Beat the spread (or butter) with an electric mixer until creamy, then beat in the icing sugar, using slow speed at first. When all the sugar has been incorporated beat at a higher speed for a minute or so until light. Stir in the ground nuts and enough lime juice to make a spreadable icing. Cover and leave at room temperature until needed.

4 Make the plain buttercream in the same way, to make a smooth icing that can be piped. Cover and leave at room temperature until needed.

5 For the 'wooden planks', first cut strips of baking paper to be used as templates for the chocolate. For the fence, cut two 6 × 30cm strips and two 6 × 21cm strips. For the veg patch, cut two 4 × 9cm strips and two 4 × 14cm strips. For the shed cut ten 2 × 14cm strips (for the long sides), five 2 × 10cm strips (for the back), ten 2 × 2.25cm strips (for the front) and one 3 × 5cm strip (for the door) as well as two triangles with a 9cm base and 6cm high (for the gable ends). Set all of these cut paper shapes on a very large sheet of baking paper.

6 The tempered chocolate should be cool and starting to thicken. Spread it fairly thickly – about 3mm – over the paper shapes using an offset palette knife. The chocolate shouldn't be too smooth – you want it to have a textured 'wooden' grain. Leave to set (the chocolate must be completely firm before you assemble the cake.)

6 When ready to assemble, turn out the cakes and trim the tops so they are completely flat. Split the larger cake in half horizontally and sandwich the 2 layers with some of the pistachio buttercream. Set on a large serving board. Spread more of the pistachio buttercream over the top of the cake.

7 Use the smaller cake to make the shed. Cut two 9 × 13cm rectangles. Split each in half horizontally to make a total of 4 layers. Sandwich 3 of the layers together with pistachio buttercream (this is the shed). Spread pistachio buttercream over the fourth layer and save to make the veg patch.

8 Make the roof with the piece of cake left over from the shed (which will be about 20.5 × 7.5cm). Cut it lengthways in half. Trim one of the pieces into a 3-sided prism shape and stick it in place on top of the shed with pistachio buttercream. Cut the remaining piece of cake in half horizontally, then cut each of these 2 slices into a triangle 6cm high with a 9cm base. These are gable ends of the roof – stick them on to the ends of the prism shape with pistachio buttercream. Cover the whole shed with a thick layer of plain buttercream. Set the shed in place near one end on the large cake, and place the veg patch near the other end.

9 Next attach the fence around the sides of the large cake and around the veg patch. First spread (or pipe) plain buttercream on to the sides of the cake and on to the cake surface where you are going to place the veg patch fence. Carefully peel the chocolate strips away from the paper and press them on to the cake (make sure your hands are clean and very dry). In the same way attach the 'planks' to the shed, slightly overlapping them, to cover the sides, and the chocolate triangles to cover the gables.

10 Fill the veg patch with poppy seeds (soil), and cover the area around the shed and veg patch with pistachios (grass). Add a pathway with the mango pieces.

11 To make the roof covering, put the caster sugar and water into a medium pan and heat gently, stirring frequently, until the sugar has dissolved. Meanwhile, arrange the flaked almonds on a silicon mat or an oiled baking sheet to make two 7 × 14cm rectangular shapes. (Leave space between the rectangles.) Once the sugar has dissolved, bring the syrup to the boil and boil rapidly until it turns to a dark caramel. Working quickly, carefully pour the caramel over the almond rectangles to cover them. Leave to set.

12 When the caramel is firm, lift each rectangle off the mat in one piece. If necessary trim it to fit, then press on to the 2 sides of the roof (if the caramel breaks or cracks, just glue it in place with plain buttercream). Add 'fruit' and 'vegetables' to the patch: we made a strawberry patch, using sliced almonds for straw, lime zest for leaves and squashed goji berries for strawberries, as well as a carrot patch made of sliced, dried apricots with sliced pistachio nuts for carrot tops!

Electric scales

Wooden spoon

Food processor

Rolling pin

Square brownie tin

Sugar thermometer

Large mixing bowl

Round cutter

Hand-held mixer

Spatula

Sieve

12-hole muffin tray

Measuring spoons

Pastry brush

Wire rack

BISCUITS AND LITTLE CAKES

These are the quickest and simplest of all bakes. So what will help them go right? Butter not only tastes good, it also helps the structure of the bake. Sugar may be caster, which has a fine grain, or a brown muscovado, which will add a darker colour and flavour and make biscuits slightly chewy. Flour is usually plain or self-raising to give a soft, crumbly texture.

When shaping biscuits, use only a little flour on the worktop and pin – too much flour could make the final result tough and dry. If the dough feels too sticky, wrap it in clingfilm and chill until it is firm.

Most biscuits need to be cooled a bit on the baking sheet before being lifted on to a wire rack. If you need to bake several batches and want to re-use the same baking sheet, rinse the sheet under the cold tap to cool it quickly, then dry and re-line.

EASY PECAN BLONDIES

These blondies – brownies made with white chocolate – look deceptively benign. But using a really good brand of white chocolate gives them a rich taste. To make them even more decadent, mix 100g dark chocolate chips into the blondie mixture with the pecan halves. Or, for a special dessert, cut the blondie cake into larger squares and serve with a warm toffee sauce (see page 254) and scoops of ice cream.

CUTS INTO 36 SQUARES
YOU WILL NEED: 1 X 20.5CM SQUARE BROWNIE TIN OR SHALLOW CAKE TIN, GREASED AND BASE-LINED

175g white chocolate (about 25% cocoa
  solids), chopped or broken up
115g unsalted butter, diced
100g caster sugar
2 medium free-range eggs, at room
  temperature

½ teaspoon vanilla extract
125g plain flour
½ teaspoon baking powder
150g pecan halves

1 Heat your oven to 180°C/350°F/gas 4. Put the chocolate and butter into a heatproof bowl large enough to hold all the ingredients. Set the bowl over a pan of hot water, off the heat, and melt gently, stirring frequently (white chocolate melts at a lower temperature than dark chocolate so watch carefully). As soon as the chocolate has nearly all melted, remove the bowl from the pan and stir until the mixture is smooth.

2 Stir in the sugar (don't worry if the mixture looks curdled at this stage). Leave to cool for 2 minutes or until barely warm.

3 While the chocolate mix is cooling, put the eggs and vanilla in a small bowl and beat with a fork until frothy. Add to the chocolate mixture and stir well with a wooden spoon to make a sleek and glossy mixture. Sift the flour and baking powder into the bowl and stir in. Add 100g of the pecan halves and stir in.

4 Transfer the mixture to the prepared tin and spread evenly. Scatter the remaining nuts over the top. Place in the heated oven and bake for 20–25 minutes until a skewer inserted into the cake

(halfway between the centre and the side of the tin) comes out clean. The centre of the cake will still be slightly soft – it will firm up as it cools.

5 Set the tin on a wire rack. Run a round-bladed knife around the cake to loosen it from the tin, then leave to cool. Once cold, turn out and cut into squares. Store in an airtight container and eat within 4 days.

VANILLA SABLÉS

Very rich, crisp, sandy-textured biscuits, sablés are the French equivalent of shortbread. The dough is traditionally rolled out and cut into rounds with a fluted cutter. The vanilla-scented biscuits here are given a glossy golden glaze with beaten egg. To ensure they colour evenly, rotate the baking sheets halfway through the baking time.

MAKES ABOUT 16
YOU WILL NEED: 1–2 BAKING SHEETS, WELL GREASED WITH BUTTER OR LINED WITH BAKING PAPER

200g plain flour
good pinch of salt
75g icing sugar
140g unsalted butter, chilled and diced

3 medium free-range egg yolks
¾ teaspoon vanilla extract
beaten egg, to glaze

1 Put the flour, salt and sugar into the bowl of a food processor and pulse to combine. Add the pieces of butter and run the machine just until the mixture looks sandy. Add the egg yolks and vanilla and process until the mixture comes together to make a firm ball of dough.

2 Remove the dough from the processor, shape it into a disc about 2.5cm thick and wrap in clingfilm. Chill for about 30 minutes until firm. Meanwhile, heat your oven to 180°C/350°F/gas 4.

3 Lightly flour the worktop and your rolling pin, then roll out the dough until it is about 4mm thick (slightly thicker than a pound coin). Try to roll the dough so it is the same thickness all over, to ensure the biscuits will cook evenly.

4 Use a 7.5cm fluted round cutter to stamp out rounds of dough. Dip the cutter in flour before you start and between each biscuit. For neat shapes firmly stamp out the rounds – don't twist the cutter. Gently knead the trimmings together, then re-roll and stamp out more rounds.

5 Set the rounds, slightly apart, on the prepared baking sheets (you may need to bake in 2 batches). Brush very lightly with beaten egg, then prick each round a couple of times with a fork. Brush again with egg. Finally, lightly score the top of each round in a cross pattern with the prongs of the fork.

6 Place in the heated oven and bake for 11–15 minutes until golden. Remove from the oven and cool on the baking sheets for 2 minutes so the biscuits can firm up, then carefully transfer them to a wire rack and leave to cool completely. Store in an airtight container and eat within a week.

COCONUT SABLÉS

These deliciously crisp biscuits are particularly good with ice cream. Make sure you use unsweetened desiccated coconut or the biscuits will quickly scorch.

MAKES ABOUT 16
YOU WILL NEED: 1–2 BAKING SHEETS, WELL GREASED WITH BUTTER OR LINED WITH BAKING PAPER

40g unsweetened desiccated coconut
160g plain flour
good pinch of salt
75g icing sugar

40g ground almonds
160g unsalted butter, chilled and diced
2 medium free-range egg yolks

1 Put the coconut, flour, salt and icing sugar into the bowl of a food processor and run the machine for 20 seconds to grind up the coconut slightly. Add the almonds and briefly pulse to combine. Add the pieces of butter and run the machine just until the mixture looks sandy. Finally, add the egg yolks and process until the mixture comes together to make a ball of dough.

2 Remove the dough from the processor bowl, shape it into a disc about 2.5cm thick and wrap in clingfilm. Chill for about 30 minutes until firm. Meanwhile, heat your oven to 180°C/350°F/gas 4.

3 Dust the worktop and your rolling pin with flour, then roll out the dough until it is about 4mm thick (slightly thicker than a pound coin). Try to roll the dough so it is the same thickness all over, to ensure the biscuits will cook evenly.

4 Use a 7.5cm fluted round cutter to stamp out rounds of dough. Dip the cutter in flour before you start and between each biscuit. For neat shapes firmly stamp out the rounds – don't twist the cutter. Gently knead the trimmings together, then re-roll and stamp out more rounds.

5 Arrange the rounds, slightly apart, on the prepared baking sheets (you may need to bake in 2 batches). Prick each round 3 times with a fork then place in the heated oven and bake for 11–14 minutes until pale golden. Rotate the baking sheets halfway through the baking time.

6 Remove from the oven and cool on the baking sheets for 2 minutes so the biscuits can firm up, then carefully transfer to a wire rack and leave to cool completely. Store in an airtight container and eat within a week.

RUM SABLÉS

Use these to make a dessert: brush the cooled biscuits with warm jam, then top with fresh berries and a swirl of whipped cream. Or sandwich 2 rounds with chilled chocolate mousse (see page 120). If you're baking in batches, quickly cool the baking sheet under the cold tap between batches, then dry – never put your carefully chilled and cut dough rounds on a warm baking sheet as they will melt.

MAKES ABOUT 20
YOU WILL NEED: 1–2 BAKING SHEETS, WELL GREASED WITH BUTTER OR LINED WITH BAKING PAPER

275g plain flour
good pinch of salt
125g icing sugar
175g unsalted butter, chilled and diced

2 medium free-range egg yolks
1 tablespoon dark rum
caster sugar, for sprinkling

1 Put the flour, salt and icing sugar into the bowl of a food processor and 'pulse' several times just to combine. Add the pieces of butter and run the machine until the mixture looks like sand. Add the egg yolks and rum and process until the mixture comes together to form a ball of dough.

2 Remove the dough from the bowl, flatten it into a disc about 2.5cm thick and wrap in clingfilm. Chill for about 30 minutes until firm.

3 Heat your oven to 180°C/350°F/gas 4. Lightly dust the worktop and rolling pin with flour, then roll out the dough to about 4mm thick. Dip a 7.5cm fluted round cutter in flour and use to stamp out rounds, re-flouring the cutter when the dough begins to stick. Gather up the trimmings and gently knead them together, then re-roll and stamp out more rounds.

4 Arrange the rounds, slightly apart, on the prepared baking sheets (you may have to bake in batches). Prick each round twice with a fork and sprinkle with sugar. Place in the heated oven and bake for 12–15 minutes until light gold. Leave to cool and firm up on the baking sheets for a couple of minutes, then transfer to a wire rack and leave to cool completely. Store in an airtight container and eat within a week.

SCANDI ALMOND COOKIES

Popular in northern Europe and Scandinavia at Christmas and Hannukah, these crumbly cookies have a rich buttery taste and a good nutty crunch.

MAKES ABOUT 14
YOU WILL NEED: 1–2 BAKING SHEETS, LINED WITH BAKING PAPER

100g walnut pieces OR roughly chopped almonds
115g unsalted butter, softened
65g icing sugar, plus extra for rolling

½ teaspoon vanilla extract OR 3 drops almond essence (if using almonds)
125g plain flour

1 Heat your oven to 180°C/350°F/gas 4. Spread the nuts in a small baking dish or tin and toast in the heated oven for 7–10 minutes until slightly darker. Leave to cool. Lower the oven temperature to 160°C/325°F/gas 3.

2 Put the soft butter into a mixing bowl and beat with an electric mixer or wooden spoon until creamy. Sift the icing sugar into the bowl and add the vanilla extract or almond essence. Beat, slowly at first, until the mixture is very light in colour and texture – about 2 minutes with an electric mixer or 3 minutes by hand.

3 Sift the flour into the bowl and work into the mixture with a wooden spoon or plastic spatula. When the flour is completely incorporated work in the nuts to make a stiff dough.

4 Dust your hands with flour. Take small pieces of dough and roll into walnut-sized balls, re-flouring your hands when the dough starts to stick. Set the balls, slightly apart, on the prepared baking sheets (if necessary bake in 2 batches). Chill for 10–15 minutes until firm – this helps the cookies keep their shape during baking.

5 Place in the heated oven and bake for 17–20 minutes until barely golden and firm. Remove from the oven and leave the cookies on the baking sheets to firm up for 2–3 minutes, then carefully transfer them to a wire rack. Leave to cool completely. When cold, gently roll the cookies in icing sugar so they look like mini snowballs. Store in an airtight container and eat within a week.

CHEWY APRICOT COOKIES

Very quick to put together and bake, these almondy cookies – rather like the British version of soft amaretti – are sandwiched with apricot conserve or butter icing. You can make the cookie dough by hand or in a food processor.

MAKES 8 SANDWICH COOKIES
YOU WILL NEED: 1–2 BAKING SHEETS, LINED WITH BAKING PAPER

125g self-raising flour
50g ground almonds
100g caster sugar
100g unsalted butter, chilled and diced
1 medium free-range egg

3–4 drops almond essence
20g flaked almonds
200g apricot conserve OR 1 x quantity
   Butter Icing (see page 84)
icing sugar, for dusting

1 Heat your oven to 160°C/325°F/gas 3. To make the dough by hand, sift the flour, ground almonds and sugar into a mixing bowl. Add the butter and rub in with your fingertips until the mixture looks like coarse crumbs. Beat the egg with the almond essence in a small bowl using a fork, just to mix, then add to the flour mixture. Beat the mixture with a wooden spoon for a few seconds so it is thoroughly combined.

2 To make the dough in a food processor put the flour, ground almonds and sugar into the processor bowl and pulse 3 or 4 times, just to combine the ingredients. Add the pieces of butter and process until the mixture looks sandy. Beat the egg with the almond essence in a small bowl using a fork, just to mix, then add to the processor through the feed tube while the machine is running. Stop the machine as soon as the dough comes together.

3 Tip the dough on to the worktop. Lightly dust your hands with flour, then roll the mixture into 16 walnut-sized balls. Arrange the balls on the prepared baking sheets, spaced well apart to allow for spreading (it may be necessary to bake in batches).

Scatter the flaked almonds on top of the balls and press in very gently. Place in the heated oven and bake for 14–17 minutes until golden and just firm when gently pressed.

4 Remove from the oven and leave the cookies to cool on the baking sheets before peeling them off the baking paper. Use the apricot conserve or butter icing to sandwich pairs of cookies together, flat sides in, then dust with icing sugar. Store in an airtight container and eat within 5 days.

BUTTER ICING

Simple but useful, butter icing can be used plain or flavoured (see below), and it can be tinted by adding edible food colouring a couple of drops at a time. The quantities here make enough icing to decorate 24 fairy cakes or 12 larger cupcakes; to fill and top a 20cm sponge cake; or to sandwich 8 pairs of cookies.

MAKES ABOUT 530G

125g unsalted butter, softened
400g icing sugar

1 Put the soft butter into a mixing bowl and beat with a wooden spoon or an electric mixer until paler in colour and very creamy.

2 Sift the icing sugar into the bowl. Add the milk and vanilla, and beat (on low speed if using an electric mixer) until very smooth and thick. To use, spread the icing with a table or palette knife, or spoon into a piping bag fitted with a star tube and pipe in swirls or rosettes.

3–4 tablespoons milk
1 teaspoon vanilla extract

Variations:
Chocolate butter icing: Replace the vanilla with 3 tablespoons cocoa powder.
Coffee butter icing: Replace the milk with cold, very strong black coffee.

BUTTERCREAM

Considerably richer, lighter and creamier than Butter Icing (above), buttercream is also slightly trickier. The quantities here make enough to decorate 24 fairy cakes or 12 larger cupcakes, or to fill and top a 20cm sponge cake.

MAKES ABOUT 350G
YOU WILL NEED: A SUGAR THERMOMETER

85g caster sugar
4 tablespoons water
2 large free-range egg yolks

1 Put the sugar and water into a small heavy-based pan and heat gently until the sugar dissolves. Bring to the boil and boil until the temperature reaches 110°C on a sugar thermometer – this will take about 5 minutes. Don't let the syrup start to caramelise.

150g unsalted butter, very soft but not runny
1 teaspoon vanilla extract

2 While the sugar syrup is coming up to temperature, put the egg yolks into a heatproof bowl and set the bowl on a damp cloth to keep it from wobbling. Whisk the egg yolks briefly with an electric mixer.

3 As soon as the sugar syrup is ready, slowly pour it into the bowl in a thin, steady stream, whisking constantly. Keep whisking until the mixture becomes very thick and mousse-like, pale in colour and completely cold.

4 Gradually whisk in the soft butter followed by the vanilla. To use, spread or pipe the buttercream on to the cakes. In warm weather, chill the decorated cakes just until the icing is firm.

Variations:
Chocolate buttercream: Replace the vanilla with 75g dark chocolate, melted and cooled.
Cofee buttercream: Replace the vanilla with 1–2 tablespoons cold, very strong black coffee.

CRUMBLY SHORTBREAD FINGERS

The ingredients for shortbread are simple – sugar, butter and flour used in the traditional proportions of 1:2:3. A mixture of caster and icing sugar make the texture sandy and crisp, and a mix of plain flour and cornflour gives lightness.

CUTS INTO 24 FINGERS
YOU WILL NEED: 1 TRAYBAKE TIN OR CAKE TIN 20.5 X 25.5 X 5CM, GREASED WITH BUTTER

220g unsalted butter, softened
30g icing sugar
80g caster sugar, plus extra for sprinkling

30g cornflour
300g plain flour

1 Heat your oven to 160°C/325°F/gas 3. Put the soft butter into a mixing bowl and beat with a wooden spoon or electric mixer until creamy.

2 Sift the icing sugar into the bowl and beat in (if using an electric mixer, use low speed to start). Beat in the caster sugar. Scrape down the sides of the bowl, then beat thoroughly for a couple of minutes until the mixture is very light and fluffy.

3 Sift the cornflour into the bowl and beat in. Sift the flour into the bowl and mix in with a wooden spoon or plastic spatula to make a crumbly mixture.

4 Tip the crumbs into the prepared tin and spread evenly. Gently press out the mixture, being sure to press it into the corners of the tin too. Prick all over with a fork. Place in the heated oven and bake for about 35 minutes until pale golden.

5 Remove the tin from the oven and set it on a heatproof surface. Cut into 24 fingers using a sharp knife, then sprinkle with sugar. Leave to cool completely before removing from the tin. Store the fingers in an airtight container and eat within a week.

LEMON SHORTBREAD

Shortbread is used here as both base and topping for an unusual filling – you'll discover bursts of sharp and sweet tastes. The filling is made from lemon slices macerated overnight with sugar, then thickened with eggs, flour and butter.

CUTS INTO 20 SQUARES
YOU WILL NEED: I TRAYBAKE TIN OR CAKE TIN 20.5 X 25.5 X 5CM, GREASED WITH BUTTER

I x quantity Shortbread mixture
  (see page 85)
I medium free-range egg yolk
caster sugar, for sprinkling

For the filling
2 medium unwaxed lemons, rinsed
150g caster sugar
2 medium free-range eggs
2 tablespoons plain flour
30g unsalted butter, melted

I First make the lemon filling mixture. Using a sharp knife (or a serrated tomato knife), cut the lemons in half lengthways, then trim off the ends. Cut the lemon halves across into the thinnest possible slices, discarding the seeds. Tip the slices and any juice into a dish.

2 Add the sugar and stir well. Cover with clingfilm and leave in the fridge for 8 hours, or overnight, stirring from time to time if possible. At the end of this time, the lemon slices will have softened and the juice and sugar formed a thick syrup.

3 Heat your oven to 160°C/325°F/gas 3. Put the eggs in a small bowl and beat with a fork, just to mix. Add to the lemon mixture along with the flour and melted butter and stir to mix.

4 Tip three-quarters of the crumbly shortbread mixture into the prepared tin and spread out, then gently press down to make an even layer. Set aside.

5 Mix the egg yolk into the remaining shortbread crumbs to make a firm dough. Turn this out on to a lightly floured worktop and roll with your hands into a sausage about 20cm long. Cut across into 30 rounds (each about the thickness of a pound coin).

6 Spoon the lemon mixture into the tin on top of the shortbread base. Make sure the lemon slices are evenly distributed. Arrange the shortbread rounds on top. Place in the heated oven and bake for 40–45 minutes until pale golden.

7 Remove from the oven and set on a wire rack. Sprinkle with sugar, then cut into 20 squares using a sharp knife. Leave in the tin to firm up for 10 minutes, then eat warm as a dessert. Or leave to cool completely in the tin. Store in an airtight container and eat within 2 days.

RASPBERRY CRUMBLE SHORTBREAD

Shortbread is all about good butter – it is what gives the biscuits their 'short' or crumbly texture and their rich flavour. These Scottish-inspired shortbread squares need to be made with top-quality jam too. Try them warm for dessert, with Fresh Egg Custard (see page 255) or ice cream.

CUTS INTO 20 SQUARES
YOU WILL NEED: I TRAYBAKE TIN OR CAKE TIN 20.5 X 25.5 X 5CM, GREASED WITH BUTTER

I x quantity Shortbread mixture (see page 85)
325g Raspberry and Redcurrant Jam (opposite) OR good bought raspberry jam or conserve

50g flaked almonds
icing sugar, for dusting

I Heat your oven to 160°C/325°F/gas 3. Set aside a quarter of the crumbly shortbread mixture for the topping, then tip the rest into the prepared tin and spread out. Press down to make an even layer. Prick well with a fork, then place in the heated oven and bake for 20 minutes. Remove and leave to cool for 10 minutes – the shortbread will still be soft as it's not completely cooked.

2 Carefully spread the jam over the shortbread base. Mix the reserved shortbread crumbs with the flaked almonds and scatter evenly over the jam.

3 Return the tin to the oven and bake for a further 20–25 minutes until the topping is lightly golden. Remove from the oven and set the tin on a heatproof surface. Cut into 20 squares using a sharp knife, then dust with icing sugar. Leave to firm up for 10 minutes before removing from the tin to eat warm, or leave to cool completely in the tin. Store in an airtight container and eat within 3 days.

RASPBERRY AND REDCURRANT JAM

A brilliantly coloured jam with a really vibrant taste of fresh fruit, this is just the thing to spread on home-made scones, muffins and crumpets or to fill sponge sandwich cakes.

MAKES ABOUT 1.6KG

500g redcurrants
500g raspberries
1kg jam sugar (sugar with pectin)

1 Rinse and thoroughly drain the redcurrants (there's no need to remove them from their stalks), then put them into a large non-aluminium pan. Set the pan over low heat and cook gently, stirring frequently, for about 10 minutes until the fruit is soft and pulpy.

2 Set a fine sieve over a large measuring jug and carefully pour in the contents of the pan to strain the juice, gently pressing on the pulp to extract all the liquid. Discard the pulp and stalks. Measure the liquid – if necessary add water to make it up to 300ml.

3 Pour the 300ml juice back into the pan and add the raspberries. Bring to the boil and simmer gently for about 5 minutes until the fruit is soft.

4 Stir in the sugar and cook gently over low heat, stirring frequently, until it has completely dissolved. Turn up the heat and boil rapidly until setting point is reached (see right), which will take 10–15 minutes.

5 Remove the pan from the heat and leave the jam to stand for 5 minutes so it cools slightly and the fruit 'settles'. Carefully ladle into hot, sterilised jam jars, then cover and label. Store in a cool spot.

HOW TO TEST FOR 'SETTING POINT'

The easiest and most accurate way to test is with a sugar thermometer: put it into the pan after the sugar has dissolved. When the temperature reaches 220°C, the jam has reached setting point.

If you don't have a thermometer, you can use a safe 'finger' test. Before you add the sugar to the pan, put several old saucers into the freezer to chill. When the boiling jam is thick, with large bubbles, start to test: carefully draw the pan off the heat, take a spoonful of jam and drop it on to a chilled saucer. Wait for 20–30 seconds so the jam cools, then draw a finger through it – if the surface wrinkles the jam will set. If it doesn't wrinkle, carry on boiling for a few more minutes, then test again.

APPLE AND OAT MUFFINS

Just a bit richer than a scone, and faster to make than a cake, a home-made muffin makes a good treat.

MAKES 12
YOU WILL NEED: 1 X 12-HOLE MUFFIN TRAY, LINED WITH PAPER MUFFIN CASES

For the topping
50g porridge oats
50g demerara (or caster) sugar
50g plain flour
50g unsalted butter, at room
 temperature

For the base
250g plain flour
25g porridge oats
175g caster sugar
2 teaspoons baking powder

finely grated zest of 1 medium
 unwaxed lemon
150g unsalted butter, diced
2 medium free-range eggs,
 at room temperature
100ml milk, at room temperature
1 large eating apple, cored and cut into
 small pieces (about 1cm)

1 Heat your oven to 190°C/375°F/gas 5. Make the crumble topping first. Put the oats, sugar and flour into a mixing bowl and combine with your hand. Cut the butter into pieces, add to the bowl and rub into the dry ingredients with your fingertips until the mixture looks like coarse crumbs. Then gently squeeze the mixture together until it forms pea-like clumps. Set aside until needed.

2 Now make the base. Put the flour, oats, sugar, baking powder and lemon zest into a mixing bowl and mix together thoroughly with a wooden spoon. Gently melt the butter in a small pan or in the microwave (use 10-second bursts); leave to cool. Beat the eggs and milk in a small bowl with a fork until just combined. Add the melted butter and the milk mixture to the flour mix in the bowl and stir gently until just combined – there's no need to beat this mixture.

3 Spoon the mixture into the 12 paper cases in the muffin tray so they are evenly filled. Top each with an equal amount of chopped apple and gently press the pieces into the muffin mixture (they should remain visible). Cover with the crumble topping, dividing it equally among the muffins, and gently press down on to the base.

4 Place in the heated oven and bake for 30–35 minutes until golden and just firm when gently pressed in the centre. Set the tray on a wire rack and cool for 3–4 minutes, then carefully lift the muffins out of the tray on to the rack. Eat warm or at room temperature the same or the next day (store in an airtight container).

MILLIONAIRE'S SHORTBREAD

Here's the classic hard-to-beat combination: crisp shortbread, sticky toffee and dark chocolate. Don't undercook the shortbread base or it will have a damp, soggy texture.

CUTS INTO 30 FINGERS
YOU WILL NEED: 1 TRAYBAKE TIN OR CAKE TIN 20.5 X 25.5 X 5CM, GREASED WITH BUTTER

1 x quantity Shortbread mixture (see page 85)

For the toffee layer
225g unsalted butter, diced
115g caster sugar
4 tablespoons golden syrup
1 x 397g tin condensed milk

For the chocolate topping
200g dark chocolate (about 70% cocoa solids), chopped or broken up
3 tablespoons water

1 Heat your oven to 160°C/325°F/gas 3. Tip the crumbly shortbread mixture into the prepared tin and spread evenly. Gently press out the mixture, being sure to press it into the corners of the tin too. Prick all over with a fork. Place in the heated oven and bake for about 35 minutes until pale golden.

2 Remove the tin from the oven and set it on a heatproof surface. Leave the shortbread in the tin until completely cold.

3 To make the toffee layer, put the diced butter, sugar, syrup and condensed milk into a medium-sized heavy-based pan. Set over low heat and stir frequently with a wooden spoon until the butter melts. Bring to the boil, then simmer, stirring constantly to prevent the mixture from catching on the base of the pan, for 3–5 minutes until it turns golden (don't let the mixture turn a darker caramel colour or it will set too hard to cut). Pour the toffee mixture over the cold shortbread and spread it evenly. Leave until cold.

4 Put the chocolate and water in a heatproof bowl, set the bowl over a pan of hot water and melt gently, stirring occasionally. Spread the chocolate evenly over the toffee.

5 Leave in a cool place – not the fridge – to set, then use a sharp knife to cut into 30 fingers. Store in an airtight container and eat within 5 days.

CLASSIC CREAM CRACKERS

Adding cream to a simple dough gives these crackers a flaky texture – there's no need for elaborate shaping or folding techniques. You can make the crackers any size you choose. They're good with cheese and pâtés.

MAKES 24–30
YOU WILL NEED: 1–2 BAKING SHEETS, LINED WITH BAKING PAPER

125g plain flour
½ teaspoon caster sugar
15g unsalted butter, cool but not hard
¾ teaspoon sea salt flakes, or to taste
1 teaspoon cumin seeds OR 2 teaspoons sesame seeds

4 tablespoons double or single cream
3 4 tablespoons water, at room temperature

1 Sift the flour and sugar into a mixing bowl. Cut the butter into flakes and add to the bowl, then rub into the flour using your fingertips until the mixture looks like very fine crumbs. Stir in the salt and seeds.

2 Add the cream and 3 tablespoons of water. Using a round-bladed knife mix everything together, adding more water a teaspoon at a time as needed, to make a soft but not sticky dough (it should look slightly rough, and feel like shortcrust pastry).

3 Lightly dust the worktop with flour. Turn out the dough and very gently knead it just for 5 seconds so it looks slightly smoother. Put the dough back into the bowl and cover the top with clingfilm. Leave to relax at room temperature for 30 minutes.

4 Towards the end of the relaxing time, heat your oven to 180°C/350°F/gas 4. Lightly dust the worktop and rolling pin with flour, then roll out the dough to a very thin sheet roughly 35 × 45cm. Cut the sheet in half and gently lift one piece on to a lined baking sheet. Prick the dough sheet all over with a fork. Using a pizza wheel cutter or large sharp knife, trim the edges so they are straight and neat (discard the trimmings), then cut the dough into squares or rectangles. Repeat with the other portion of dough (if you only have one sheet then bake in 2 batches).

5 Place in the heated oven and bake for 14–17 minutes until the crackers are a light gold colour (they will shrink a little). To make sure they cook evenly, it's a good idea to rotate the baking sheet halfway through the baking time.

6 Remove from the oven and firm up on the baking sheets for 2 minutes, then transfer the crackers to a wire rack and leave to cool. Store in an airtight container and eat within 5 days.

CHEESE AND MUSTARD CRACKERS

Serve these crisp and crumbly biscuits with cheese and wine or for a savoury snack. The dough can be kept in the fridge, tightly wrapped, for up to 2 days, so you can slice and bake to order. For a simple starter, top the warm biscuits with slices of tomato or roasted peppers plus crumbled blue cheese.

MAKES 36
YOU WILL NEED: 1–2 BAKING SHEETS, LINED WITH BAKING PAPER

200g plain flour
½ teaspoon salt
½ teaspoon baking powder
100g unsalted butter, chilled and diced
1 medium free-range egg yolk

200g extra-mature Cheddar
    cheese, grated
2 tablespoons wholegrain mustard

1 Put the flour, salt and baking powder into a food processor and 'pulse' a couple of times just to combine. Add the butter and run the machine for a few seconds until the mixture looks like fine crumbs. Add the egg yolk, cheese and mustard and run the machine just until the mixture comes together to form a ball of dough.

2 Remove the dough from the bowl and set in the middle of a sheet of clingfilm. With lightly floured hands shape the dough into a log 18 x 6cm. Wrap the clingfilm around the log. Chill for 1 hour until firm.

3 Towards the end of the chilling time, heat your oven to 180°C/350°F/gas 4. Unwrap the log and set it on a cutting board. Cut across into slices 5mm thick. Arrange them on the lined baking sheets, spacing well apart to allow for spreading. (If you have only one sheet, wait for it to cool down before baking the second batch of biscuits.) Place in the heated oven and bake for 15–18 minutes until a good golden colour.

4 Leave the biscuits to cool and firm up on the baking sheet for 2–3 minutes before transferring to a wire rack. Eat warm or leave to cool. Store in an airtight container and eat within 4 days.

FRESH TOMATO AND PEACH SALSA

Serve this colourful fresh sauce as a dip for crackers and bread or with quiches and cold pies. For a deeper flavour, roast the whole chillies under a very hot grill until the skin is charred; leave to cool in a paper bag, then carefully peel off the skin.

SERVES 4–6

2 large, ripe tomatoes
1 large, ripe peach
1–2 moderately hot jalapeño chillies,
    to taste

salt
½–1 tablespoon lemon juice, to taste

1 Bring a medium pan of water to the boil. With the tip of a small knife, make a tiny nick in the skin of the tomatoes and peach at the stalk end. Lower the tomatoes and peach into the boiling water using a slotted spoon. Leave for 10 seconds, then lift out and put into a bowl of cold water. Leave until cool enough to handle.

2 Drain the tomatoes and peach, and slip off their skins. Quarter the tomatoes and discard the seeds. Halve the peach and remove the stone. Cut the tomatoes and peach into small chunks. Put into a mixing bowl.

3 Halve the chillies, then carefully cut out the core, seeds and white ribs. Chop the chillies very finely. (Take care you don't touch your eyes or any delicate skin until you've finished and thoroughly washed your hands, because all the 'heat' in the chillies is in the seeds and ribs and can sting.)

4 Add the chillies to the bowl with a little salt and lemon juice. Mix gently, then taste and add more salt and lemon juice if needed. Cover and chill for at least 1 hour before serving. Best eaten the same day, icy cold.

OLIVE OIL AND ROSEMARY CRACKERS

Very thin and crisp, these crackers are good with dips. During baking it's a good idea to rotate the baking sheets about halfway through so the crackers cook evenly.

MAKES 20
YOU WILL NEED: 1–2 BAKING SHEETS, LINED WITH BAKING PAPER

200g plain flour
¾ teaspoon baking powder
½ teaspoon icing sugar
½ teaspoon sea salt flakes, or to taste
1 teaspoon finely chopped
   fresh rosemary

4 teaspoons extra virgin olive oil, plus
   extra for brushing
about 100ml water, at room
   temperature

1 Sift the flour, baking powder and icing sugar into a mixing bowl. Add the salt and rosemary and stir them in with your hand. Add the oil to the bowl plus enough water to make a soft but not sticky dough – you can use a wooden spoon, round-bladed knife or your hand to mix the dough.

2 Turn out the dough on to a very lightly floured worktop and shape it with your hands to a sausage 20cm long. Wrap it in clingfilm and chill for 1 hour until firm.

3 Towards the end of the chilling time, heat your oven to 220°C/425°F/gas 7. Unwrap the dough and set it on a cutting board. Cut across into 20 equal pieces. Lightly dust the worktop and rolling pin with flour, then roll out each piece into a long oval as thin as possible – aim for about 15cm long. The ovals should look fairly rustic rather than neat and even in shape.

4 Arrange the ovals slightly apart on the lined baking sheets (you may need to bake in batches). Brush very lightly with olive oil, then place in the oven and bake for 8–10 minutes until the crackers are a light golden colour with slightly darker edges

that curl up. Watch them carefully to be sure they don't get too dark. They will bubble up in places so no two crackers will look the same.

5 Remove from the oven and firm up on the baking sheets for 2 minutes, then transfer the crackers to a wire rack and leave to cool. Store in an airtight container and eat within 5 days.

BITTER CHOCOLATE BROWNIES

Rich and fudge-like, these dark chocolate brownies are a gluten-free treat. Finish simply with a dusting of icing sugar or add a fudge icing plus a decoration of walnut halves if you feel like it. Make a day ahead because, as with most chocolate bakes, the chocolate flavour will develop and mature. The cake will slice better too.

CUTS INTO 36 SQUARES
YOU WILL NEED: 1 X 20.5CM SQUARE BROWNIE TIN OR SHALLOW CAKE TIN, GREASED AND BASE-LINED

225g dark chocolate (about 70% cocoa
   solids), chopped or broken up
110g unsalted butter, diced
35g cocoa powder
good pinch of salt
3 medium free-range eggs, at room
   temperature

150g light brown muscovado sugar
100g walnut pieces
icing sugar, for dusting, OR 1 x quantity
   Quick Fudge Icing (opposite)

1 Heat your oven to 180°C/350°F/gas 4. Put the chocolate and butter in a heatproof bowl, set the bowl over a pan of hot water and melt gently, stirring occasionally. Remove the bowl from the pan and sift the cocoa and salt on top of the melted mixture. Stir in until completely smooth, then leave to cool until just barely warm.

2 While the mix is cooling, put the eggs into a large mixing bowl and whisk with an electric mixer until frothy. Make sure there are no lumps in the sugar, then add to the eggs and continue whisking until the mixture is very thick and mousse-like, and will make a ribbon trail on itself.

3 Pour the chocolate mixture into the bowl and fold in with a large metal spoon. When you can no longer see any streaks, add the nuts and fold them in.

4 Transfer the mixture to the prepared tin and spread evenly. Place in the heated oven and bake for about 30 minutes until a skewer inserted into the mixture – halfway between the side of the tin and the centre – comes out clean. The centre will still be slightly soft; the brownie cake will continue cooking for a few minutes after it comes out of the oven.

5 Set the tin on a wire rack and run a round-bladed knife around the brownie cake to loosen it from the tin. Leave until cold, then carefully turn out and cut into squares. Dust with icing sugar just before serving. Alternatively, cover the brownie cake with fudge icing before cutting into squares. Store the brownies in an airtight container and eat within 5 days.

QUICK FUDGE ICING

This easy melt-and-mix topping can be used to ice Bitter Chocolate Brownies (opposite) and Easy Pecan Blondies (see page 76) as well as to fill a sponge sandwich cake. For a salted caramel icing add ¼–½ teaspoon sea salt flakes (to taste) after the icing sugar has been worked in; for a vanilla fudge icing add ½ teaspoon vanilla extract with the icing sugar.

MAKES ENOUGH TO ICE A 20.5CM SQUARE CAKE

125g dark brown muscovado sugar
75g unsalted butter
3 tablespoons single or double cream

125g icing sugar, sifted
50g walnut halves (optional)

1 Press any lumps out of the sugar, then put it in a small, heavy-based pan with the butter. Set over low heat and stir until melted and smooth, then bring to the boil and simmer for 1 minute.

2 Stir in the cream and simmer for 1 more minute, stirring constantly so the mixture doesn't catch on the base of the pan. Remove from the heat and add the icing sugar, then beat well with a wooden spoon until the mix is smooth and thick.

3 Spread the icing on top of the turned-out brownie or blondie cake. If adding walnut halves, arrange them on the icing. Leave to set before cutting into squares.

DOUBLE CHOCOLATE BISCOTTI

Just the thing for dunking into hot chocolate or good coffee – and a boxful makes an excellent gift. For the ultimate triple chocolate biscotti, coat one end with melted dark chocolate.

MAKES ABOUT 34
YOU WILL NEED: 1–2 BAKING SHEETS, LINED WITH BAKING PAPER

100g whole blanched almonds or hazelnuts
100g unsalted butter
3 medium free-range eggs, at room
 temperature
200g caster sugar
½ teaspoon vanilla extract
325g plain flour
2 teaspoons baking powder
good pinch of salt

3 tablespoons cocoa powder
110g dark chocolate (about 70% cocoa
 solids), coarsely chopped

To finish (optional)
150g dark chocolate (about 70% cocoa
 solids), chopped into even pieces

1 Heat your oven to 180°C/350°F/gas 4. Put the nuts into a small baking dish or tin and toast in the heated oven for 6–8 minutes until they turn a light golden brown. Leave to cool a bit, then chop each nut in half. Set aside until needed. Don't turn off the oven.

2 Gently melt the butter in a small pan over low heat, or in the microwave (use 10-second bursts). Leave to cool until lukewarm but still fluid.

3 While the butter is cooling, put the eggs in a large mixing bowl and whisk with an electric mixer until frothy. Add the sugar and vanilla extract and whisk for 3–4 minutes until very thick. Pour the melted butter into the bowl while whisking at medium speed (to avoid splattering). Once all the butter has been added, whisk for 10 seconds on high speed.

4 Sift the flour, baking powder, salt and cocoa into the bowl and stir in with a wooden spoon. When you can no longer see any specks of flour (or cocoa), mix in the toasted nuts and chopped chocolate. The dough will be stiff and heavy.

5 Dust your hands with a little flour, then divide the dough into 2 equal portions. Set each piece on a prepared baking sheets (if using just one large baking sheet, set the pieces of dough well apart to allow for spreading). Flour your hands again, then gently mould and shape each piece of dough into a log about 23cm long and 7cm wide.

6 Place in the heated oven and bake for 25–30 minutes until barely firm when gently pressed in the centre (the dough will continue cooking for a few minutes after it comes out of the oven). Remove from the oven but leave the logs on the baking sheets until completely cold – if you try to cut the logs while they are still warm you'll end up with a sticky mess. Turn off the oven now.

7 When the dough is ready for slicing and the second bake, reheat the oven to 180°C/350°F/gas 4. Put one log on to a cutting board and, using a serrated bread knife, gently cut across into diagonal slices 1cm thick – for best results use a sawing motion rather than chopping straight down. Arrange the slices,

cut-side down, on the lined baking sheet – they can be set close together now as they won't need room to spread. Repeat to slice the second log, baking the biscotti in batches if necessary (line the baking sheet with fresh baking paper each time).

8 Place in the heated oven and bake for 10–15 minutes until firm and dry. Remove from the oven and allow to firm up for 5 minutes, then slide the biscotti off the lining paper on to a wire rack and leave until completely cold.

9 To finish your biscotti with an optional chocolate dip, put the chopped chocolate into a heatproof bowl, set over a pan of hot water and melt gently. Remove the bowl from the pan and stir the chocolate until smooth. Dip one end (about a third) of each biscotti into the chocolate to coat lightly, then place on a sheet of baking or wax paper and leave to set. Store in an airtight container and eat within a week.

ITALIAN CHOCOLATE TRAYBAKE

An easy, but deeply flavoured all-in-one sponge, this doesn't need an icing. You could also eat it warm for dessert, with a hot chocolate sauce (see opposite) and vanilla ice cream.

CUTS INTO 20 SQUARES
YOU WILL NEED: I TRAYBAKE TIN OR CAKE TIN 20.5 X 25.5 X 5CM, GREASED AND BASE-LINED

150g blanched hazelnuts
150g unsalted butter, softened
150g caster sugar
170g self-raising flour
3 medium free-range eggs, at room temperature

2 tablespoons milk
100g dark chocolate (about 70% cocoa solids)
cocoa powder and icing sugar, for dusting

1 Heat your oven to 180°C/350°F/gas 4. Tip the nuts into a small baking dish or tin and toast in the heated oven for 6–8 minutes until golden. Allow to cool (leave the oven on), then put 100g of the nuts on a cutting board and chop each one in half. Finely grind or finely chop the remaining 50g nuts.

2 Put the ground nuts into a mixing bowl and add the soft butter, sugar, flour, eggs and milk. Beat well with a wooden spoon or an electric mixer until smooth and creamy.

3 Chop the chocolate into large, thin shards and add to the bowl with the halved nuts. Gently stir in with a plastic spatula or large metal spoon.

4 Transfer the mixture to the prepared tin and spread evenly. Place in the heated oven and bake for 25–30 minutes until the sponge is golden and feels just firm when gently pressed in the centre.

5 Set the tin on a wire rack. Run a round-bladed knife around the sponge to loosen it from the tin, then carefully turn out on to the rack. Leave to cool before cutting into squares. Dust with cocoa and then lightly with icing sugar just before serving. Store in an airtight container and eat within 5 days.

HOT CHOCOLATE SAUCE

A jug of hot chocolate sauce makes a bowl of ice cream a real treat, or you can pour it over profiteroles, meringues and all manner of puds – try it with a piece of warm Italian Chocolate Traybake (opposite) or Chestnut Meringue Roulade (see page 270). Any leftover sauce can be kept, covered, in the fridge, then gently reheated to serve the next day.

SERVES 4–6

100g dark chocolate (about 70% cocoa
   solids), broken up
25g unsalted butter

2 tablespoons icing sugar
100ml water

1 Simply put all the ingredients into a small pan, preferably non-stick, and heat gently, stirring frequently, until melted and smooth. Serve warm.

FRESH BERRY SCONES

An old trick for making feather-light scones is to use buttermilk, a low-fat, slightly acidic by-product of butter-making. Adding fresh rather than dried fruit to the scones gives bursts of flavour as you eat – be sure to pick firm berries and mix in lightly to prevent them from breaking up too much.

MAKES 8–9
YOU WILL NEED: I BAKING SHEET, GREASED WITH BUTTER

250g self-raising flour
good pinch of salt
60g caster sugar
50g unsalted butter, chilled and diced
I medium free-range egg, at room
   temperature

about 100ml buttermilk, at room temperature
50g fresh blueberries
40g fresh raspberries
a little extra buttermilk or milk, for brushing
demerara or caster sugar, for sprinkling

1 Heat your oven to 220°C/425°F/gas 7. Sift the flour, salt and caster sugar into a mixing bowl. Add the pieces of butter and rub them into the flour using your fingertips until you can no longer see any lumps of butter, and the whole mixture looks like fine crumbs.

2 Put the egg and 100ml buttermilk in a small bowl and beat with a fork, just to mix. Pour into the crumbs and mix in with a round-bladed knife to make a rough-looking dough. Add the berries and use your hands to bring the mixture together to make a ball of slightly soft dough, with the berries evenly distributed – try not to squash the berries too much as you mix. If there are any dry crumbs at the bottom of the bowl, work in a little more buttermilk.

3 Lightly dust the worktop and your hands with flour. Turn out the dough on to the worktop and gently pat out to about 3cm thick. Dip a 6cm plain round cutter in flour and use it to stamp out rounds, re-flouring it when it starts to stick. Press the trimmings together, pat out and cut more rounds as before.

4 Set the scone rounds slightly apart (to allow for spreading) on the prepared baking sheet. Lightly brush the top of each scone with buttermilk, then sprinkle with demerara sugar. Place in the heated oven and bake for 12–14 minutes until a good golden brown (undersides too) – these fresh berry scones will take slightly longer to bake than regular or dried fruit scones.

5 Transfer immediately to a wire rack and leave to cool slightly, then eat warm, split and spread with butter or clotted cream. These are best eaten the same day.

BISCUITS AND LITTLE CAKES

P.106

CHOCOLATE CHIP SCONES

Try these scones – flavoured with bittersweet marmalade and milk chocolate – for brunch, split and spread with butter or more marmalade. To ensure a crisp and golden exterior, your oven needs to be fully up to temperature before you put the scones in to bake.

MAKES 8
YOU WILL NEED: 1 BAKING SHEET, GREASED WITH BUTTER

250g self-raising flour
good pinch of salt
50g caster sugar
50g unsalted butter, chilled and diced
1 medium free-range egg, at room
  temperature

about 100ml buttermilk, at room temperature
2 tablespoons marmalade (see page 168 for
  an easy home-made marmalade recipe)
60g milk chocolate chips or chopped
  chocolate

1 Heat your oven to 220°C/425°F/gas 7. Sift the flour, salt and sugar into a mixing bowl. Add the pieces of butter and rub them into the flour using your fingertips until you can no longer see any lumps of butter, and the whole mixture looks like fine crumbs.

2 Put the egg and 100ml buttermilk in a small bowl and beat with a fork, just to mix. Pour into the crumbs and add the marmalade and chocolate chips. Mix with a round-bladed knife to make a rough-looking dough, then use your hands to bring the mixture together into a ball of slightly soft dough. If there are dry crumbs at the bottom of the bowl work in a little more buttermilk.

3 Lightly dust the worktop and your hands with flour. Turn out the dough on to the worktop and gently knead for a couple of seconds. Flour your hands again, then pat out the dough to about 3cm thick. Dip a 6cm plain round cutter in flour and use it to stamp out rounds, re-flouring it when it starts to stick. Press the trimmings together, pat out and cut more rounds as before.

4 Set the scone rounds slightly apart (to allow for spreading) on the prepared baking sheet. Place in the heated oven and bake for about 12 minutes until a good golden brown (undersides too). Immediately transfer to a wire rack to cool slightly. These are best eaten warm the same day.

TWO-CHEESE AND DILL SCONES

The tastier the cheese you use to make these savoury scones, the better their flavour will be. A straight-sided cutter will make scone rounds with good, neat sides that rise well.

MAKES 8–9
YOU WILL NEED: I BAKING SHEET, GREASED WITH BUTTER

250g self-raising flour
a couple of pinches each salt and cayenne
   pepper
50g unsalted butter, chilled and diced
25g pecorino cheese, grated

100g extra-mature Cheddar cheese, grated
I teaspoon finely chopped fresh dill
I medium free-range egg, at room temperature
about 100ml buttermilk, at room temperature

I Heat your oven to 220°C/425°F/gas 7. Sift the flour, salt and cayenne into a mixing bowl. Add the pieces of butter and rub them into the flour using your fingertips until you can no longer see any lumps of butter, and the whole mixture looks like fine crumbs. Stir in the pecorino cheese. Set aside a heaped tablespoon of the grated Cheddar (for sprinkling) and add the rest to the bowl with the dill. Mix in with a round-bladed knife.

2 Put the egg and 100ml buttermilk in a small bowl and beat with a fork, just to mix. Pour into the crumbs and mix with the round bladed knife to make a shaggy-looking dough, then use your hands to bring the mixture together into a ball of soft but not sticky dough. If there are dry crumbs at the bottom of the bowl work in a little more buttermilk.

3 Lightly dust the worktop and your hands with flour. Turn out the dough on to the worktop and gently knead for a couple of seconds. Flour your hands again, then pat out the dough to about 3cm thick. Dip a 6cm plain round cutter in flour and use it to stamp out rounds, re-flouring it when it starts to stick. Press the trimmings together, pat out and cut more rounds as before.

4 Set the scone rounds slightly apart (to allow for spreading) on the prepared baking sheet. Sprinkle the top of each scone with some of the reserved Cheddar. Place in the heated oven and bake for about 12 minutes until a good golden brown (undersides too). Immediately transfer to a wire rack to cool slightly. Eat warm the same day, or split and toast the next day (when cold, store in an airtight container).

RED PEPPER AND GOATS' CHEESE MUFFINS

If you like feta cheese, you can use that instead of the goats' cheese. These are perfect with a bowl of soup or a salad.

MAKES 12
YOU WILL NEED: 1 X 12-HOLE MUFFIN TRAY, LINED WITH PAPER MUFFIN CASES

135g log-style goats' cheese
1 medium red pepper (about 100g), cored and cut into 1cm chunks
300g plain flour
2 teaspoons baking powder
$\frac{1}{2}$ teaspoon bicarbonate of soda
$\frac{1}{2}$ teaspoon salt, or to taste

$\frac{1}{4}$ teaspoon cayenne pepper, or to taste
1 tablespoon coarsely chopped fresh basil or parsley
225ml buttermilk, at room temperature
1 medium free-range egg, at room temperature
100ml extra virgin olive oil

1 Heat your oven to 190°C/375°F/gas 5. Cut or crumble the goats' cheese into pieces about the same size as the red pepper chunks.

2 Sift the flour, baking powder, bicarbonate of soda, salt and cayenne into a mixing bowl. Add the chopped herbs, red pepper and cheese and stir into the dry ingredients using a wooden spoon.

3 Lightly beat the buttermilk with the egg and olive oil in a measuring jug, just to mix, then pour into the bowl. Mix everything together with the wooden spoon until just combined – there's no need to beat the mixture. Spoon into the paper muffin cases, making sure they are evenly filled.

4 Place in the heated oven and bake for 25–30 minutes until the muffins are golden brown and feel just firm when pressed in the centre. Leave the muffins to cool in the tray for 2 minutes, then lift out on to a wire rack. Eat warm or at room temperature the same or the next day. Once cold store in an airtight container.

WEEKEND BAKING

Recipes from Mary, Paul and the bakers

- Apricot and Pistachio Tiffin

- Mary's Ginger and Treacle Spiced Traybake

- Mary's Tuiles with Chocolate Mousse

APRICOT AND PISTACHIO TIFFIN

A glamorous version of a much-loved family favourite: pistachio digestives plus home-made marshmallows, apricots and more nuts glued together with lots of dark chocolate.

CUTS INTO 20 SQUARES
YOU WILL NEED: 2 BAKING SHEETS, LINED WITH BAKING PAPER; 1 BROWNIE TIN ABOUT 20.5 X 25CM, OILED AND LINED WITH BAKING PAPER, A SUGAR THERMOMETER

For the marshmallows
5 gelatine leaves (8g total weight)
225g white granulated sugar
100ml water
1 teaspoon liquid glucose
1 large free-range egg white, at room temperature
1 teaspoon vanilla extract
about 200g icing sugar, for dusting
100g soft, ready-to-eat dried apricots, roughly chopped

For the digestives
200g shelled unsalted pistachios (slivered or kernels)
100g unsalted butter, at room temperature

50g light brown muscovado sugar
80g plain flour
¼ teaspoon salt
1 teaspoon baking powder
100g fine oatmeal

For the chocolate mixture
100g golden syrup
200g salted butter, diced
600g dark chocolate (about 70% cocoa solids), broken up
200g shelled unsalted pistachios (slivered or roughly chopped kernels)
200g soft, ready-to-eat dried apricots, roughly chopped
good pinch of sea salt flakes

1 To make the marshmallows, put the sheets of gelatine into a bowl, cover with cold water and leave to soak and soften until needed. Combine the granulated sugar, water and glucose in a small pan over low heat and dissolve the sugar, stirring frequently, without letting the mixture boil. Meanwhile, put the egg white into a large, very clean bowl and whisk with an electric mixer until the egg white will form stiff peaks.

2 Bring the sugar syrup to the boil, then boil rapidly, without stirring, until it reaches 127°C on a sugar thermometer. Pour the hot syrup on to the whisked egg white in a thin, steady stream while whisking constantly at high speed – the mixture will turn

quite liquid. Lift the gelatine sheets out of the water and gently squeeze them to remove excess water, then add to the meringue along with the vanilla and whisk for 5–7 minutes until the mixture cools and thickens enough to hold a shape (like a soft peak).

3 Heavily dust an oiled baking sheet or large tin with icing sugar, then spoon half the marshmallow mixture into the centre. Using a palette knife dipped in cold water, gently spread the marshmallow out to a rectangle 1cm thick. Scatter the apricots evenly over it, then spoon the rest of marshmallow on top and spread it in a very smooth, even layer. Dust with more icing sugar. Place in the fridge to chill for about 1 hour until firm.

4 Cut the marshmallow into 2cm cubes using a pizza wheel-cutter or large knife. Toss the cubes in icing sugar to prevent them from sticking together, then set aside in a cool spot until needed.

5 To make the digestives, heat your oven to 180°C/350°F/gas 4. Grind the nuts in a food processor to a fairly coarse powder – don't let the mixture turn sticky. Using a wooden spoon or electric mixer, cream the butter with the sugar in a mixing bowl until soft and fluffy. Sift the flour, salt and baking powder into the bowl. Add the oatmeal and ground nuts and mix everything together – first with a wooden spoon or plastic spatula, then with your hands.

6 Turn the dough on to the worktop and gently knead with your hands until it holds together (if the mixture feels very oily wrap it in clingfilm and chill for about 20 minutes until firm). Divide the dough in half and roll out each portion on the very lightly floured worktop to 4mm thick. Cut into squares about 5cm (they are going to be broken up, so they don't have to be neat) and arrange slightly apart on the lined baking sheets. Place in the heated oven and bake for about 12 minutes until golden brown. Allow the digestives to cool on the sheets for a few minutes to firm up, then transfer to a wire rack and leave until cold.

7 To make the chocolate mixture measure the syrup, butter and chocolate into a large pan (preferably non-stick). Set over very low heat and stir gently until melted and smooth. Remove from the heat. Pour 250g of the mixture into a small heatproof jug or bowl and set aside for the topping. Leave the rest in the pan until it has cooled to room temperature – if the chocolate is warm it will melt the marshmallows.

8 Set aside 5 digestive biscuits for the decoration and roughly break the remainder into the cooled chocolate mixture. Add half the pistachios, half the apricots and the salt. Mix thoroughly, then gently stir in half the marshmallow cubes. Tip into the prepared brownie tin and spread evenly, then compress the mixture with the back of a spoon or spatula, making sure the surface is flat. Pour over the reserved chocolate mixture (gently warmed if necessary) to give a smooth, even covering. Scatter the rest of the pistachios and apricots over the surface. Cover the top of the tin with clingfilm, then chill for about 4 hours until firm and set.

9 Carefully turn out the tiffin and cut into squares. Decorate with the remaining marshmallow cubes and reserved digestives, broken up.

MARY'S GINGER AND TREACLE SPICED TRAYBAKE

Dark, moist and spicy, this is studded with tiny pieces of stem ginger. Treacle can be difficult to weigh accurately – it tends to stick to the scales pan – so weigh all the ingredients directly in the mixing bowl set on the scales.

CUTS INTO 15–20 PIECES
YOU WILL NEED: 1 TRAYBAKE OR BAKING TIN 23 X 30 X 4CM (OR A ROASTING TIN OF ABOUT THIS SIZE), GREASED AND LINED WITH BAKING PAPER

For the sponge
225g baking margarine or unsalted butter, softened
175g light brown muscovado sugar
200g black treacle
300g self-raising flour
2 teaspoons baking powder
1 teaspoon ground mixed spice
1 teaspoon ground allspice
4 medium eggs, at room temperature

4 tablespoons milk
3 lumps (about 60g) stem ginger in syrup, drained and finely chopped

For the icing
75g icing sugar
3 tablespoons ginger syrup from the jar
3 lumps (about 60g) stem ginger in syrup, drained and coarsely chopped

1 Heat your oven to 160°C/325°F/gas 3. Measure all the ingredients for the sponge straight into a large bowl. Beat well with an electric mixer or wooden spoon for about 2 minutes until well blended; scrape down the sides of the bowl from time to time to be sure everything is thoroughly combined.

2 Using a plastic spatula, scrape the mixture into the prepared tin, then use the back of the spatula to gently level the surface. Place in the heated oven and bake for 35–40 minutes until the centre of the sponge springs back when pressed lightly with a finger, and the edges of the sponge are beginning to shrink away from the sides of the tin.

3 Leave the traybake to cool slightly in the tin before removing it to a wire rack: first ease the paper away from the sides of the tin, then turn out

the sponge on to the rack and remove the lining paper. Turn the cake over so it is right way up. Leave to cool completely.

4 To make the icing, sift the icing sugar into a small bowl, add the ginger syrup and stir together until smooth. Pour the icing over the cake and spread out gently to the edges using a small palette knife. Sprinkle the chopped stem ginger over the surface. Leave to set before serving in squares or slices.

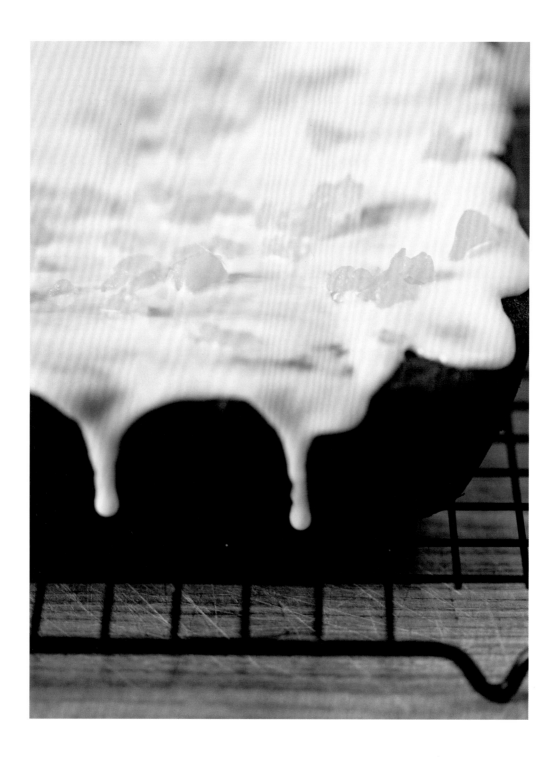

MARY'S TUILES WITH CHOCOLATE MOUSSE

Pretty and delicately decorated, these biscuits are baked quickly and shaped as soon as they come out of the oven. If they start to harden, becoming too firm to bend before you have a chance to shape them all, just return the sheet to the oven for 30–60 seconds to soften. This recipe will make loads of tuiles – you can bake them all and then freeze some, or keep the mix in the fridge for 3–4 days to make fresh tuiles when wanted.

SERVES 8 (1 BASKET OF MOUSSE, 4 TUILES AND 1 CIGAR PER SERVING – WITH A LITTLE LEFTOVER MIXTURE)
YOU WILL NEED: 1 BAKING SHEET, LINED WITH BAKING PAPER; A SILICONE SHEET

For the tuiles
200g unsalted butter, softened
180g icing sugar, sifted
1 teaspoon vanilla extract
6 large egg whites, at room temperature, lightly beaten
200g plain flour
3 teaspoons cocoa powder
50g dark chocolate (your favourite), broken into even pieces

For the chocolate mousse
300ml double cream
200g dark chocolate (about 36% cocoa solids), broken into even pieces
1 large egg white, at room temperature
50g caster sugar
raspberries, to serve

1 Heat your oven to 180°C/350°F/gas 4. To make the tuile mixture, put the soft butter, icing sugar and vanilla into a mixing bowl and whisk together with an electric mixer to make a paste. Gradually add the egg whites, whisking constantly. Fold in the flour, a little at a time, stirring between each addition.

2 Transfer a sixth of the mixture to a small bowl, add the cocoa powder and beat with a spatula or wooden spoon until well mixed. Cover both bowls with clingfilm and leave to rest at room temperature for 30 minutes.

3 Meanwhile, make the chocolate mousse. Heat 150ml of the cream in a small pan until just simmering. Remove the pan from the heat, add the chocolate pieces and stir gently until the chocolate has melted and the mixture is smooth. Pour into a bowl and leave to cool for 15 minutes.

4 Add the remaining cream and beat with an electric mixer until the mixture will stand in soft peaks when the whisk is lifted out. Put the egg white into another bowl and whisk (with a clean whisk or beaters) until it will stand in stiff peaks. Whisk in the sugar, a tablespoon at a time, then keep whisking to make a soft, smooth and glossy meringue. Gently fold the meringue into the chocolate mixture. Cover the bowl and chill until set.

5 While the mousse is chilling, make the tuiles. First make a template for the round tuiles using a plastic sheet or the lid of an old ice cream carton. Cut out holes 7cm in diameter. Set the template on the lined baking sheet. Spread plain tuile mixture over the cut-out shapes using a palette knife, then draw the blade across the template to scrape off the surplus tuile mixture. Carefully remove the template by peeling it away from the sheet.

6 Spoon the cocoa tuile mixture into a small piping bag fitted with a writing tube (or a disposable bag with the end snipped off) and pipe patterns – dots/squiggles/wavy or straight lines – on the tuiles. Place in the heated oven and bake for 5–6 minutes until the tuiles are just turning golden around the edges. Remove the sheet from the oven and, working very quickly, lift each warm tuile off the baking sheet with a palette knife and drape over a rolling pin so the tuile cools in a curved shape. Leave to cool and set.

7 To make tuile cigars, spread the plain tuile mix over the template as before, but don't add the cocoa decorations. Bake as in step 6. While the tuiles are baking, gently melt the 50g dark chocolate. Remove the sheet from the oven and, working quickly, lift the warm tuiles off the sheet and gently curl them around wooden spoon handles to make neat cigar shapes. Leave to cool and set, then slide them off the spoon handles and dip both ends in the melted chocolate. Leave to set on a sheet of baking paper. (The baked tuiles – both curved and cigars – can be frozen or kept in an airtight tin for 3–4 days.)

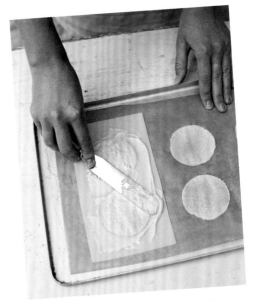

Spread the tuile mixture over the cut-out shapes

Shape curved tuile 'roof tiles', cigars and baskets

8 To make a tuile basket, line the baking sheet with a silicone sheet. Drop a spoonful of the tuile mixture on to the sheet and spread out with the back of the spoon to an uneven circle about 13cm across. Bake for 5–6 minutes until pale golden. Remove the baking sheet from the oven, carefully lift off the tuile and quickly mould it over an upturned pudding mould or ramekin to make a basket shape. Leave to cool and firm up before gently lifting the basket off the mould. Fill with the chocolate mousse and serve as soon as possible with the curved tuiles and tuile cigars.

Small
mixing bowl

Small sharp knife

Flameproof
casserole

Box grater

Spatula

Round cutter

Small loaf tin

Electric scales

Large loaf tin

Wooden spoon

Sieve

Baking sheet

Rolling pin

Free-standing
electric mixer

BREAD

Breads that use chemical raising agents rather than yeast – 'quick' breads – can be made in minutes rather than hours. But yeast-raised breads are still the champions of the baking world.

For yeast-raised doughs, you need higher-protein flours labelled 'strong' or 'for bread'. The different types of flours vary in the amount of liquid they can absorb, so be prepared to add a bit more or a bit less liquid than the recipe specifies. Quick breads rely on a combination of acidic and alkaline ingredients to produce the bubbles of gas that make the dough expand and give a good, light-textured result. Buttermilk and bicarbonate of soda are a combination that works well.

Slashing a loaf across the top just before baking helps it rise evenly as the air escapes. For a good-looking result lightly oil the blade of the sharp knife first, so it won't stick to the surface of the dough and drag the loaf out of shape.

CRUNCHY BACON SODA BREAD

The light texture of this bread comes not from yeast and kneading but a combination of acidic buttermilk and bicarbonate of soda (alkali). Adding crisp-fried bacon and plenty of parsley to the basic dough makes a savoury loaf with bags of flavour. Don't fall into the trap of adding extra bicarb to make a lighter, bigger loaf, because this will give the bread an unpleasant aftertaste. Be sure to use top-quality plain flour, not cheap 'bargain' flour.

MAKES 1 MEDIUM LOAF
YOU WILL NEED: 1 BAKING SHEET, LINED WITH BAKING PAPER

4 rashers (about 85g) smoked back bacon
1 shallot, finely chopped
handful of parsley sprigs, finely chopped
450g plain white flour
1 teaspoon bicarbonate of soda
1 teaspoon salt
25g unsalted butter, chilled and diced
about 350ml buttermilk

1 Snip the bacon rashers across into thin strips (about 5mm) with kitchen scissors – the strips don't have to be neat or even-sized. Put into a cold non-stick frying pan, set over fairly low heat and cook, stirring occasionally, until the fat starts to melt. Turn up the heat to medium and cook until the bacon starts to colour. Add the shallot and parsley and cook, stirring constantly, until the shallot turns golden. Remove from the heat and leave to cool.

2 Heat your oven to 220°C/425°F/gas 7. Sift the flour, bicarbonate of soda and salt into a mixing bowl. Add the pieces of butter and toss in the flour to separate them and coat them in flour. Then rub the butter into the flour until the mixture looks like breadcrumbs.

3 Stir in the cooled bacon mixture using a round-bladed knife. Make a well in the centre of the mixture and pour in the buttermilk. Mix everything together (with the same knife, or your hands) to make a soft, slightly sticky, rough-looking dough. If the dough feels dry and won't come together, work in more buttermilk a tablespoon at a time.

4 Lightly dust your hands and the worktop with flour, then turn out the dough and shape it into a ball, using no more than 3 or 4 kneading movements – the dough shouldn't look smooth. Set the ball of dough on the lined baking sheet and gently flatten with your fingers so the dough is 3–4cm tall. Using a table knife, cut a deep cross in the top of the dough and dust it with flour.

5 Place in the heated oven and bake for about 35 minutes until the bread is a good golden brown and sounds hollow when tapped on the base. Transfer to a wire rack to cool. Best eaten warm the same day, or toasted the next.

NO-KNEAD COMTÉ LOAF

Eggs give this easy, one-rise loaf a rich and golden crumb – like a brioche without the work. It's good freshly baked or toasted. Try it with baked beans.

MAKES 1 LARGE LOAF
YOU WILL NEED: 1 X 900G LOAF TIN (ABOUT 26 X 12.5 X 7.5CM), GREASED WITH BUTTER

500g strong white bread flour
1½ teaspoons salt
¼ teaspoon English mustard powder
½ teaspoon dried chilli flakes (or to taste)
1 x 7g sachet fast-action dried yeast

100g Comté cheese, grated
4 medium free-range eggs, at room temperature
about 250ml milk, at room temperature

1 Put the flour, salt, mustard powder, chilli flakes and yeast into a large bowl and mix thoroughly with your hand. Add the grated cheese and mix in so it is evenly distributed and no longer in clumps.

2 Beat the eggs and milk in a small bowl with a fork, just to combine, then add to the big bowl. Mix everything together with your hand to make a soft, sticky dough. Work the dough in the bowl, using your hand like a paddle to slap and beat the dough, for 3 minutes until it feels very stretchy and elastic.

3 Scoop the dough into the prepared tin and press it out evenly, into the corners too, to make a neat loaf shape. Slip the tin into a large plastic bag. Slightly inflate the bag so the plastic doesn't stick to the dough, then secure the end. Leave at normal room temperature for 1½–2 hours until the dough has risen to 1cm below the rim of the tin. Towards the end of this time heat your oven to 190°C/375°F/gas 5.

4 Remove the tin from the bag and place in the heated oven. Bake for 40–45 minutes until the loaf is a good golden brown and sounds hollow when tapped on the base. Turn out and cool on a wire rack. Best eaten within 5 days.

QUICK RYE

Rye flour is very low in gluten (different to wheat gluten) so it makes a very sticky dough that bakes to a more dense, moist loaf than one made with wheat flour. Using an acidic ingredient like buttermilk in this rye soda bread, rather than regular milk or water, helps to give a lighter texture. If you can, bake a day or so before slicing to give the flavour time to develop. To make a sweeter loaf you can replace the caraway seeds with cumin seeds and add 2 tablespoons raisins.

MAKES 1 MEDIUM LOAF
YOU WILL NEED: 1 X 450G LOAF TIN (ABOUT 19 X 12.5 X 7.5CM), WELL GREASED WITH BUTTER

2½ tablespoons rye flakes
400g stoneground wholemeal rye flour
1 teaspoon caraway seeds
1½ teaspoons bicarbonate of soda
½ teaspoon baking powder

1 teaspoon salt
1 tablespoon runny honey
400ml buttermilk OR 200ml each low-fat
    natural yoghurt and milk

1 Heat your oven to 180°C/350°F/gas 4. Spoon 1½ tablespoons of the rye flakes into the buttered tin and give the tin a shake to spread out the flakes, then press them all over the base and sides. Save the rest of the flakes for the top.

2 Put the flour, seeds, bicarbonate of soda, baking powder and salt into a mixing bowl and mix well with your hand. Make a well in the centre of the mixture. Stir the honey into the buttermilk (or yoghurt/milk mixture), then pour into the well in the flour. Mix with a wooden spoon or your hand to make a heavy, sticky dough. If the dough is dry and stiff, work in more buttermilk or milk a spoonful at a time.

3 Scrape the dough into the loaf tin and spread it out evenly with a dampened rubber spatula, or your fingers, into the corners too, to make a neat loaf. Scatter the rest of the rye flakes on top and gently press them on to the surface of the dough.

4 Place in the heated oven and bake for 50–60 minutes until a skewer inserted into the centre of the loaf comes out clean. Turn out the loaf on to a wire rack and leave until cold. Wrap in foil and leave overnight before cutting into thin slices. Best eaten within 5 days.

CARAMELISED ONION PISSALADIÈRE

This is the pissaladière of Provence – a yeasted dough base flavoured with thyme and olive oil covered with a rich mix of onions, anchovies and olives (and sometimes slices of tomato). The long, slow cooking of the onions with a seasoning of thyme and anchovies renders them meltingly soft and mild. Cut into large squares for lunch, or into fingers for a starter or to serve with drinks.

MAKES 1 LARGE TART
YOU WILL NEED: 1 LARGE BAKING SHEET (ABOUT 38 X 32CM), LIGHTLY GREASED WITH OLIVE OIL

For the onion topping
5 tablespoons virgin olive oil
1 x 50g tin anchovies in olive oil (30g drained weight), drained and finely chopped
4 large sprigs of fresh thyme
10 medium onions, very thinly sliced
freshly ground black pepper

For the dough
400g strong white bread flour
1 teaspoon salt

1 x 7g sachet fast-action dried yeast
1 teaspoon fresh thyme leaves, chopped
3 tablespoons virgin olive oil, plus extra for kneading
about 275ml water, at room temperature

To finish
75g stoned black olives, halved
few sprigs of fresh thyme

1 Heat the oil in a deep, heavy flameproof casserole or pan over low heat. Add the anchovies with the sprigs of thyme and cook gently for about 10 minutes, stirring frequently, until they have softened and broken down almost to a purée.

2 Add the onions and stir to coat thoroughly in the anchovy oil. Season with a few grinds of black pepper and stir in. Cover the pan and cook very gently for about 30 minutes, stirring occasionally, until the onions are very tender and reduced to about a fifth of their original volume.

3 Pick out the thyme twigs (the leaves will have been mixed into the onions). Turn up the heat to medium, then stir-fry the onions until they become sticky and lightly golden, and all the moisture has

evaporated. Be ready to turn down the heat if they look like they are browning too much. Remove from the heat and leave to cool.

4 Make up the dough while the onions are cooking slowly. Mix the flour with the salt, dried yeast and thyme in a mixing bowl or the bowl of a large free-standing electric mixer. Make a well in the centre of the mixture and pour in the oil. Add the water and mix everything together with your hand, or the dough hook attachment of the mixer on the lowest speed, to make a very soft and slightly sticky dough. If it feels dry and firm, or there are dry crumbs in the base of the bowl, work in more water a tablespoon at a time. If the dough seems very wet and sticky, and won't leave the sides of the bowl, work in a little more flour.

5 Lightly oil your hands and the worktop with olive oil (only use a teaspoon). Turn out the dough from the mixing bowl and knead it for about 10 minutes until it feels firmer and is very smooth, elastic and stretchy (or knead in the mixer with the dough hook for about 5 minutes on the lowest speed).

6 Return the dough to the bowl and cover tightly with clingfilm or a snap-on lid. Leave on the worktop to rise for 1–1½ hours until doubled in size.

7 Oil your hands and the worktop again. Punch down the dough (still in the bowl) to deflate it, then turn it out on to the oiled surface. Roll it out to a rectangle to fit your baking sheet. Lift the dough on to the sheet and press it out evenly with your fingers so it completely covers the sheet.

8 Spoon the cold onion mixture on to the dough and spread evenly over the surface to within 1cm of each edge. Scatter the olives over the top. Cover loosely with a large sheet of clingfilm and leave on the worktop to rise for 15 minutes.

9 Meanwhile, heat your oven to its maximum setting. Uncover the tart and put it into the very hot oven. Immediately turn down the temperature to 220°C/425°F/gas 7 and bake for 20 minutes until the crust is a good golden brown. Remove from the oven and scatter over the thyme sprigs. Leave to cool for 5 minutes before cutting into squares with a pizza wheel-cutter. Eat while warm. Any leftover tart can be wrapped in foil and kept in the fridge overnight; next day, reheat on a heated baking sheet in the oven at 180°C/350°F/gas 4 for about 10 minutes.

ROSEMARY POTATO BREAD

Here's an old Irish recipe with a new twist. The mashed floury potatoes give the bread a light texture, and chunks of potato and rosemary add wonderful flavour. You can use all the dough to make rolls, or make 8 rolls plus 1 medium loaf or 2 medium loaves.

MAKES 16 ROLLS
YOU WILL NEED: 1–2 BAKING SHEETS, LINED WITH BAKING PAPER

450g floury or baking potatoes
2 tablespoons olive oil
1 tablespoon young rosemary leaves
500g strong white bread flour
300g wholemeal bread flour
1 x 7g sachet fast-action dried yeast
about 425ml lukewarm milk
salt and freshly ground black pepper

1 Heat your oven to 220°C/425°F/gas 7. Scrub about 150g of the potatoes and cut into 2.5cm chunks. Put them in an ovenproof dish, add the oil and toss gently until coated. Place in the heated oven and roast for 15 minutes until lightly golden – they will be half-cooked and will finish cooking as the loaf is baked. Remove from the oven. Add the rosemary and some salt and pepper, and toss gently. Leave to cool (turn off the oven for now).

2 While the potatoes are roasting, peel the remaining potatoes and halve or quarter them so the pieces are all about the same size. Place in a pan of cold water, bring to the boil and cook for about 15 minutes until tender. Drain thoroughly, then return to the pan, cover with a tea towel and dry for a couple of minutes, then mash until smooth. Leave to cool.

3 Combine the flours and 1 teaspoon salt in a large mixing bowl or the bowl of a large free-standing electric mixer. Add 200g of the cooled mashed potato (if there is any left over, keep it for another use) and mix in with your fingers until thoroughly combined. Mix in the dried yeast.

4 Make a well in the flour mixture and pour in the milk. Using your hand, or the dough hook attachment of the mixer on the lowest speed, mix everything together to make a firm dough. If there are dry crumbs or the dough feels stiff and dry, work in a little more milk a tablespoon at a time; if the dough feels very sticky work in a little more flour.

5 Turn out the dough on to a lightly floured worktop and knead thoroughly for 10 minutes until smooth and stretchy (or for 4 minutes in the mixer using the dough hook on the lowest possible speed). Add the roast potatoes, with the rosemary and oil, and gently work into the dough by hand. Return the dough to the bowl and cover with clingfilm, a damp tea towel or a snap-on lid. Leave in a warm spot to rise for about 1 hour until doubled in size.

6 Gently press down the risen dough to deflate it, then turn out on to the lightly floured worktop. Divide the dough in half: each half will make 8 rolls or a loaf. To make rolls, press the dough into a thick disc about 20cm across, then cut it into 8 wedges using a sharp knife. Set the wedges well apart on a lined baking sheet. To make a loaf, shape the dough into a ball – it doesn't have to be neat – and set on a lined baking sheet. Cut a deep cross into the top of the loaf.

7 Slip each baking sheet into a large plastic bag, slightly inflate it and secure the opening. Leave in a warm place to rise until doubled in size – allow about 30 minutes for rolls or 1 hour for a loaf. Towards the end of the rising time heat your oven to 220°C/425°F/gas 7.

8 Uncover the dough and place in the heated oven. Bake until the rolls or loaves are a good golden brown and sound hollow when tapped on the base – 15–20 minutes for rolls or about 35 minutes for a loaf. Cool on a wire rack and eat warm.

NUT LOAF

Good with cheese, this bread is made with both white and wholemeal flours so you get plenty of flavour, a chewy texture and a light crumb. For a really crisp crust, add a burst of steam at the start of baking.

MAKES 2 MEDIUM LOAVES
YOU WILL NEED: 1–2 BAKING SHEETS, LINED WITH BAKING PAPER

300g strong white bread flour
100g stoneground wholemeal bread flour
1 teaspoon salt
1 x 7g sachet fast-action dried yeast
about 300ml lukewarm water

125g mixed nuts (shelled pistachios,
    pine nuts and roughly chopped blanched
    hazelnuts and almonds)
25g large raisins

1 Put both flours into a large mixing bowl or the bowl of a large free-standing electric mixer. Add the salt and dried yeast and mix well with your hand or the dough hook attachment of the mixer on the lowest speed.

2 Make a well in the centre. Add the lukewarm water and mix everything together, with your hand or the dough hook (on lowest speed), to make a soft and slightly sticky dough – wholemeal flour takes slightly longer than white flour to absorb water and stiffens up as it is worked, so you have to mix a bit longer. If the dough feels dry and stiff, or there are dry crumbs at the base of the bowl, work in more water a tablespoon at a time.

3 Lightly flour your hands and the worktop, then turn out the dough. Knead for about 7 minutes until it is stretchy (or in the mixer with the dough hook for about 4 minutes at lowest speed). Add the nuts and raisins and work into the dough, then knead for a further 1–2 minutes to make sure they are evenly distributed and the dough is elastic.

4 Return the dough to the bowl and cover tightly with clingfilm or a snap-on lid. Leave on the worktop to rise for about 1 hour until the dough has doubled in size.

5 Punch down the risen dough with your knuckles to deflate it, then turn it out on to the lightly floured worktop. Divide the dough into 2 equal pieces. Gently knead one piece for a minute, then shape into a ball and then into an oval about 20cm long, 7.5cm wide in the middle and about 6cm high. Do the same with the other piece of dough.

6 Set the shaped loaves on the lined baking sheet or sheets (if using one baking sheet make sure the loaves are placed well apart to allow for spreading). Cover the loaves loosely with a sheet of clingfilm or a dry tea towel and leave on the worktop to rise for about 1 hour until doubled in size. Towards the end of this time heat your oven to 220°C/425°F/gas 7.

7 Uncover the loaves. Using a small, sharp knife, make a few slashes across the top of each loaf. Place in the heated oven and bake for 10 minutes, then turn down the temperature to 200°C/400°F/gas 6. Bake the loaves for a further 20–25 minutes until they are a good golden brown and they sound hollow when tapped on the base. Cool on a wire rack. Best eaten within 4 days.

THYME FOUGASSE

Smelling deliciously of herbs and wild mushrooms, this is a bread you can't wait to eat straight from the oven – perfect for tearing into pieces to dip in good olive oil and balsamic vinegar.

MAKES 1 MEDIUM BREAD
YOU WILL NEED: 1 BAKING SHEET

15g dried porcini mushrooms
200ml boiling water
250g strong white bread flour
100g stoneground wholemeal wheat or
    spelt flour for bread
1 teaspoon salt

1 x 7g sachet fast-action dried yeast
1 teaspoon roughly chopped fresh thyme
    leaves

To finish (optional)
fresh thyme leaves
sea salt flakes

1 Put the mushrooms into a heatproof bowl, breaking up any very large pieces, and pour over the boiling water. Leave the mushrooms to soak until the water has cooled to room temperature.

2 Put both flours, the salt, yeast and thyme into a large mixing bowl or the bowl of a large free-standing electric mixer. Mix well with your hand or the dough hook attachment on the lowest speed. Make a well in the flour mixture.

3 Drain the mushrooms in a sieve set over a measuring jug, pressing down on the mushrooms to extract all the liquid. Add the mushrooms to the well in the flour. Measure the mushroom liquid and make it up to 225ml with lukewarm water. Pour into the well. Mix everything together with your hand or the dough hook attachment (on lowest speed) to make a soft but not sticky dough. If the dough feels dry and is hard to bring together, or there are dry crumbs in the bottom of the bowl, work in more water a tablespoon at a time; if the dough is very sticky, work in a little more flour.

4 Lightly dust your hands and the worktop with flour, then turn out the dough. Knead for about 10 minutes until it feels very stretchy and elastic (or for 5 minutes in the mixer with the dough hook on lowest speed). Flour your fingers again, then pat out the dough to an oval about 25 x 20cm. Carefully lift

it on to a sheet of baking paper. Cover loosely with a dry tea towel or clingfilm. Leave on the worktop to rise for about 1 hour until doubled in size.

5 Towards the end of the rising time, heat your oven to 230°C/450°F/gas 8. Put in the baking sheet to heat up plus an empty roasting tin on the floor of the oven.

6 Uncover the loaf. If using, scatter the thyme leaves and sea salt flakes evenly over the surface. With a small, sharp knife cut 5 slits, about 10cm long, in the dough (rather like veins in a leaf), then gently open them out to make lozenge-shaped holes about 6cm wide.

7 Remove the hot baking sheet from the oven and set it on a heatproof surface. Carefully lift the loaf, on the sheet of baking paper, on to the baking sheet and place it back in the oven. Add a cup of cold water or handful of ice cubes to the hot roasting tin, then quickly shut the oven door. Bake for about 12 minutes until the bread is a good golden brown and sounds hollow when tapped on the base. Transfer the bread to a wire rack to cool for a few minutes, then eat warm.

ROQUEFORT LOAF

Roquefort, a blue cheese made from raw sheep's milk, works well in a bread dough. The taste of the cheese comes through, but without making the crumb, or crust, heavy or greasy. Make sure the oven is properly heated before you start to bake the loaves or the crust will be tough.

MAKES 2 MEDIUM LOAVES
YOU WILL NEED: 1 BAKING SHEET, LINED WITH BAKING PAPER

350g strong white bread flour
150g white spelt flour
1 ½ teaspoons salt
few grinds of black pepper

1 x 7g sachet fast-action dried yeast
150g Roquefort cheese, at room temperature
about 300ml water, at room temperature

1 Put both flours, the salt, pepper and yeast into a large bowl and mix well with your hand. Crumble the cheese into the bowl and mix in. Make a well in the middle of the mixture. Pour the room-temperature water into the well (not warm water, which would make the dough greasy) and mix everything together with your hand to make a very soft dough. If the dough is dry and difficult to bring together, work in more water a tablespoon at a time; if the dough is very sticky work in more flour.

2 Dust your hands and the worktop with flour, then turn out the dough. Knead it gently for 2 minutes – the cheese will start to break up – then return to the bowl. Cover with clingfilm or a snap-on lid and leave on the worktop to rise for an hour – the dough will look puffy.

3 Flour your hands and the worktop again. Turn out the dough and knead for about 5 minutes until the dough feels stretchy and elastic. Return to the bowl, cover and leave as before for about 45 minutes until doubled in size.

4 Turn out the dough on to the lightly floured worktop and divide in half. With your hands, flatten each portion to a rectangle about 15 x 20cm. Roll up each rectangle tightly from one short side and pinch the seam to seal. Move one roll of dough to an unfloured part of the worktop and, using your

hands, roll back and forth to make a fat sausage-shaped loaf about 30cm long with neat tapered ends. Repeat to shape the other loaf.

5 Set the 2 loaves, well apart, on the lined baking sheet. Cover loosely with a dry tea towel and leave on the worktop to rise for about 45 minutes until doubled in size. Towards the end of the rising time, heat your oven to 220°C/425°F/gas 7. Put an empty roasting tin on the floor of the oven to heat up.

6 Uncover the risen loaves and brush them lightly with water. With a sharp knife slash each loaf across several times on a slight diagonal, then put them into the heated oven. Pour a jug of cold water into the hot roasting tin to create a burst of steam, then quickly close the oven door. Bake the loaves for about 25 minutes until a rich golden brown and they sound hollow when tapped on the base. Transfer to a wire rack and leave to cool. Best eaten the same day or the next.

BAGUETTES

To make a good 'French stick' with its distinctive open texture, you need a very lively dough that's just slightly soft, rather than slightly firm. A bit of steam at the start of baking will help give the baguettes the traditional glossy, razor-sharp crust.

MAKES 2
YOU WILL NEED: I LARGE BAKING SHEET OR PIZZA BAKING STONE

300g strong white bread flour
200g plain white flour
1 x 7g sachet fast-action dried yeast
about 300ml lukewarm water

1 teaspoon salt
½ teaspoon salt dissolved in 4 tablespoons
 cold water, for brushing

1 Mix together both flours in a large bowl, then tip about half into another, smaller bowl and put on one side. Stir ½ teaspoon of the yeast into the flour in the large bowl, then work in the lukewarm water, using your hand like a paddle, to make a smooth, thick batter. Cover the bowl with clingfilm and leave on the worktop for 3–4 hours until the surface of the batter is covered with tiny bubbles (if you use water from the cold tap you can leave the batter for 8 hours or overnight).

2 Uncover the bowl and stir 1 tablespoon of lukewarm water into the batter. Mix the rest of the yeast and the salt into the flour in the second bowl. Gradually work this mixture into the batter, using your hand, to make a dough that's slightly soft but not sticky. If the dough feels very sticky or doesn't hold its shape, work in a little more of either type of flour; if the dough feels tough and dry once all the flour has been added (or there are dry crumbs that can't be worked into the dough), work in more lukewarm water a tablespoon at a time.

3 Lightly dust your hands and the worktop with flour, then turn out the dough. Thoroughly knead it for about 10 minutes until it feels smooth and very stretchy. Put the dough back into the mixing bowl, cover with clingfilm and leave to rise on the worktop for about 1 hour until doubled in size.

4 Lightly dust your hands and the worktop with flour, then gently turn out the ball of dough – don't punch it down to deflate it. Use a sharp knife to cut it in half. Without handling the dough too much, shape each piece into a rough ball. Cover loosely with a dry tea towel or sheet of clingfilm and leave for 15 minutes.

5 Move one piece of dough to the side. Dust your rolling pin with flour, then gently roll out the other piece of dough to a rectangle about 25 x 30cm. Roll up the rectangle fairly tightly from one long side, like a swiss roll. Tuck in the ends and pinch the seam together firmly. Move the roll of dough to an unfloured part of the worktop and roll back and forth with your hands to make a sausage-shaped loaf 40cm long with gently tapering ends.

6 Lay a large, dry tea towel on a large tray or board and lightly dust the towel with flour. Gently lift the shaped loaf and place on one side of the cloth-topped tray. Repeat to shape the second loaf, pleating the cloth in between the loaves and at the sides to make a barrier and a support (you could use the rolling pin under the cloth along one side as a wall, and tins of food or a thin bottle as the other). Cover the whole lot with a large sheet of clingfilm and leave on the worktop to rise for about 45 minutes until doubled in size.

7 While the loaves are rising, heat your oven to 230°C/450°F/gas 8. Put the baking sheet or pizza stone in the oven to heat up, and place an empty roasting tin on the floor of the oven.

8 When the loaves are ready for baking, quickly remove the hot baking sheet from the oven. Slide and roll the loaves on to the baking sheet. Brush them with the salty water, then make several slashes along the loaves with a sharp knife. Put the baking sheet back into the oven. Pour a jug of cold water into the roasting tin to create plenty of steam, then quickly shut the oven door. Bake the loaves for about 20 minutes until golden brown and crisp. Cool on a wire rack and eat the same or next day.

WHOLEMEAL OATY SODA BREAD

A farmhouse recipe, this soda bread has plenty of texture thanks to the flakes of wheat and porridge oats. Mixing plain flour with stoneground wholemeal gives a lighter, softer texture. You could add a tablespoon each of wheat germ and wheat bran if you like the flavour. For the best texture, mix and bake the dough quickly.

MAKES 1 MEDIUM LOAF
YOU WILL NEED: 1 BAKING SHEET, LINED WITH BAKING PAPER

200g plain white flour
200g plain stoneground wholemeal flour
1 teaspoon bicarbonate of soda
1 teaspoon salt

25g unsalted butter, chilled and diced
50g porridge oats
50g wheat or spelt flakes
about 375ml buttermilk

1 Heat your oven to 220°C/425°F/gas 7. Put both flours, the bicarbonate of soda and salt into a mixing bowl and mix well with your hand. Add the pieces of butter and rub in until the mixture looks like fine crumbs. Stir in the oats and flakes, distributing them evenly.

2 Make a well in the centre of the mixture and pour in the buttermilk. Mix everything together, using a round-bladed knife or your hand, to make a soft, slightly sticky, shaggy-looking dough. If the mixture feels dry and won't come together, or there are dry crumbs in the bowl, work in more buttermilk a tablespoon at a time.

3 Lightly dust your hands and the worktop with flour, then turn out the dough and shape it into a ball, using no more than 3 or 4 kneading movements – the dough shouldn't look smooth. Set the ball of dough on the lined baking sheet and gently flatten with your fingers so the ball is 3–4cm tall. Using a table knife, cut a deep cross in the top of the dough and dust it with flour.

4 Place in the heated oven and bake for about 35 minutes until the bread is a good golden brown and sounds hollow when tapped on the base. Transfer to a wire rack to cool. Best eaten warm the same day, or toasted the next.

WEEKEND
BAKING

Recipes from Mary, Paul and the bakers

- Paul's Olive Breadsticks

- Paul's English Muffins

- Mexican Breadsticks

- Paul's Rye Bread

- Paul's Pretzels

PAUL'S OLIVE BREADSTICKS

These breadsticks are packed with green olives and taste so good.

MAKES 36
YOU WILL NEED: 3 BAKING SHEETS, LINED WITH BAKING PAPER

1kg strong white bread flour, plus
  extra for dusting
20g salt
20g fast-action dried yeast
800ml tepid water
4 tablespoons olive oil
1kg good-quality pitted green olives,
  well drained
fine semolina, for dusting (optional)

1 Put the flour into the bowl of a large free-standing electric mixer fitted with a dough hook. Add the salt to one side of the bowl and the yeast to the other side. Pour in three-quarters of the water and begin mixing on slow speed. As soon as the dough starts to come together, slowly add the rest of the water, still mixing.

2 Turn up to medium speed and mix for a further 5–8 minutes. The dough should now be wet and easy to stretch when pulled. Add the olive oil and mix for a further 2 minutes, then add the olives and mix with your hand or a spoon just until evenly distributed in the dough.

3 Grease two 2–3 litre square plastic tubs or containers with oil. Divide the dough equally between the tubs and cover with clingfilm. Leave on the worktop until the dough has at least tripled in size – about 1 hour. Towards the end of the rising time heat your oven to 220°C/425°F/gas 7.

The wet dough will be stretchy

4 Heavily dust the worktop with flour, plus some semolina if you have it, then carefully tip the dough from one of the tubs on to the floury surface. The dough will be very loose and flowing, but don't worry! Rather than knock it back to deflate, you should handle it gently to keep in as much air as possible. Dust the top of the dough with flour, then gently stretch it out with your fingertips to a rough rectangle about 25 x 36cm and 1cm thick.

5 Starting at one long side, cut the dough rectangle into about 18 strips using a large knife or pizza wheel-cutter. Lay the strips, spaced well apart, on the lined baking sheets – 6 strips to each sheet.

6 Place in the heated oven and bake for 10–15 minutes until golden. Transfer to a wire rack to cool. Meanwhile, shape and bake the second batch of breadsticks. Store the baked breadsticks in an airtight container for up to a week.

Gently stretch out the dough with your fingertips to a rectangle

PAUL'S ENGLISH MUFFINS

English muffins have a soft, tender crumb and very little crust – they are not baked but are quickly cooked on a griddle or hot plate. Use them for Eggs Benedict, topped with a poached egg, slice of ham and Hollandaise Sauce (see the recipe for the sauce on page 211).

MAKES 8
YOU WILL NEED: GRIDDLE (NON-RIDGED), HOT PLATE OR FLAT, HEAVY SHALLOW PAN

300g strong white bread flour
6g fast-action dried yeast
6g salt
15g caster sugar
15g unsalted butter, softened and cut in
   small pieces

1 medium egg, lightly beaten to mix
about 170ml milk, at room temperature
15g semolina or fine polenta

1 Tip the flour into a large mixing bowl. Sprinkle the yeast on one side of the flour and the salt on to the other side of the flour. Add the sugar, the pieces of butter, beaten egg and milk to the bowl. Mix everything together with your hand to make a soft dough, adding more milk if necessary.

2 Sprinkle the worktop with a little flour, then turn out the dough and thoroughly knead for 10 minutes until soft, smooth and stretchy. Put the ball of dough into a clean, lightly oiled bowl. Cover it with clingfilm and leave to rise on the worktop for about 1 hour until doubled in size.

3 Tip the dough out on to the lightly floured worktop and roll out to about 1.5cm thick. Leave the dough on the worktop, uncovered, to relax for 15 minutes (this will help prevent the muffins from shrinking).

Mix with your hands to make a soft dough

4 Sprinkle half of the semolina or polenta on to 2 baking sheets. Using a 9cm straight-sided cutter, stamp out 8 muffins. (If you need to, gather up the trimmings and knead gently, then re-roll and stamp out more muffins.) Arrange 4 muffins, evenly spaced apart, on each of the baking sheets. Sprinkle the remaining semolina or polenta over the top of the muffins. Leave to rise, uncovered, for 30 minutes – the muffins will expand but will not double in size.

5 Heat the griddle over a low heat. Place the muffins on the heated griddle and cook for 5–6 minutes: as the heat rises up and the muffins cook, you'll see their texture and colour change – a bit like a fillet of salmon does when pan-fried. When the colour change has reached halfway up the muffins,

Flip over the muffins to cook on the other side

MEXICAN BREADSTICKS

Two doughs – one white and one coloured with spices – are sandwiched with chopped Mexican chillies, then cut into strips and twisted. The resulting breadsticks are tongue-tinglingly good!

MAKES 36
YOU WILL NEED: 1–2 BAKING SHEETS, SPRINKLED WITH CORNMEAL

90g fine cornmeal, plus extra for
   dusting
370g strong white bread flour
1½ teaspoons salt
5g (1 teaspoon) fast-action dried yeast
½ teaspoon chilli powder (mild or hot
   to taste)
½ teaspoon ground cumin
2 teaspoons paprika

2 teaspoons smoked sweet paprika
¼ teaspoon garlic powder or fine
   granules
¼ teaspoon onion powder
4 teaspoons virgin olive oil
300ml lukewarm water
100g drained sliced jalapeño chillies
   (from a jar)

1 Put the cornmeal, flour, salt and yeast into a mixing bowl and mix thoroughly with your hand. Tip half of the mixture into another bowl and add the chilli powder, cumin, both types of paprika and the garlic and onion powders. Mix well. Make a well in the dry ingredients in each bowl.

2 Add half the oil and half the water to one bowl and mix to a soft but not sticky dough. Sprinkle the worktop and your hands with cornmeal, then turn out the dough and knead it thoroughly for about 5 minutes until very smooth and elastic. Return it to the bowl and cover the top with clingfilm. Repeat all this for the other bowl. Leave the 2 doughs to rise in a warm spot for about 1 hour until doubled in size.

3 Towards the end of the rising time, heat your oven to 180°C/350°F/gas 4. Chop the chillies finely. Put them on a clean tea towel (or thick kitchen paper) and squeeze them dry.

4 Sprinkle cornmeal on your worktop Place the white dough on this and sprinkle it with a little cornmeal. Roll out to a rectangle about 18 × 16cm and 1cm thick. Cover the dough evenly with the chopped chillies and gently press them into the dough. Roll out the dark pink dough to a rectangle exactly the same size as the white one, then set it on top and gently press the 2 doughs together.

5 Roll out the layered dough to a rectangle 36 × 20cm and 5mm thick. Using a pizza wheel-cutter or a large sharp knife, cut the rectangle in half to make 2 pieces each 36 × 10cm. Cut each piece across into strips 2cm wide and 10cm long.

6 One at a time, roll each strip with your hands back and forth on the worktop to make a thin pencil shape about 25cm long. Twist the strip to give a striped candy-cane effect, then roll in a little extra cornmeal. As the breadsticks are shaped, set them slightly apart on the baking sheets.

7 As soon as they are all shaped, place in the heated oven and bake for 30–35 minutes until golden and crisp; give the baking sheets a little shake halfway through the baking time so the breadsticks turn over slightly. Cool on a wire rack and store in an airtight container.

PAUL'S RYE BREAD

Dark and slightly chewy, this wheat-free loaf has a good crust. The dough is only risen once, but it does take a while to double in size.

MAKES 1 LOAF
YOU WILL NEED: 1 BAKING SHEET, LINED WITH BAKING PAPER

500g rye flour
10g salt
10g fast-action dried yeast

20ml black treacle
350ml cool water
olive oil, for kneading

1 Tip the flour into a large mixing bowl. Add the salt to one side of the bowl and the yeast to the other. Add the treacle and three-quarters of the water, then turn the mixture round with your fingers. Continue adding the rest of the water, a little at a time, turning the mixture until you've picked up all the flour from the sides of the bowl (you may not need all the water, or you may need to add a little more: you want a dough that is soft but not soggy). Use the mixture to clean the inside of the bowl, and keep turning and mixing until you have a rough dough.

2 Coat the worktop with a little olive oil, then tip the dough on to it. Knead for 5–10 minutes: work through the initial 'wet' stage until the dough starts to form a soft skin. You will find that this dough feels different from a conventional wheat-flour dough – less smooth and stretchy.

3 Form the dough into a smooth round cob by turning it on the worktop and tucking the edges underneath until the top is smooth and tight. Generously dust the inside of a large round proving basket with rye flour. Put the dough in it, smooth top side down. Cover with a slightly damp tea towel to protect the dough and prevent a skin from forming. Leave to prove for about 8 hours (ideally overnight) – the rye dough will eventually double in size, but will take considerably longer than a wheat-flour dough.

4 When you are ready to bake, heat your oven to 220°C/425°F/gas 7, and put a roasting tin on the floor of the oven to heat. Carefully invert the rye loaf on to the lined baking sheet: the basket should have imprinted a pattern on the surface of the dough. Slash a deep cross-hatch pattern on the top with a sharp knife.

5 Place the loaf in the heated oven. Pour cold water, or throw a handful of ice cubes, into the hot roasting tin and quickly close the oven door to trap the resulting steam inside. Bake for about 30 minutes until the loaf sounds hollow when tapped on the base. Cool on a wire rack.

PAUL'S PRETZELS

A soft white dough is shaped and twisted into 2 flavours of pretzel – a savoury pretzel with salt and sesame seeds and a sweet one flavoured with orange zest and poppy seeds, then glazed after baking with a sweet orange syrup.

MAKES 6 SAVOURY AND 6 SWEET
YOU WILL NEED: 2 LARGE BAKING SHEETS, LINED WITH BAKING PAPER

For the dough
500g strong white bread flour
10g salt
1 x 7g sachet fast-action dried yeast
40g unsalted butter, softened
1 tablespoon malt extract
280ml milk, at room temperature
finely grated zest of 2 oranges
50g poppy seeds

For cooking
7 litres water
21g bicarbonate of soda

To finish
20g rock salt
50g sesame seeds
finely shredded zest of 1 orange
juice of 3 oranges
125g caster sugar

1 To make the dough, put the flour, salt, yeast and butter into a large mixing bowl. Add the malt extract to the milk and stir well until dissolved. With your hand, gradually work the milk mixture into the flour, and keep mixing to make a stiff, non-sticky dough.

2 Turn out the dough on to a worktop (the dough shouldn't need any extra flour for kneading). Knead for about 10 minutes until the dough is smooth and glossy. Divide it in half and put one half into an oiled bowl. Add the orange zest and poppy seeds to the other portion of dough and work in until evenly distributed. Put this dough into another oiled bowl. Cover both bowls with clingfilm and leave to prove for about 45 minutes until doubled in size.

3 Heat your oven to 200°C/400°F/gas 6. Turn out the plain dough on to the worktop and divide into 6 equal pieces. Take one piece and, using your hands, roll it back and forth to make a rope shape 40–50cm long, tapering the ends and creating a slight bulge in the centre. As you roll the dough rope, apply pressure to work it from the middle outwards, pushing out any air bubbles. You may find it easier to roll the rope part of the way, then leave it for a few minutes to relax before continuing the rolling to the full length – this helps prevent the rope from springing back and creating misshapen pieces. Shape the remaining pieces of plain dough, then divide and roll the sweet orange dough in the same way.

4 The traditional – and quickest – way to shape a pretzel is to take hold of each tapered end of the rope and lift them up to create a U shape, then – without letting go of the ends (and in one swift movement) – flip the centre of the U, propelling it to form a double twist. Lay the twist back on the worktop and lightly press the tapered ends on to the opposite sides of the pretzel, attaching them at either side of central bulge. (You may find a little dab of water helps stick the ends to the pretzel.) Carefully flip the pretzel over and on to a lined baking sheet so the ends are face down. You should now have a classic pretzel shape with 3 equally spaced sections.

5 Another, simpler, way to shape a pretzel is flat on the worktop. Curve the rope into a U shape, then take the 2 tapered ends and twist them around each other twice before fixing the ends to the opposite sides of the pretzel, pressing down lightly to seal. Whichever method you use, work speedily to shape all 12 pretzels.

6 Bring the water to the boil in a large pan, then add the bicarbonate of soda. Gently drop a pretzel into the boiling water and leave for 5 seconds, then carefully remove with a slotted spoon and set on a lined baking sheet. Continue blanching all the pretzels, keeping the differently flavoured pretzels separate. While the plain dough pretzels are still wet from the pan sprinkle over the rock salt and sesame seeds.

7 Make a deep slash into the thickest part of the dough (the central bulge of the pretzel) using a small sharp knife. Place the pretzels in the heated oven and bake for 20–25 minutes until they are a deep brown.

8 Meanwhile, make the glaze for the sweet pretzels. Put the orange zest and juice and 100g of the sugar into a small pan. Bring to the boil, stirring to dissolve the sugar, and boil for 1 minute. Lift out the zest with a slotted spoon and roll in the rest of the sugar in a small bowl. Boil the orange syrup until reduced and sticky, then strain through a fine sieve.

9 As soon as the pretzels are baked, transfer them to a wire rack. Quickly brush the sweet pretzels with the syrup glaze and scatter over the candied zest. Leave to cool.

Twist the ends together, then flip to the opposite side

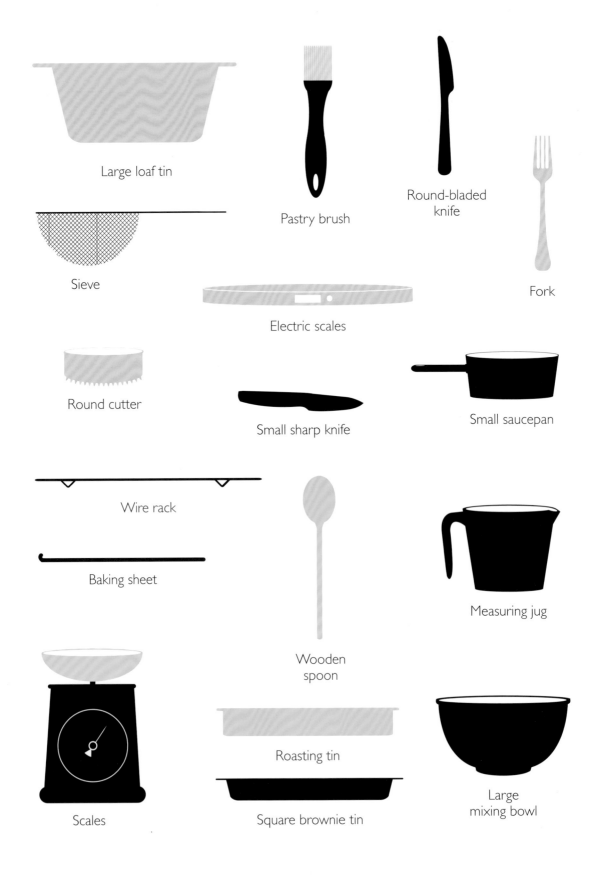

Large loaf tin

Pastry brush

Round-bladed knife

Fork

Sieve

Electric scales

Round cutter

Small sharp knife

Small saucepan

Wire rack

Baking sheet

Wooden spoon

Measuring jug

Scales

Roasting tin

Square brownie tin

Large mixing bowl

SWEET BREAD

Sweet breads are richer than everyday loaves, with a more tender crumb and crust plus a fancier finish — plenty of scope for invention then. Adding sugar and butter to a yeast dough slows down the yeast action, so the dough will take more time to rise. Using milk instead of (or in addition to) water gives a softer, more tender crumb that will keep slightly longer.

For a deep golden-brown crust and perfectly cooked crumb, a hot oven is vital. You can give quick breads a glossy 'professional' finish by brushing the hot, baked sweet loaves with melted butter.

CHOCOLATE SODA BREAD

No time to bake a cake? Try this very quick, very simple sweet bread flavoured with milk chocolate chunks, pecans and dried cherries. Serve thick slices spread with butter or creamy goats' cheese.

MAKES 1 MEDIUM LOAF
YOU WILL NEED: 1 BAKING SHEET, LINED WITH BAKING PAPER

450g plain white flour
1 teaspoon bicarbonate of soda
1 teaspoon salt
2 teaspoons caster sugar
25g unsalted butter, chilled and diced

75g good-quality milk chocolate, roughly chopped
75g dried sour cherries
75g pecan halves, broken in half
about 350ml buttermilk

1 Heat your oven to 220°C/425°F/gas 7. Sift the flour, bicarbonate of soda, salt and sugar into a mixing bowl. Add the pieces of butter and rub in until the mixture looks like fine crumbs. Stir in the pieces of chocolate, cherries and nuts.

2 Make a well in the centre of the mixture and pour in the buttermilk. Mix everything together quickly, using a round-bladed knife or your hand, to make a soft, slightly sticky, rough-looking dough. If the dough feels dry and won't come together, work in more buttermilk a tablespoon at a time.

3 Lightly dust your hands and the worktop with flour, then turn out the dough and shape it into a ball, using no more than 3 or 4 kneading movements – the dough shouldn't look smooth. Set the ball of dough on the lined baking sheet and gently flatten with your fingers so the ball is 3–4cm tall. Using a table knife, cut a deep cross in the top of the dough and dust it with flour.

4 Place in the heated oven and bake for about 35 minutes until the bread is a good golden brown and sounds hollow when tapped on the base. Transfer to a wire rack to cool. Best eaten warm the same day, or toasted the next.

MALTY, STICKY DATE LOAF

An all-in-one loaf that couldn't be easier – the dough is made in a saucepan. It's low in fat and sugar but packed with flavour.

MAKES 1 MEDIUM LOAF
YOU WILL NEED: 1 X 900G LOAF TIN (ABOUT 26 X 12.5 X 7.5CM), GREASED WITH BUTTER AND LINED WITH A LONG STRIP OF BAKING PAPER TO COVER THE BASE AND 2 SHORT SIDES

3 tablespoons malt extract
1 tablespoon golden syrup
2 tablespoons dark muscovado sugar
300g stoned dates, chopped
25g unsalted butter
150ml water
1 medium free-range egg, at
  room temperature

100g walnut pieces
225g wholemeal plain flour
2 teaspoons baking powder
½ teaspoon bicarbonate of soda
good pinch of salt

1 Measure the malt extract, syrup, sugar, dates, butter and water into a saucepan large enough to hold all the ingredients. Set over low heat and stir occasionally with a wooden spoon until the butter has melted. Bring the mixture to the boil, then give it a good stir and remove the pan from the heat. Leave to cool for about 15 minutes until lukewarm.

2 While the date mixture is cooling heat your oven to 160°C/325°F/gas 3.

3 Beat the egg in a small bowl with a fork, just to mix, then add to the warm date mixture. Stir in the egg, followed by the walnuts. Sift the flour, baking powder, bicarbonate of soda and salt into the pan (add any bits of bran left in the sieve) and mix everything together.

4 Scrape the mixture into the prepared tin and spread it evenly, into the corners too. Place in the heated oven and bake for about 50 minutes until a skewer inserted into the centre of the loaf comes out clean.

5 Remove from the oven and set the tin on a wire rack. Run a round-bladed knife down the long sides of the loaf to loosen it from the tin, then leave until cold before turning out. The loaf will be richer in flavour and easier to cut if you wrap it in foil and leave it overnight before slicing. Best eaten within 5 days.

BAKED CHOCOLATE DOUGHNUTS

This is a quick and very easy way to make doughnuts – there's no kneading and rising nor any deep-frying. Chunks of white chocolate make a good contrast to the slightly fudgy doughnut but you could also use your favourite dark, milk or flavoured chocolate (try coffee or butterscotch), or even slightly crushed malt-honeycomb chocolate balls. Try the doughnuts warm from the oven with a scoop of ice cream and Mocha Sauce (see page 201).

MAKES 6
YOU WILL NEED: I X 6-HOLE NON-STICK DOUGHNUT TRAY OR 6 SMALL SAVARIN MOULDS, WELL BUTTERED (SEE RECIPE)

100g plain flour
30g cocoa powder
½ teaspoon baking powder
½ teaspoon bicarbonate of soda
good pinch of salt
125g light brown muscovado sugar
75g white chocolate, coarsely chopped
1 medium free-range egg,
   at room temperature

½ teaspoon vanilla extract
2 tablespoons buttermilk OR
   low-fat natural yoghurt
4 tablespoons milk, at room temperature
50g unsalted butter, melted
icing sugar, for dusting

1 Heat your oven to 190°C/375°F/gas 5. Even if your doughnut tray (or moulds) are non-stick it's a good idea to butter them well so the doughnut mixture doesn't stick. Brush them with melted butter, paying particular attention to the raised centre, then chill in the freezer or fridge for a couple of minutes to set the butter. Repeat to add a second coating of butter.

2 Sift the flour, cocoa, baking powder, bicarbonate of soda, salt and sugar into a mixing bowl. Stir in the pieces of chocolate.

3 In another bowl whisk the egg with the vanilla, buttermilk (or yoghurt), milk and melted butter until thoroughly combined. Pour into the flour mixture and mix everything together with a wooden spoon.

4 Spoon the soft, sticky mixture into the prepared moulds to fill evenly. Place in the heated oven and bake for about 15 minutes until the doughnuts are well risen and spring back when lightly pressed. Turn out on to a wire rack and dust with icing sugar. Best eaten the same or the next day.

SPELT, MAPLE AND PECAN LOAF

Spelt flour has a richer, more nutty taste than wheat flour and makes bread that toasts well. Adding maple syrup and rapeseed oil (for a soft, moist crumb) and lightly toasted pecans makes this a good loaf for breakfast as well as for sandwiches.

MAKES I LOAF
YOU WILL NEED: I BAKING SHEET, LINED WITH BAKING PAPER

150g pecan halves
500g stoneground wholegrain spelt flour
1½ teaspoons salt
1 x 7g sachet fast-action dried yeast

3 tablespoons maple syrup
1 teaspoon rapeseed oil
about 300ml lukewarm water

1 Heat your oven to 180°C/350°F/gas 4. Tip the nuts into a heatproof dish or small tin and toast in the heated oven for about 8 minutes until lightly coloured. Remove from the oven (you can turn it off for now) and leave to cool.

2 Put the flour, salt and yeast into a mixing bowl, or the bowl of a large free-standing electric mixer, and mix together with your hand or the dough hook attachment (on low speed). Make a well in the flour and pour in the maple syrup, oil and water. Mix everything together with your hand (or the dough hook on lowest speed) to make a soft but not sticky dough – stoneground wholegrain flours take longer to absorb liquid than white flours, so the dough will take more time to mix. If the dough feels dry and stiff or won't come together, work in more water a tablespoon at a time.

3 Lightly flour your hands and the worktop, then turn out the dough. Knead well for 3 minutes (or for 2 minutes in the mixer with the dough hook on lowest speed). The dough will feel a bit firmer. Cover it with the upside-down bowl or a sheet of clingfilm and leave to rest on the worktop for 5 minutes.

4 Scatter the cooled nuts over the dough (there's no need to chop them as they will get broken up during kneading). Thoroughly knead the dough for

3 minutes (or 2 minutes in the mixer) until the nuts are evenly mixed in and the dough feels stretchy. Put the dough back into the bowl, cover it with clingfilm or a snap-on lid and leave on the worktop to rise for 1–1½ hours until doubled in size.

5 Uncover the bowl and punch down the risen ball of dough with your knuckles to deflate it. Dust your hands and the worktop with flour again, then turn out the dough and knead a couple of times. Shape into a neat ball. Set it on the lined baking sheet and cover loosely with a dry tea towel or sheet of clingfilm. Leave on the worktop to rise for about 1 hour until doubled in size. Towards the end of this time heat your oven to 220°C/425°F/gas 7.

6 When the loaf is ready to bake, uncover it and cut a couple of deep slashes into the top with a small, sharp knife. Place in the heated oven and bake for 15 minutes, then turn down the temperature to 190°C/375°F/gas 5. Bake for a further 20 minutes until the loaf is a good golden brown and sounds hollow when tapped on the base. Transfer to a wire rack and leave until completely cold before slicing. Best eaten within 4 days.

MARMALADE TEA CAKES

Not just for teatime, these tea cakes are good split and toasted for breakfast too. Be sure to use a well-flavoured Seville bitter orange marmalade with plenty of chunky peel – if you want to make your own see the recipe on page 168.

MAKES 8
YOU WILL NEED: 1–2 BAKING SHEETS, LINED WITH BAKING PAPER

500g strong white bread flour
1 teaspoon salt
50g unsalted butter, at room temperature
1 x 7g sachet fast-action dried yeast

100g sultanas
150g good marmalade
about 250ml lukewarm milk

1 Mix the flour and salt in a large mixing bowl or the bowl of a large free-standing electric mixer. Cut the butter into small pieces and add to the flour. Toss until the butter is coated in flour, then rub in until the mixture looks like fine crumbs. Stir in the dried yeast and then the sultanas, breaking up any clumps. Make a well in the mixture.

2 Combine the marmalade with the milk and pour into the well. Mix with your hand, or the dough hook of your mixer on the lowest speed, to make a soft, slightly sticky dough. If there are dry crumbs at the bottom of the bowl or the dough feels dry and is tough to bring together, work in more milk a tablespoon at a time; if the dough feels very wet and sticky work in more flour a tablespoon at a time.

3 Lightly dust your hands and the worktop with flour, then turn out the dough. Knead it thoroughly for 10 minutes (or for 4 minutes in the mixer with the dough hook on the lowest speed) until smooth and elastic. Put the ball of dough back into the bowl and cover with clingfilm or a snap-on lid. Leave on the worktop to rise for about 1 hour until doubled in size.

4 Uncover the bowl and punch down the risen dough to deflate it. Dust your hands and the worktop with flour again, and turn out the dough. Divide it into 8 equal portions. Shape each into a neat ball, then gently flatten with your hand to make a disc about 10cm across and 2.5cm high. Arrange the discs, well apart to allow for spreading, on the lined baking sheet(s). Cover loosely with a dry tea towel and leave on the worktop to rise for about 45 minutes until doubled in size. Towards the end of this time, heat your oven to 200°C/400°F/gas 6.

5 Uncover the tea cakes and brush lightly with milk. Place in the heated oven and bake for about 20 minutes until a good golden brown. Transfer the cakes to a wire rack and leave to cool. Best eaten the same or next day.

EASY ORANGE AND GINGER MARMALADE

Here is a simple, very good way to make marmalade when Seville oranges are available. The orange peel is quickly chopped in a food processor, then soaked overnight (along with the pulp and pips) so it softens, which reduces the cooking time and gives the marmalade a fresher taste. You can add a little more or less stem ginger as you like – or leave it out altogether.

MAKES ABOUT 3KG

1kg Seville oranges
juice of 1 large lemon
2.5 litres cold water
2kg granulated sugar

5 lumps (about 100g) preserved
   stem ginger in syrup, drained
3 tablespoons ginger syrup from the jar

1 Rinse the oranges well, then dry with kitchen paper. Score the skin of each orange into quarters with the tip of a small, sharp knife, then peel these off. Put the peel quarters into the bowl of a food processor and chop as finely or as coarsely as you like; alternatively, chop or shred the peel with a large sharp knife. Tip the peel into a large stainless steel pan or a large china or glass bowl.

2 Chop the orange pulp roughly, removing all the pips. Put the pips into the centre of a small piece of muslin or fine, clean cloth and tie securely into a loose bag with string. Add to the chopped peel together with the chopped pulp and its juice. Add the lemon juice and cold water. Stir well, then cover the pan or bowl and leave to soak overnight.

3 Next day, pour everything (including the bag of pips) into a large pan or preserving pan. Bring slowly to the boil, stirring occasionally – this will take about 25 minutes. Simmer gently for about 1 hour until the peel is quite tender (remove a teaspoonful and, when it is cool enough to handle, check that you can easily pierce the peel with your thumbnail) – the cooking time will depend on how finely the peel is chopped.

4 Remove from the heat. Lift out the bag of pips and cool it on a plate, then squeeze all the juice from the pips back into the pan (press the bag between 2 small plates). Put several saucers or small plates into the freezer to chill.

5 Add the sugar to the pan and stir gently. Chop the ginger as coarsely or finely as you like and stir in with the ginger syrup. Set the pan over low heat and stir until the sugar has completely dissolved. Turn up the heat so the mixture boils rapidly and boil, stirring frequently, until the marmalade reaches setting point (see page 89) – this may take up to 45 minutes, depending on the heat and your pan, but start testing after 25 minutes.

6 Once setting point has been reached remove from the heat. Leave the marmalade to cool and settle for 10–15 minutes before ladling it into warm sterilised jars. Cover and label. Store in a cool spot.

EARL GREY TEA LOAF

Soaking the dried fruit in delicately scented Earl Grey tea adds a distinctive flavour to this loaf. For a stronger, more malty flavour you could use Assam tea bags instead. Try slices toasted for Welsh rarebit, or in a bread-and-butter pudding.

MAKES I LARGE LOAF
YOU WILL NEED: I X 900G LOAF TIN (ABOUT 26 X 12.5 X 7.5CM), GREASED WITH BUTTER

2 Earl Grey tea bags
150ml boiling water
125g mixed dried fruits (raisins,
    sultanas, currants)
finely grated zest of ½ medium
    unwaxed lemon
500g strong white bread flour

I teaspoon salt
2 tablespoons caster sugar
50g unsalted butter, at room
    temperature
I x 7g sachet fast-action dried yeast
about 175ml milk, at room
    temperature, plus extra for brushing

I Put the tea bags into a heatproof bowl and pour over the boiling water, then leave to steep for 5 minutes. Remove the bags, squeezing them well. Add the dried fruit and lemon zest to the tea in the bowl and stir well. Leave to soak for an hour.

2 Put the flour, salt and sugar into a large mixing bowl, or the bowl of a large free-standing electric mixer, and mix well with your hand. Cut the butter into small pieces and add to the bowl. Toss the butter in the flour to coat the pieces, then rub in until the mixture looks like fine crumbs. Stir in the dried yeast.

3 Drain the soaked fruit in a sieve set over a bowl or wide-necked measuring jug. Measure the strained liquid and make up to 275ml with the milk.

4 Add the drained fruit to the flour mixture and stir in, then work in the tea/milk liquid with your hand (or the dough hook of your mixer, on lowest speed) to make a soft but not sticky dough. If there are dry crumbs, or the mixture feels stiff and dry and won't come together, work in more milk a tablespoon at a time; if the dough feels sticky and 'claggy', work in more flour.

5 Lightly flour your hands and the worktop, then turn out the dough. Knead for 5 minutes (or for 3 minutes in the mixer with the dough hook on the lowest speed). The fruit will start to break up. When the dough is smooth and stretchy, shape it into a ball and put it back into the mixing bowl. Cover with clingfilm or a snap-on lid and leave on the worktop to rise for 1–1½ hours until doubled in size.

6 Uncover the bowl and punch down the dough with your knuckles to deflate it. Flour your hands and the worktop again, then pat out the dough to a rectangle the length of your tin. Roll up the dough fairly tightly from one short end, like a swiss roll. Tuck the ends under.

7 Lift the roll into the prepared tin with the seam underneath. Slip the tin into a large plastic bag, slightly inflate it (so the plastic doesn't stick to the dough) and secure the ends; or cover the tin lightly with a damp tea towel. Leave on the worktop to rise for about I hour until doubled in size (not more). Towards the end of this time heat your oven to 200°C/400°F/gas 6.

8 Uncover the loaf and brush the top with milk. Place in the heated oven and bake for about 35 minutes until the loaf is a good golden brown and sounds hollow when tapped on the base. Leave to cool on a wire rack before slicing. Best eaten within 4 days.

SIMNEL 'CHELSEA' BUNS

If you're partial to sticky, spicy Chelsea buns, have a go at making these for Easter. The same bun dough is used, with dried fruit kneaded in, to echo traditional Simnel cake flavours. A thin layer of marzipan is rolled up with the dough, in place of the usual fruit, butter and sugar filling, and the baked buns are topped with a lemon icing.

MAKES 16
YOU WILL NEED: 1 CAKE TIN OR BROWNIE TIN 20.5 X 25CM, WELL GREASED WITH BUTTER

200ml milk (full-fat or semi-skimmed)
50g unsalted butter
450g strong white bread flour
1 teaspoon salt
3 tablespoons light brown muscovado sugar
1 x 7g sachet fast-action dried yeast
finely grated zest of 1 medium unwaxed lemon
150g luxury dried mixed fruit

1 medium free-range egg, at room temperature
400g white marzipan

To finish
100g icing sugar, sifted
2 teaspoons lemon juice
mini Easter eggs and chicks, to decorate (optional)

1 Put the milk and butter into a small pan and warm gently over low heat just to melt the butter (or heat in the microwave). Leave to cool until lukewarm.

2 Put the flour, salt, sugar, dried yeast, lemon zest and dried fruit in a large mixing bowl or the bowl of a large free-standing electric mixer. Mix thoroughly with your hand, or the dough hook attachment on the lowest speed. Make a well in the middle of the mixture.

3 Beat the egg into the milk/butter mixture, then pour into the well. Using your hand, or the dough hook (on lowest speed), work everything together to make a soft but not sticky dough. If there are dry crumbs and the mixture won't come together, work in more milk a tablespoon at a time; if the dough feels very sticky work in a little more flour.

4 Lightly dust your hands and the worktop with flour, then turn out the dough. Knead thoroughly for 10 minutes (or for 4 minutes in the mixer with the dough hook on lowest speed). Return the dough to

the bowl, cover with clingfilm or a snap-on lid and leave on the worktop to rise for about 1 hour until doubled in size.

5 Uncover the bowl and punch down the dough with your knuckles to deflate it. Turn out on to the lightly floured worktop and divide the dough in half. Roll out one piece to a rectangle about 36 x 18cm.

6 Gently knead the marzipan to make it more supple, then cut it in half. Roll out one half on the lightly floured worktop to a thin rectangle to fit your rolled-out dough. Set the marzipan on top of the dough and gently press it on to the surface. Starting from one long side, roll up like a swiss roll. Repeat with the other portion of dough and the rest of the marzipan.

7 Using a large, sharp knife cut each roll across into 8 even slices. Arrange them, cut side up, in the tin so they are barely touching – they will join up as the dough rises. Cover the tin loosely with a dry tea towel or sheet of clingfilm and leave on the worktop to rise for 35–45 minutes until doubled in size.

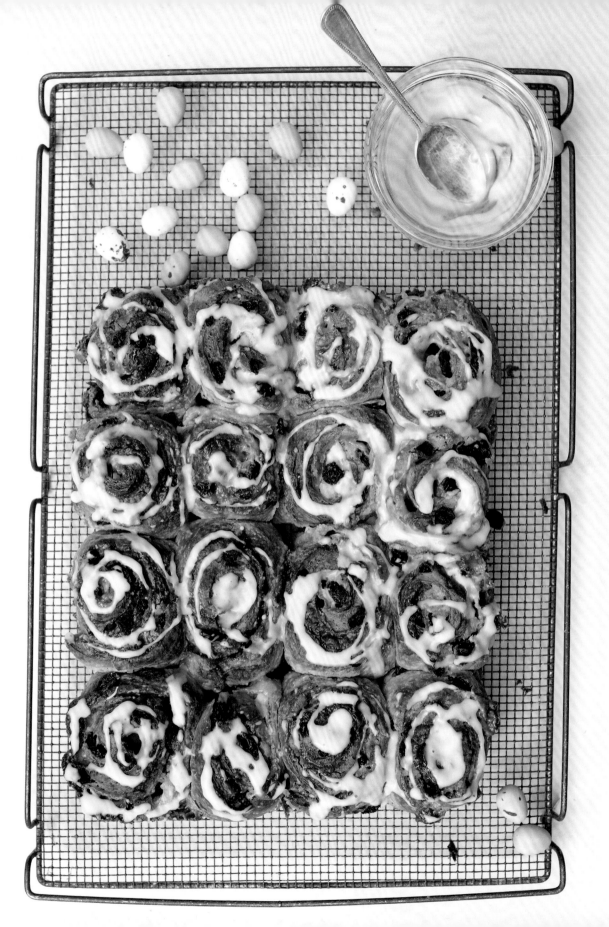

8 Towards the end of the rising time heat your oven to 200°C/400°F/gas 6. Uncover the tin and place in the heated oven. Bake for about 25 minutes until the buns are a good golden colour.

9 While the buns are baking, make up the icing. Mix the icing sugar with the lemon juice to make a smooth, thick but spreadable icing.

10 Remove the tin from the oven and set it on a wire rack. Leave to cool for 10 minutes, then run a round-bladed knife around the inside edge of the tin and carefully turn out the buns on to the wire rack. Spoon on the lemon icing and spread it evenly over the warm buns. Leave to cool completely and set before gently pulling them apart. If you like, decorate with Easter chicks and tiny eggs just before serving. Beat eaten the same or next day.

CARDAMOM STOLLEN

For many, stollen is the quintessential German Christmas cake – a rich and spicy yeasted bread studded with fruit, nuts and citrus peel and finished with a coating of butter and sugar. Bake a week or two in advance to give the loaf time to mature.

MAKES 1 LARGE LOAF
YOU WILL NEED: 1 BAKING SHEET, LINED WITH BAKING PAPER

125g large raisins
50g chopped mixed peel, chopped more finely
finely grated zest and juice of 1 medium unwaxed lemon
4 teaspoons dark rum
about 125ml milk
freshly grated nutmeg
seeds from 2 cardamom pods, crushed
250g strong white bread flour
½ teaspoon salt
3 tablespoons caster sugar

1 x 7g sachet fast-action dried yeast
2 medium free-range egg yolks, at room temperature
100g unsalted butter, softened but not runny
50g whole blanched almonds, lightly toasted and roughly chopped
75g white marzipan

To finish
50g unsalted butter, melted
icing sugar, for dusting

1 Put the raisins, chopped peel, lemon zest and juice, and rum into a small bowl. Stir well, then cover tightly and leave to soak overnight.

2 Next day, uncover the bowl and stir again. Gently warm the milk with half a dozen gratings of nutmeg and the cardamom, then remove from the heat and leave to infuse for 15 minutes.

3 Sift the flour, salt and sugar into a large mixing bowl or the bowl of a large free-standing electric mixer. Stir in the dried yeast. Make a well in the centre and add the lukewarm milk and egg yolks. Work in with your hand, or the dough hook attachment of the mixer on low speed, to make a very soft dough that holds its shape. If the dough feels dry and firm work in more milk a tablespoon at a time; if the dough seems sloppy work in a little more flour.

4 Turn out the dough on to a lightly floured worktop and knead for 10 minutes (or for 5 minutes in the mixer with the dough hook on the lowest speed) until the dough feels firmer and very elastic.

Return the dough to the bowl, cover with a snap-on lid or clingfilm and leave in a warm place to rise for about 1½ hours until doubled in size.

5 Cut the butter into small pieces and work into the dough (still in the bowl) with your hands, squeezing the dough between your fingers, until the butter is completely amalgamated. Turn out the dough on to the lightly floured worktop and pat out to a rectangle about 1cm thick. Scatter the fruit mixture (drain off any excess liquid, if necessary) and the almonds along the centre of the dough.

6 Fold in the two long edges of the dough so they meet in the centre, then fold in the two short ends to the centre. Fold the dough parcel in half. Lightly dust your hands and the worktop with flour, then pat out the dough again and fold up 2 or 3 more times until the fruit and nuts are evenly distributed. The dough will feel very soft and sticky.

7 Return the dough to the bowl, cover as before and leave on the worktop to rise for 1½–2 hours until doubled in size. Don't put the dough to rise in a warm place because the butter will start to ooze out.

8 Flour your hands and the worktop again, then turn out the dough. Pat out to a rectangle about 20 × 15cm. With the side of your hand make a shallow groove down the centre of the dough. Roll the marzipan with your hands to make a sausage shape 18cm long and set it into the long groove in the dough. Fold the dough in 3: fold one long edge over to cover the marzipan, then fold over the other long edge to make a three-layer sandwich with the marzipan under 2 layers of dough. Tuck the ends under neatly.

9 Transfer the dough to the prepared baking sheet and gently shape the loaf with your hands to make a neat oval. Cover loosely with a sheet of clingfilm and leave on the worktop to rise for about 1 hour until doubled in size. Towards the end of this time heat your oven to 180°C/350°F/gas 4.

10 Uncover the risen loaf and place in the heated oven. Bake for about 40 minutes until a good golden brown; cover the loaf loosely with foil or baking paper after 25 minutes if it is browning too quickly. Remove from the oven and transfer, on the lining paper, to a wire rack. Brush the stollen with melted butter and dust with plenty of icing sugar. Leave until cold, then wrap in greaseproof paper and foil and allow to mature for at least a week. Dust with more icing sugar just before serving, cut into thick slices.

WEEKEND BAKING

Recipes from Mary, Paul and the bakers

- Paul's Brioche Têtes

- Paul's Tea Loaf

- Paul's Apricot Couronne

- Chai Tea Loaf

PAUL'S BRIOCHE TÊTES

The dough, rich with butter and eggs, for these tiny, soft-textured brioches is easy to make in a food processor. The dough needs to spend the night in the fridge – to prove and firm up – so you can have brioche warm from the oven for breakfast!

MAKES 16 (WITH A LITTLE DOUGH LEFTOVER)
YOU WILL NEED: 16 INDIVIDUAL NON-STICK BRIOCHE MOULDS; 1–2 BAKING SHEETS

500g strong white bread flour
50g caster sugar
10g fast-action dried yeast
7g salt
140ml full-fat milk,
    at room temperature

5 medium free-range eggs, at room
    temperature
250g unsalted butter, softened

To finish
1 medium egg, beaten, to glaze

1 Put the flour, sugar, yeast, salt, milk and eggs into the bowl of a food processor or a large mixing bowl. Mix thoroughly to make smooth dough – this will take about 5 minutes using the processor or 8 minutes if you are mixing with your hand. Add the butter to the dough and mix in until completely amalgamated – about 5 minutes in the processor or 10 minutes by hand. Transfer the dough to a large bowl, cover with clingfilm and leave in the fridge overnight.

2 Next day, the dough will have risen and will feel like playdough. It will be easy to shape. Cut the dough into 16 x 50g pieces. From each 50g piece of dough cut off 45g for the body, leaving 5g for the head (tête).

3 Using your hands, shape each 45g piece into a neat ball and put into a mould. Use your finger or thumb to make a dent in the centre of the ball. Shape each 5g piece of dough into a small ball and press into the dent in the large ball. Set the moulds on 1–2 baking sheets, slide into a plastic bag and leave to rise in a warm place for 45 minutes to 1 hour until doubled in size.

4 Towards the end of the rising time, heat your oven to 200°C/400°F/gas 6. Remove the baking sheets from the plastic bag. Carefully brush each brioche with beaten egg to glaze, then place in the heated oven and bake for about 20 minutes until a good golden brown. Turn out on to a wire rack and leave to cool.

PAUL'S TEA LOAF

A colourful fruity loaf, flavoured with orange and cinnamon, this is baked on a sheet rather than in a loaf tin. Eat it at teatime with lashings of butter.

MAKES 1 MEDIUM LOAF
YOU WILL NEED: 1 BAKING SHEET, GREASED

400g strong white bread flour
1½ teaspoons salt
40g caster sugar
40g unsalted butter, softened
10g fast-action dried yeast
120ml milk, at room temperature
120ml water, at room temperature
50g sultanas

60g glacé cherries, cut into quarters
1 teaspoon ground cinnamon
finely grated zest of 3 oranges

To finish
75g icing sugar

1 Put the flour, salt, sugar, butter, yeast, milk and water into a large bowl and mix everything together with your hands to make a dough. Tip out on to a lightly floured worktop and knead for about 10 minutes until smooth and pliable. Return the dough to the bowl, cover with clingfilm and leave to rest for about an hour until doubled in size.

2 Add the sultanas, cherries, cinnamon and orange zest to the dough and work in well with your hands (or the dough hook of your electric mixer). When the fruit is evenly distributed, turn the dough out on to the lightly floured worktop. Flatten with your hands to a rectangle about 15 x 30cm.

3 Roll up the dough from one long side to make a sausage shape. Set it seam side down on the baking sheet. Slide the sheet into a large plastic bag, to protect the loaf from draughts, and leave to rise for about an hour until doubled in size.

4 Towards the end of the rising time heat your oven to 200°C/400°F/gas 6. Uncover the loaf and place in the heated oven. Bake for 20 minutes until the loaf is a good golden brown and sounds hollow when tapped on the base. Cool on a wire rack.

5 To finish the loaf, sift the icing sugar into a small bowl and gradually stir in enough cold water to make a runny icing that coats the back of the spoon. Drizzle the icing over the loaf. Leave to set before cutting into thick slices to serve.

PAUL'S APRICOT COURONNE

A soft, rich dough filled with fruit and nuts is rolled, split and twisted to make this pretty crown-shaped bread. It is packed with flavour.

MAKES 1 LARGE CROWN LOAF
YOU WILL NEED: 1 LARGE BAKING SHEET, LINED WITH BAKING PAPER

For the dough
250g strong white bread flour
5g salt
1 x 7g sachet fast-action dried yeast
50g unsalted butter, softened
105ml full-fat milk, at room temperature
1 medium egg, at room temperature

For the filling
90g unsalted butter, softened
70g light brown muscovado sugar

120g ready-to-eat dried apricots,
   chopped and soaked in 100ml orange juice
35g plain flour
60g raisins
65g walnut pieces
finely grated zest of 1 orange

To finish
50g apricot jam
100g icing sugar, sifted
25g flaked almonds

1 To make the dough, tip the flour into a large mixing bowl. Add the salt to the bowl on one side and the yeast to the other. Add the soft butter, milk and egg and turn the mixture round with your fingers, using them like a paddle. Keep doing this, mixing until you've picked up all the flour from the sides of the bowl. Use the mixture to clean the inside of the bowl, picking up all the scraps, and keep going until you have a ball of soft dough.

2 Turn the dough out on to a lightly floured worktop and knead for 10–12 minutes: work through the initial 'wet' stage until the dough starts to develop a soft, smooth skin. When the dough feels smooth and silky put it into a lightly oiled large bowl. Cover the bowl with a dry tea towel and leave to rise for about 1 hour until doubled in size.

3 While the dough is rising, make the filling. Put the soft butter, sugar, drained apricots, flour, raisins, walnuts and zest into a bowl and mix thoroughly. Set aside until needed.

4 Turn the risen dough on to the lightly floured worktop. Without punching it down to deflate, roll it out to a rectangle about 25 × 33cm. If necessary turn the dough around so you have a long edge closest to you. Spread the apricot filling mixture evenly over the dough, then roll up like a swiss roll – tack down the edge nearest to you, so it won't move, then roll up the dough from the other long edge towards you so get a really tight roll. Roll it back and forth slightly to seal the 'seam', then cut it lengthways in half. (You can keep one end attached, which will make it easier to shape).

5 Twist the two strands of dough together, then twist the 2 ends together to finish the 'crown'. Carefully transfer the crown to the prepared baking sheet. Put the sheet inside a large plastic bag and leave to prove for 30–45 minutes until the dough springs back quickly when you prod it lightly with a fingertip.

6 While the dough is rising heat your oven to 200°C/400°F/gas 6. When the couronne is ready for baking, uncover the baking sheet and place in the oven. Bake for 25–35 minutes until risen and golden. Transfer to a wire rack.

7 Gently heat the apricot jam with a splash of water, then push it through a sieve into a bowl. Quickly brush over the warm loaf to glaze. Mix the icing sugar with enough water to make a thin icing. Drizzle over the loaf and sprinkle with the flaked almonds. Leave to cool.

Split open the rolled dough

Twist the strands together

CHAI TEA LOAF

A light-textured but richly flavoured loaf infused with spices, served with home-made butter and 'teaspoons' of caramel. You can buy cinnamon-infused sugar or make your own: shake 250g golden caster sugar with 1 cinnamon stick and 1 teaspoon ground cinnamon in a lidded container and leave for a few days to infuse, if possible.

MAKES 1 LARGE LOAF
YOU WILL NEED: 1 BAKING SHEET, LINED WITH BAKING PAPER; A SILICONE SET OF 6 SPOON MOULDS

For the dough
300ml full-fat milk
2 Chai tea bags
1 cinnamon stick
6 cardamom pods, crushed
good pinch of ground ginger
450g strong white bread flour
50g unsalted butter, at room
    temperature, diced
50g cinnamon-infused sugar
10g salt
10g fast-action dried yeast
1 medium free-range egg, at room
    temperature

For the filling
75g unsalted butter, softened
50g light brown muscovado sugar
2 teaspoons ground cinnamon

For the butter 'sugar cubes'
300ml double cream
3 cardamon pods, crushed
pinch of sea salt flakes
about 50g cinnamon-infused sugar

For the caramel 'spoons'
150g cinnamon-infused sugar
50ml water

1 To make the bread dough, pour the milk into a small pan and add the tea bags, cinnamon stick, cardamom pods and ground ginger. Heat until the milk is steaming hot, then stir well and remove from the heat. Leave to infuse for about 30 minutes until the milk is barely lukewarm, then strain into a jug (discard the spices etc).

2 Put the flour into a large mixing bowl, add the butter and rub in. Stir in the sugar. Make a well in the middle of the mixture. Put the salt on one side of the mixture and the yeast on the other. Lightly beat the egg in a bowl with a fork, just to mix, then pour into the well. Mix everything together with your hand, or with an electric mixer fitted with the dough hook attachment, adding enough of the strained milk to make a soft dough.

3 Turn out on to a very lightly floured worktop and knead by hand for about 10 minutes until the dough is very smooth and elastic (or knead for 5 minutes with the dough hook of the mixer). Return the dough to the bowl (if necessary), then cover tightly with clingfilm and leave to rise in a warm spot for about 1 hour until doubled in size.

4 While the dough is rising, make the filling by creaming the butter with the sugar and cinnamon until smooth. Set aside at room temperature until needed.

5 Punch down the risen dough to deflate it, then turn it out on to a lightly floured worktop. Roll out to a 22cm round that is 1cm thick. Spread the butter mixture over the dough, leaving a 1cm border clear all around. Fold the dough in half to make a semi-circle, then fold it in on itself to make a cone shape before gently forming a neat ball. Take care that all the seams are well pinched together so the filling is sealed in. Set the ball, rounded side up, on the lined baking sheet and cover with an upturned mixing bowl. Leave to rise for 40–50 minutes until almost doubled in size. Towards the end of this time, heat your oven to 200°C/400°F/gas 6.

6 Remove the upturned bowl and place the baking sheet in the heated oven. Bake for about 35 minutes until the loaf is a deep, rich brown colour and sounds hollow when tapped on the base. Cool on a wire rack.

7 While the loaf is rising and baking, make the butter 'sugar cubes'. Pour the cream into a small pan, add the cardamom and heat gently until starting to boil. Remove the pan from the heat and leave to cool for about 30 minutes, then transfer to the fridge and chill thoroughly.

8 Strain the cream into a large mixing bowl (discard the spices) and whisk with an electric mixer on high speed for several minutes until the mixture separates to form lumpy curds of butter and watery buttermilk (be patient). Pour the mixture into a strainer set over a jug. Discard the liquid in the jug. Tip the butter, which will be in a lump in the sieve, into a bowl of very cold water and rinse it well, using your hand to swish it about. Drain off the water and repeat with fresh water until the water stays clear.

9 Gently squeeze as much water out of the butter as possible, then work in the salt with a round-bladed knife. Press the butter into a dish lined with baking paper to make a layer about 1.5cm thick. Cover and chill until firm, then cut into cubes and toss in the cinnamon sugar. Chill until needed.

10 To make the caramel 'spoons', put the sugar and water into a small pan and set over low heat. Heat gently, stirring frequently, until the sugar dissolves, then turn up the heat and boil until the syrup turns to a thick, dark caramel – the cinnamon will make

the syrup dark to begin with, but it will turn a richer chestnut brown. Remove the pan from the heat and wait a few seconds for the bubbles to subside, then pour into the clean, dry spoon moulds. Leave to set at room temperature before carefully unmoulding.

11 Serve the loaf with the butter 'sugar cubes' and caramel 'spoons'.

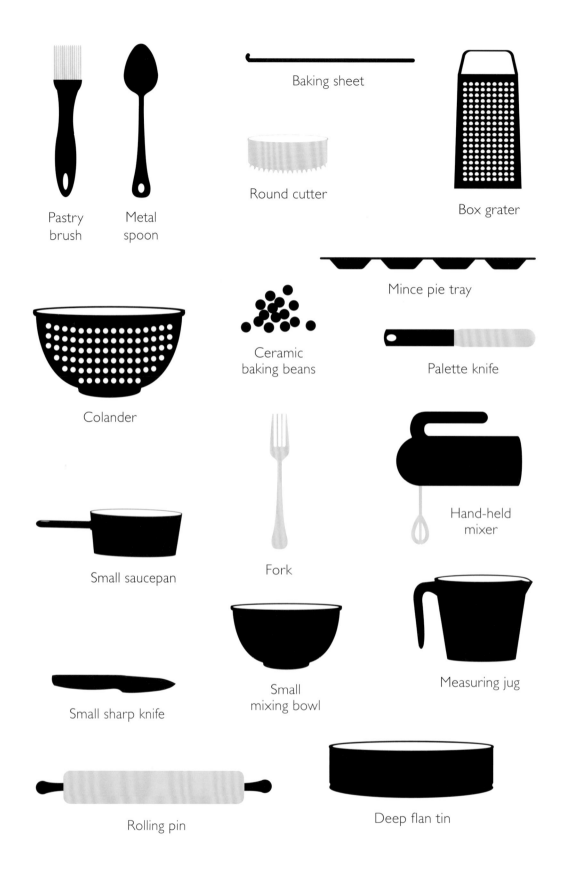

Pastry brush

Metal spoon

Baking sheet

Round cutter

Box grater

Mince pie tray

Colander

Ceramic baking beans

Palette knife

Small saucepan

Fork

Hand-held mixer

Small sharp knife

Small mixing bowl

Measuring jug

Rolling pin

Deep flan tin

PASTRY

Most pastries use butter for its special flavour. It also helps give the pastry a good colour. Butter to be rubbed in needs to be at the right temperature: cold yet pliable.

Once made, many pastry doughs are left to 'relax' in the fridge before rolling out. If your kitchen is warm the dough may need extra chilling until it firms up. If you forget your pastry is in the fridge, just leave it (still wrapped) on the worktop to 'come to' – if you try to roll out very hard pastry it just cracks.

To ensure individual pastries turn out crisp and golden, don't overcrowd the baking sheet: leave plenty of room around the pastries so the air can circulate and they can expand.

For neat slices leave quiches and custard-filled tarts to cool and firm up before cutting. Cheesecakes are better after a day and night in the fridge. Choux buns (cooled and unfilled) can be made ahead and stored in an airtight container, or frozen. Just warm through in the oven to re-crisp before serving.

MAPLE APPLE PUFFS

As soon as they come out of the oven, these flaky puffs get a brushing of maple syrup glaze for a classy pastry-shop finish. You can use home-made or bought puff pastry.

MAKES 6
YOU WILL NEED: I BAKING SHEET, LINED WITH BAKING PAPER

I large Bramley cooking apple
  (about 325g)
3 tablespoons maple syrup
I tablespoon water
I small cinnamon stick
½ x quantity Puff Pastry (see page 192)
  OR 375g ready-made all-butter
  puff pastry, thawed if frozen

For the glaze
3 tablespoons icing sugar
2 teaspoons maple syrup

1 Make the filling first as it has to cool before using. Peel and quarter the apple. Cut out the core, then cut each quarter across into 6 slices. Put them into a medium pan with the maple syrup, water and cinnamon stick. Set over medium-low heat and simmer gently, stirring every minute or so, until the apples feel soft when you prod them with the spoon and all the liquid has evaporated. (If the apples are ready but there is still liquid in the pan, turn up the heat and cook for another minute, stirring carefully so the apples don't burn.) Leave the apples until completely cold.

2 Lightly dust the worktop and rolling pin with flour, then roll out the pastry to a 23 x 34cm rectangle. Using an 11cm plain round biscuit cutter, cut out 6 circles (or cut around a saucer of this size using a small sharp knife).

3 Remove the cinnamon stick from the apples (leave it to dry on kitchen paper and use to add flavour to a curry). Spoon a sixth of the apple filling on to one half of each pastry circle, leaving a 1cm border of pastry around the edge.

4 Dip a pastry brush in cold water and lightly brush the 1cm border of each pastry circle to dampen it. Fold the uncovered half of each circle over the filling, so the edges meet neatly. Seal the edges firmly together with your fingers, then press them with the back of a fork to make a neat pattern.

5 Place the half-moon pastries, slightly apart, on the lined baking sheet. Make a small hole in the centre of each pastry with the tip of a small knife. Put the baking sheet in the fridge so the pastry can firm up for 15 minutes. While the puffs are chilling, heat your oven to 200°C/400°F/gas 6.

6 Place the apple puffs in the heated oven and bake for about 15 minutes until a good golden brown. Meanwhile, put the icing sugar and maple syrup into a small bowl and stir well to make a smooth, runny mixture.

7 Remove the baking sheet from the oven and set it on a heatproof surface. Gently brush the maple glaze over the hot puffs. If the glaze seems too stiff to brush on easily (it will melt on contact with the hot pastry) stir in a teaspoon of water. Leave to cool for 10 minutes, then transfer to a wire rack. Serve warm, or cool completely and store in an airtight container. Eat the same or the next day.

PUFF PASTRY

What makes puff pastry so delicious is its butteriness – it's made with as much butter as flour – and what makes it so flaky is the way the butter is rolled into the initial dough to make literally hundreds and hundreds of layers. The lightness is the result of the water in the dough turning to steam in the oven and puffing up the fragile layers.

It's difficult to make puff pastry in small quantities, but after it has had four 'turns' it can be kept in the fridge for 4 days or frozen – the last two 'turns' can then be done when you want to use the dough. Save any pastry trimmings: stack on top of each other and then re-roll; don't knead them together. Chill thoroughly, then use to make Crunchy Tapenade Straws (see page 209).

MAKES ABOUT 750G

300g plain flour
½ teaspoon salt
300g unsalted butter, cold
   but not rock-hard

1 teaspoon lemon juice
about 140ml ice-cold water

1 Put the flour and salt into the bowl of a food processor and 'pulse' a few times just to combine and aerate the flour. Cut 50g of the cold butter into small pieces and add to the bowl, then process until the mixture looks like fine crumbs.

2 Mix the lemon juice with the water. With the machine running, add to the bowl through the feed tube to make a ball of slightly moist dough. (This initial dough can also be made by rubbing the butter into the flour and then stirring in the lemon and water mix with a round-bladed knife.) Turn out and cut a deep cross in the top of the dough ball. Wrap in clingfilm and chill for 15 minutes.

3 Sprinkle a little flour on the remaining piece of butter, then set it between two sheets of clingfilm. Pound it with a rolling pin until it is half the original thickness. Remove the film and fold the butter in two, then cover with the film and pound again. Keep doing this until the butter has a pliable texture (it should still be very cold – if it gets warm it will be hard to handle, so if necessary put it back in the fridge to firm up slightly). Beat it into a 13cm square.

4 Put the ball of dough on the floured worktop and roll out in four directions (north, south, east and west) to make a shape with four flaps and a thicker square in the centre. Lightly dust the beaten butter with flour, then set it on the centre square and fold the flaps of dough over to enclose it. Gently press the seams with the rolling pin to seal in the butter. Flip the dough over and lightly press with the rolling pin to flatten it – not too hard because you don't want to squeeze out the butter.

5 Gently roll out the dough away from you into a rectangle about 54 × 18cm. Fold the dough in three like a business letter: fold the bottom third up to cover the centre third, then fold the top third down to cover the other two layers and make a neat square. (Before completing each fold, brush off excess flour with a dry pastry brush.) Lightly press the open edges with the rolling pin to seal. This is your first 'turn'.

6 Lift up the dough and give it a quarter turn anti-clockwise so the folded edges are now on the right and left. Roll out the dough into a rectangle and fold it in three again, just as before. This is your second 'turn'. Wrap and chill the dough for 15 minutes, then give it two more 'turns'.

7 Wrap and chill the dough as before, then give it two more 'turns' to make a total of six before a final chilling. It is now ready to use.

AMARETTI APRICOT TARTS

For these mini fruit tarts there's no need to bake the pastry cases 'blind' – setting the tray on a heated baking sheet will ensure crisp pastry. Choose apricots that will fit neatly into the holes in the mince pie or bun tray.

MAKES 12
YOU WILL NEED: 1 X 12-HOLE MINCE PIE OR BUN TRAY, VERY LIGHT GREASED WITH BUTTER IF NOT NON-STICK

½ x quantity Puff Pastry (see opposite) OR 375g ready-made all-butter puff pastry, thawed if frozen

For the topping
50g unsalted butter, softened
50g caster sugar

1 medium free-range egg, at room temperature
50g ground almonds
40g amaretti biscuits
6 medium apricots

1 Sprinkle your worktop with flour and roll out the pastry to a rectangle about the size of your mince pie tray. Dip a 7.5cm plain round cutter in flour, then stamp out rounds of pastry, re-flouring the cutter when it starts to stick. Pile up the trimmings, re-roll and cut out more rounds until you have 12.

2 Press a round into each hole in the tray, making sure the pastry edge comes up above the rim of the hole. Prick the base of each pastry case with a fork, then cover the tray lightly with clingfilm and chill for 20 minutes while you make the topping.

3 Heat your oven to 200°C/400°F/gas 6 and put a baking sheet in to heat up. Put the soft butter and sugar into a mixing bowl and beat with a wooden spoon until creamy. Lightly beat the egg in a small bowl with a fork, just to mix, then add to the butter mix along with the ground almonds. Beat until thoroughly combined.

4 Put the amaretti into a plastic bag and tie closed, then bash the bag with a rolling pin to crush the amaretti into crumbs. Tip into the bowl and stir in.

5 Cut the apricots in half and remove the stones. Set one half, cut side up, in each pastry case. Spoon the amaretti mixture into the hollow where the stone was.

6 Place in the heated oven and bake for 20–25 minutes until the topping is a good golden brown and just firm when gently pressed. Serve just warm, or at room temperature, the same day, with cream.

APPLE 'CAKE'

You can use a mix of apple varieties for this deeply filled, Yorkshire pie – it's a really good use of windfalls. The soft, slightly spongy pastry is made with milk and baking powder.

MAKES 1 LARGE PIE
YOU WILL NEED: 1 X 26CM PIE PLATE OR DEEP OVENPROOF PLATE

1 Put the flour, salt, baking powder and caster sugar into the bowl of a food processor and 'pulse' a few times just to mix the ingredients. Add the pieces of butter and run the machine until the mixture looks like fine crumbs. Add the lemon zest and 'pulse' a couple of times. Mix the egg yolk with the milk. With the machine running, add the yolk mix through the feed tube. Stop the machine as soon as the dough comes together in a ball. If there are dry crumbs and the dough feels dry and hard, add more milk, a teaspoon at a time. (Alternatively, make the pastry dough by hand – see page 204.) Turn out the dough, flatten into a disc about 3cm thick and wrap in clingfilm. Chill for about 20 minutes until firm.

2 Meanwhile, make the filling. Put the soft butter, sugar, and lemon zest and juice in a bowl and beat with a wooden spoon until soft and creamy – don't worry if it looks a bit curdled. Set aside until needed. Peel, core and thinly slice the apples into a mixing bowl. If you are using different varieties make sure they are well mixed.

3 Heat the oven to 190°C/375°F/gas 5 and put a baking sheet into the oven to heat up. Lightly dust the worktop and your rolling pin with flour. Cut off one-third of the pastry for the base (rewrap the rest and set aside on the worktop) and roll out to a circle about 1cm larger than your pie plate. Wrap the pastry loosely around the rolling pin and lift it over the plate. Unroll to drape over the plate, then flour your fingers and gently press the pastry on to the base and rim. Leave any excess pastry hanging over the rim for now.

4 Carefully arrange the apples slices in neat layers on the pastry, mounding them up and adding dabs of the butter mixture, evenly spaced, between each layer. Finish with a layer of apples, and leave the pastry rim clear of filling. Brush the rim with cold water.

5 Roll out the rest of the pastry to a circle that is large enough to cover the mound of apples. Roll it around the pin, as before, and drape it over the pie. Gently but firmly press the pastry on to the dampened rim to seal the two layers together.

6 Use a sharp knife to trim off any pastry hanging over the rim of the plate. With the back of a small knife, 'knock up' the edge by making small horizontal cuts into the pastry rim so it looks like the pages of a book. Then scallop the pastry edge: place 2 fingers on the edge and gently draw a knife between them; continue doing this all the way round. Cut a small slit or steam hole in the centre of the pastry lid. If you like, gather up the pastry trimmings, re-roll and cut out leaves, small apples or other fancy shapes for decoration. Stick them on to the pie lid with a dab of water. Lightly brush the pastry with water and sprinkle with sugar.

7 Set the pie plate on the heated baking sheet in the oven and bake for about 20 minutes until the pastry is starting to colour. Turn down the oven to 180°C/350°F/gas 4 and bake for a further 20–25 minutes until the pastry is a good golden colour. Leave to cool for 15 minutes, then serve with custard or ice cream. If there are any leftovers, gently warm them before serving so the buttery filling starts to melt again.

For the pastry

300g plain flour

good pinch of salt

3/4 teaspoon baking powder

3 tablespoons caster sugar

200g unsalted butter, chilled and diced

finely grated zest of 1 small lemon

1 medium free-range egg yolk

4 tablespoons milk

For the filling

50g unsalted butter, softened

3 tablespoons caster sugar,
  plus extra for sprinkling

finely grated zest of 1 small lemon

1 tablespoon lemon juice

850g dessert apples (about 8 medium)

REDCURRANT GLAZE

Tarts filled with red fruits – raspberries, strawberries, cherries, tayberries and loganberries, and redcurrants – look and taste wonderful if you brush them with a glossy 'red' glaze. Redcurrant jelly, from a jar, makes the simplest and best jelly glaze as it adds a clear pink colour and is slightly sharp rather than sickly sweet. The quantity here makes enough glaze for a tart filled just with fruit; if there is a layer of crème pâtissière or other filling in the tart case under the fruit, you'll only need about 6 tablespoons to glaze the surface of the fruit.

MAKES ABOUT 225ML

225g redcurrant jelly
1 tablespoon water

1 Put the jelly and water in a small pan and gently melt, stirring constantly with a wooden spoon. Once melted, beat well with the spoon to make a smooth, thick syrup. Remove the pan from the heat before the syrup boils and immediately brush over the fruit.

2 If the syrup cools and thickens before you've finished glazing the tart, gently reheat. Any leftover glaze can be cooled and then kept in a covered container in the fridge for up to a week. Reheat before using.

APRICOT GLAZE

For tarts filled with golden or yellow fruits – peaches, apricots, apples, gooseberries, mangoes, banana – you need an apricot jam glaze. You can find ready-made apricot glaze in supermarkets, but it's easy to make your own with a jar of good apricot jam. If you want to be extravagant, add ½–1 tablespoon apricot liqueur to the hot glaze before using. You'll need about 4 tablespoons glaze for a medium – about 23cm – fruit-filled tart.

MAKES ABOUT 300ML

1 x 340g jar apricot jam
1 tablespoon lemon juice

2 tablespoons water

1 Gently warm the jam with the lemon juice and water in a small pan until melted, stirring with a wooden spoon, then bring to the boil. Pour and scrape the jam into a sieve set over a clean pan and press through the sieve to remove the lumps of fruit and skin.

2 Bring the sieved jam back to the boil, stirring, and boil to make a thick syrup. If it is too thick to brush

on thinly, add another tablespoon of water and bring back to the boil; if the syrup is too thin then gently boil it, stirring constantly, until it is thick enough to cover the fruit without running off.

3 Brush the hot glaze over the fruit. Any leftover glaze can be cooled and then stored in a covered container in the fridge for a week. Reheat before using.

RHUBARB AND GINGER TART

Early spring is the time for tender, delicate pink forced rhubarb. Try this crumble-in-a-tart warm from the oven with a jug of custard.

MAKES 1 MEDIUM TART
YOU WILL NEED: 1 X 23CM DEEP LOOSE-BASED FLAN TIN

1 x quantity Rich Sweet Shortcrust Pastry
  (see page 205)

For the filling
50g gingernut biscuits (about 5)
600g tender young pink rhubarb, cut into
  1.5cm pieces
2 tablespoons cornflour
3 tablespoons caster sugar, or to taste
2 lumps (about 25g) stem ginger in syrup,
  drained and finely chopped

For the topping
70g plain flour
80g light muscovado sugar
60g unsalted butter, chilled and diced
50g gingernut biscuits (about 5)
2 lumps (about 25g) stem ginger in syrup,
  finely chopped
icing sugar, for dusting (optional)

1 Sprinkle the worktop and your rolling pin lightly with flour, then roll out the pastry and use to line the flan tin (see page 12). Prick the base of the pastry case well, then chill for 15 minutes.

2 Heat your oven to 190°C/375°F/gas 5. Bake the pastry case 'blind' (see page 12). Remove from the oven, set on a heatproof surface and leave to cool for 10 minutes. Put a baking sheet into the oven to heat up.

3 Make the filling and topping while the pastry case is baking. Finely crush the gingernuts in a food processor, or put into a plastic bag and bash with a rolling pin. Put the rhubarb in a mixing bowl, sprinkle over the cornflour, sugar and chopped ginger, and mix well. Set aside.

4 To make the topping, mix the flour with the sugar in another bowl. Add the butter and rub in to make very coarse, slightly lumpy, crumbs. Roughly crumble the gingernuts into the bowl so there are some fine crumbs and some larger pieces. Add the chopped ginger and mix well.

5 When ready to assemble the tart scatter the gingernut crumbs in the base of the pastry case (this helps keeps the pastry crisp). Stir the rhubarb mixture once more, then spoon on top of the crumbs and spread evenly. Scatter the crumbly topping mixture over the fruit, making sure the fruit is completely and evenly covered.

6 Set the flan tin on the heated baking sheet in the oven and bake for about 35 minutes until the topping is golden and crisp, and the fruit is just tender when prodded with the tip of a sharp knife. Remove from the oven and leave to firm up for about 5 minutes before carefully unmoulding. Serve warm, dusted with icing sugar, if using. Best eaten the same day.

COFFEE AND CHOCOLATE CHOUX BUNS

Here choux pastry is sweetened and flavoured with cocoa, then used to make large puffs. To ensure the puffs turn out crisp and light, you need to get rid of the steam, so follow the method carefully. When cold, split the puffs and fill with an easy white chocolate and coffee mousse, and serve with a mocha or chocolate sauce.

MAKES 8

YOU WILL NEED: I BAKING SHEET, LINED WITH BAKING PAPER

1 Heat your oven to 200°C/400°F/gas 6. Spoon the choux pastry in 8 large mounds, about 6cm across and 4cm high, on the lined baking sheet, spacing the mounds well apart to allow for spreading. Place in the heated oven and bake for 20 minutes.

2 Reduce the oven temperature to 180°C/350°F/gas 4. Quickly open and close the oven door, just to let out the steam, then bake for a further 15 minutes until the puffs are crisp.

3 Remove the baking sheet from the oven. Carefully make a small hole in the side of each puff using a cocktail stick or skewer to let out the steam. Return to the oven and bake for a further 5–10 minutes until the pastry is completely crisp. Transfer to a wire rack and leave to cool.

4 Meanwhile, make up the mousse filling. Put the chocolate in a heatproof bowl, set over a pan of hot water and melt very gently, stirring frequently. Remove the bowl from the pan and leave to cool until needed.

5 Heat the double cream in a saucepan until steaming hot but not boiling. Sprinkle over the coffee and stir or whisk in until dissolved. Leave to cool to the same temperature as the chocolate, then whisk the cream into the chocolate (the mixture will darken in colour) until smooth. Leave on the worktop until cooled to room temperature.

6 Whip the whipping cream until it will stand in soft peaks when the whisk is lifted out of the bowl. Whisk in the mocha cream mixture (on the lowest speed possible if using an electric mixer). Stop whisking as soon as the mixtures are combined. Cover and chill until firm.

7 To assemble, split the buns open horizontally and spoon in the mousse. Dust with icing sugar and serve as soon as possible with hot mocha or chocolate sauce.

1 x quantity Choux Pastry
   (see page 200) - add 1 tablespoon cocoa powder and
   1 teaspoon caster sugar, sifting them with the flour
icing sugar, for dusting
1 x quantity Mocha Sauce
   (see page 201) or Hot Chocolate Sauce
   (see page 105), to serve

For the mousse
   100g good-quality white chocolate,
      broken into small pieces
   100ml double cream
   2 teaspoons instant coffee
      granules or powder
   125ml whipping cream, well chilled

CHOUX PASTRY

It's quite amazing that a lump of thick, sticky paste made in a saucepan can be transformed in the heat of the oven to a crisp and light ball of air, but that is just what happens with choux pastry. Make sure you don't underbake the shaped dough, otherwise it will turn out flabby rather than crisp.

MAKES ENOUGH FOR ABOUT 12 ÉCLAIRS, 48 PROFITEROLES OR 8 CREAM PUFFS

100g plain flour
175ml water
¼ teaspoon salt
75g unsalted butter, diced

3 medium free-range eggs,
   at room temperature

1 Sift the flour on to a sheet of greaseproof paper. Put the water, salt and butter into a medium-sized pan and heat gently until the butter has completely melted – don't let the water boil and begin to evaporate. Then quickly bring the mixture to the boil and tip in the flour all in one go. Remove the pan from the heat and beat furiously with a wooden spoon. The mixture will look a mess at first but don't worry – as you beat it will turn into a smooth, heavy dough.

2 Set the pan back on low heat and beat the dough for about 2 minutes to slightly cook it, until it comes away from the sides of the pan to make a smooth, glossy ball of dough. Tip the dough into a large mixing bowl and leave to cool until barely warm.

3 Beat the eggs in a small bowl with a fork, just to mix. Using an electric mixer (a wooden spoon won't give the same result), gradually beat the eggs into the dough, beating well after each addition, until it is very shiny and paste-like and just falls from a spoon when lightly shaken. You may not need to add the last tablespoon or so of beaten egg: the dough needs to be stiff enough to pipe or spoon into shapes – if it is too wet it will spread out rather than puff up in the oven.

4 The dough is now ready to shape. Use immediately or cover the bowl tightly, keep at cool room temperature and use within 4 hours.

MOCHA SAUCE

Enjoy this coffee-chocolate sauce with profiteroles and choux buns as well as coffee ice cream. Any leftover sauce can be cooled and kept, covered, in the fridge overnight. Gently reheat before serving.

MAKES ABOUT 300ML

1 tablespoon instant coffee
  granules or powder
1 tablespoon boiling water
100g dark chocolate (about 70% cocoa
  solids), chopped or broken up

175ml single cream
1 tablespoon icing sugar

1 Dissolve the coffee granules or powder in the boiling water in a small pan (off the heat), then allow to cool until warm.

2 Add the chocolate pieces, cream and sugar. Warm gently – on the lowest heat – stirring frequently, until the chocolate has melted and the sauce is smooth and hot. Do not let the sauce come to the boil. Serve hot or warm.

CARAMELISED LEMON CHEESECAKE SLICES

Baking puff pastry a second time with a dusting of icing sugar turns it a shiny, deep golden-brown and adds a nutty, sweet flavour. Instead of the usual cream or custard cream filling, these millefeuille pastries are sandwiched with creamy cheese and lemon curd.

MAKES 6
YOU WILL NEED: 2 LARGE BAKING SHEETS, LINED WITH BAKING PAPER

1 Lightly dust the worktop and rolling pin with flour, then roll out the pastry into a thin 31cm square. Trim the edges to neaten using a pizza wheel-cutter or large sharp knife (take care not to drag the knife as this can give the pastry sheet wonky sides).

2 Loosely roll the pastry square around the rolling pin, then lift it over on to one of the lined baking sheets and gently unroll so the pastry is upside down on the sheet. Brush off the excess flour with a dry pastry brush, then prick the pastry well with a fork. Cover with a second sheet of baking paper. Place in the fridge to chill for 20 minutes.

3 While the pastry is chilling, heat your oven to 180°C/350°F/gas 4. Gently set the second baking sheet on top of the paper on the pastry square (if you don't have a second baking sheet use an upturned wire rack). This is to make sure the pastry cooks and puffs evenly.

4 Place in the heated oven and bake for about 25 minutes until the pastry is crisp and an even golden brown. If it needs more baking, check it every couple of minutes so it doesn't get too dark. Remove from the oven and set on a wire rack. Carefully lift off the top baking sheet (or rack) and the covering paper. Leave the pastry square to cool completely on its lining paper on the baking sheet, which will take about an hour. You can turn off the oven for now.

5 When ready to finish, heat the oven again, to 230°C/450°F/gas 8. Using a pizza wheel-cutter or large sharp knife, cut the pastry square into 3 strips, each about 10 x 30cm, then cut each strip across into 6 rectangles. Leave them exactly where they are on the baking sheet. Dust the pastry with a thick, even layer of icing sugar.

6 Place in the heated oven and bake for 3–4 minutes until the sugar melts and caramelises – watch carefully and rotate the sheet after 2 minutes so the pastry colours evenly; don't let the edges catch. As soon as the pastry is a shiny rich brown, remove the baking sheet from the oven and set it on a wire rack. Leave the pastry to cool before gently separating the rectangles, using the tip of the knife or pizza cutter to help.

7 To make the filling stir the lemon curd until smooth. In another bowl stir the mascarpone and fromage frais together until thoroughly combined, then stir the lemon curd through the mixture so it looks marbled. If not using immediately, cover and chill for up to 6 hours.

8 To assemble, first choose the 6 best-looking rectangles for the tops. For each slice, layer up 3 pastry rectangles with the lemon cheese filling. Serve within an hour with fresh berries or fresh raspberry sauce.

½ x quantity Puff Pastry
  (see page 192) OR 375g ready-made
  all-butter puff pastry, thawed if frozen
40g icing sugar, for dusting

For the filling
½ x quantity Lemon Curd (see page 38)
  OR 175g ready-made lemon curd
150g mascarpone
150g fromage frais
fresh berries or Fresh Raspberry Sauce
  (see page 275), for serving (optional)

SWEET SHORTCRUST PASTRY

Crumbly, buttery and slightly sweet this is the pastry for your apple pies, jam tarts or mince pies. Use good butter, well chilled for the best results, and don't skip the chilling stages before and after rolling out – the pastry will thank you! The quantity here is enough for 12 jam tarts or 6 mince pies; to line a 23cm deep flan tin; or to cover a deep (about 1 litre) pie dish.

MAKES ABOUT 350G

200g plain flour
pinch of salt
2 tablespoons caster sugar

125g unsalted butter, chilled and diced
about 2½ tablespoons ice-cold water

1 To make the pastry by hand, sift the flour, salt and sugar into a large mixing bowl. Add the pieces of cold butter and toss them lightly in the flour so they become coated. Using a round-bladed knife cut the butter into the flour so the pieces get smaller, coating them with flour as you go. Then rub the butter into the flour with your fingertips until the pieces of butter have disappeared and you are left with a bowl of fine crumbs.

2 Sprinkle the water over the crumbs. Stir the mixture with the round-bladed knife, gradually adding more water, a teaspoon at a time, if needed, until the crumbs come together into a dough. Gather the dough into a ball, kneading it gently in the bowl just for a couple of seconds until smooth. (Don't over-handle the dough or it will start to become greasy.)

3 Alternatively, make the pastry in a food processor. Put the flour, salt and sugar into the processor bowl and 'pulse' a couple of times until combined. Add the pieces of cold butter and process for about a minute – just until the mixture looks like fine crumbs. With the machine running pour in the water through the feed tube. The crumbs should come together in a ball of dough within a minute. If this doesn't happen, and there are dry crumbs in the bottom of the processor bowl, add more water a teaspoon at a time.

4 Wrap the ball of dough in clingfilm and chill for 15–20 minutes until firm but not hard. The dough is now ready to be rolled out as needed in your recipe.

RICH SWEET SHORTCRUST PASTRY

Reduce the sugar to 1 tablespoon and replace the water with a mix of 1 medium free-range egg yolk lightly beaten with about 2 tablespoons ice-cold water.

SAVOURY SHORTCRUST PASTRY

Omit the sugar and add a bit more salt (a good pinch) plus a good pinch of pepper.

RICH SAVOURY SHORTCRUST PASTRY

Omit the sugar. Increase the butter to 150g and replace the water with a mix of 1 medium free-range egg yolk lightly beaten with 1½ tablespoons ice-cold water.

CHOCOLATE HAZELNUT TART

You only need a small slice of this ultra-rich, heavenly match of toasted nuts, ganache and biscuit-like pastry. For the best flavour use fresh nuts from an unopened bag (hazelnuts quickly go off because of their oils) and a mixture of chocolates – you could use all dark chocolate, but milk chocolate adds a nice rounded flavour – in the filling. The rich pastry is best made in a food processor.

MAKES 1 MEDIUM TART
YOU WILL NEED: 1 X 23CM LOOSE-BASED DEEP FLAN TIN

For the biscuit pastry
200g plain flour
good pinch of salt
80g icing sugar
100g unsalted butter, chilled
    and diced
4 medium free-range egg yolks
½ teaspoon vanilla extract

For the filling
250g blanched (skinless) hazelnuts
400ml double cream
150g good-quality milk chocolate
    (about 34% cocoa solids)
150g dark chocolate
    (about 70% cocoa solids)
¼ teaspoon sea salt flakes,
    slightly crushed

1 Put the flour, salt and icing sugar into the bowl of a food processor and 'pulse' a couple of times just to combine. Add the pieces of cold butter and process until the mixture looks like fine crumbs. With the motor running, add the yolks and the vanilla through the feed tube. Stop the machine as soon as the dough comes together in a ball, which will take about 1 minute. Remove the dough from the bowl, flatten it into a disc about 3cm thick and wrap in clingfilm. Chill for 30 minutes to firm it up.

2 Lightly dust the worktop and your rolling pin with flour, then roll out the pastry to a circle about 32cm across. Use to line the flan tin (see page 12). Prick the base of the pastry case well, then chill for 15 minutes.

3 Heat your oven to 180°C/350°F/gas 4. Bake the pastry case 'blind' (see page 12); after removing the paper and beans, turn down the temperature

to 160°C/325°F/gas 3 and bake for a further 7–9 minutes. (The pastry isn't going to be baked any more after this so it needs to be cooked through.) Remove from the oven and set the tin on a wire rack to cool. Turn the oven back up to 180°C/350°F/gas 4.

4 While the pastry case is cooling, make a start on the filling. Tip the nuts into an ovenproof dish or tin and toast in the oven for 8–10 minutes until golden brown. Remove from the oven and leave the nuts to cool.

5 Set aside 12 nuts for decoration, then weigh out 50g of the remainder and process until very finely chopped (don't let them start to form a sticky paste). Heat the cream in a medium pan until steaming hot. Remove from the heat and stir in the finely chopped nuts. Cover and leave to infuse for at least 45 minutes (up 2 to hours if possible), stirring from time to time.

6 Finely chop or break up both types of chocolate and put into a heatproof bowl. Gently reheat the cream/nut mixture until steaming hot, then pour through a sieve on to the chocolate. Gently stir until melted and smooth. Discard the chopped nuts in the sieve.

7 Roughly chop the rest of the hazelnuts (not the 12 saved for the decoration) and add to the chocolate mixture with the salt. Beat well with a wooden spoon for about a minute until the mixture is thick, then scrape it into the cooled pastry case and spread evenly. Scatter the reserved whole nuts over the top. Lightly cover the tart (still in the tin) with clingfilm and chill for 20 minutes to firm up.

8 Carefully unmould the tart and leave at room temperature for 20 minutes before serving. Store in an airtight container in a cool place or the fridge; bring back to room temperature before serving. Best eaten within 4 days.

CRUNCHY TAPENADE STRAWS

The best puff pastry straws should be thin, crisp and flaky so they just melt in the mouth, and should taste of butter and something deliciously savoury. Here, the flavouring is tapenade, a speciality of Provence, made from black olives, anchovy fillets, garlic and capers.

MAKES 30
YOU WILL NEED: 2 BAKING SHEETS, LINED WITH BAKING PAPER

½ x quantity Puff Pastry (see page 192) OR 375g ready-made all-butter puff pastry, thawed if frozen

4 tablespoons ready-made tapenade or black olive paste

1 Lightly flour the worktop and your rolling pin, then roll out the pastry to a thin rectangle about 40 x 25cm (if the pastry sticks to the worktop as you are rolling, sprinkle with a little more flour).

2 Spread the tapenade evenly over the pastry, right to the edges, using a palette knife. Fold the pastry lengthways in half to make a rectangle 40 x 12.5cm. Gently roll the rolling pin over the pastry, just to seal the layers – you don't want to make it any thinner.

3 Using a large, sharp knife or a pizza-wheel cutter, cut the rectangle across into 30 even strips each 1.5cm wide and 12.5cm long. Try not to drag the knife or pull the dough out of shape as this can spoil the flaky pastry layers.

4 Hold one end of a pastry strip and, with the other hand, twist the strip several times. Lay it on a lined baking sheet. Repeat with the rest of the strips. Lightly cover with clingfilm and chill for 20 minutes to firm up and 'relax' so the pastry doesn't shrink or toughen in the heat of the oven.

5 Heat your oven to 200°C/400°F/gas 6. Uncover the pastry strips and place in the heated oven to bake for about 15 minutes until crisp and a good golden brown. Carefully transfer to a wire rack and leave to cool. Serve warm the same day, or store in an airtight container and gently reheat the next day (in an oven heated to 180°C/350°F/gas 4, for about 5 minutes).

Variation: Mustard Cheese Straws
Instead of tapenade, spread 3 tablespoons mild mustard, or herb-flavoured mustard, over the rolled-out pastry. Mix 90g grated Parmesan cheese with 2 teaspoons mild smoked paprika and sprinkle over the mustard. Press the cheese into the mustard, then fold the pastry in half and continue as above. When you twist the pastry strips, sprinkle any cheese that drops off back on the straws.

SMOKY HADDOCK SOUFFLÉ TART

A rich combination of crisp pastry and a classic smoked fish soufflé. Most of the preparation – the pastry case baked blind, the fish poached and the sauce made – can be done up to 12 hours ahead. Keep the fish and sauce, covered, in the fridge until needed, then gently warm the sauce before continuing with the recipe.

MAKES 1 MEDIUM TART
YOU WILL NEED: 1 X 23CM LOOSE-BASED DEEP FLAN TIN

1 x quantity Rich Savoury Shortcrust Pastry (see page 205) – sift ¼ teaspoon salt and 2 good pinches of cayenne pepper or smoked hot paprika with the flour

For the filling
1 x 250g piece undyed smoked haddock fillet
250ml milk (full-fat or semi-skimmed)

25g unsalted butter
25g plain flour
125g Gruyère cheese, grated
½–1 teaspoon wholegrain mustard
salt, pepper and cayenne pepper to taste
3 medium free-range eggs, separated, plus 1 egg white, at room temperature

1 Lightly dust the worktop and your rolling pin with flour, then roll out the pastry and use to line the flan tin (see page 12). Prick the base well, then chill for about 20 minutes.

2 Heat your oven to 190°C/375°F/gas 5. Bake the pastry case 'blind' (see page 12); after removing the paper and beans, turn down the temperature to 180°C/350°F/gas 4 and bake for a further 7 minutes. Remove from the oven and set aside on a wire rack to cool. Turn the oven back up to 190°C/375°F/gas 5 and put a baking sheet into the oven to heat up.

3 Make the filling while the pastry case is being baked blind and then cooling. Put the fish into a medium-sized pan and pour over the milk. Bring to the boil, then turn down the heat, cover the pan and simmer for 2 minutes. Remove from the heat and leave the fish to cool in the milk. Lift out the fish (keep the milk for later) and flake on to a plate, discarding the skin and any bones. Set aside.

4 Melt the butter in a large pan. Stir in the flour with a wooden spoon and cook over low heat for a minute. Stir in the saved milk, then cook, stirring constantly, until the mixture comes to the boil and thickens to make a thick, smooth sauce. Simmer, stirring, for a minute to cook out any floury taste.

5 Remove the pan from the heat and set it on a heatproof surface. Stir in 100g of the grated cheese, the mustard and seasoning. Taste and add more mustard, salt, pepper and cayenne as needed (make sure the sauce isn't bland). Stir in the 3 egg yolks.

6 Put the 4 egg whites in a large, very clean bowl with a pinch of salt and whisk with an electric mixer until they will stand in stiff peaks. Using a large metal spoon or rubber spatula, fold about a third of the whites into the cheese sauce mixture. Then carefully fold in the remaining whites in 2 batches.

7 Arrange the flaked fish in the cooled pastry case (still in the tin), then spoon the cheese soufflé mixture on top. Scatter the remaining cheese over the filling. Set the tin on the heated baking sheet in the oven and bake for about 25 minutes until the top is a good golden brown and feels firm when touched in the centre (it should be much firmer than a normal soufflé as it has to be cut in slices).

8 Remove the tin from the oven and leave the tart to cool and firm up for about 10 minutes before carefully unmoulding. Serve warm. Best eaten the same day.

HOLLANDAISE SAUCE

The classic sauce for Eggs Benedict (poached eggs plus a slice of ham or bacon on a toasted English muffin), as well as steamed asparagus or poached salmon, hollandaise is really a warm mayonnaise made with melted butter instead of oil. This easy method uses a food processor or blender, and the result is a very light, but rich-tasting buttery sauce. You can flavour it with chopped fresh herbs added to the processor at the last minute.

MAKES ABOUT 250ML

3 medium free-range egg yolks,
   at room temperature
2 tablespoons water

juice of ½ medium lemon, or to taste
175g unsalted butter
salt and pepper

1 Put the egg yolks, water and lemon juice into the bowl of a food processor or blender. Add a little salt and pepper and process briefly until just combined – about 10 seconds.

2 Melt the butter in a small pan over low heat. Skim the froth off the surface with a small spoon, then heat the clear butter until very hot but not quite boiling.

3 With the motor running, pour the hot butter into the processor bowl through the feed tube in a thin, steady stream. Stop the machine as soon as all the butter has been added and the sauce is creamy and thick. Taste and add more salt, pepper or lemon juice, if needed. Serve as soon as possible.

FILO-TOPPED VENISON RENDANG

This slow-cooked venison curry – spiced with coarsely ground black pepper and flavoured with tamarind (an essential ingredient in Worcestershire sauce) and soy sauce – has an easy topping of crisp, golden filo pastry. The filling can be cooled, then covered and kept in the fridge for up to 48 hours. Bring back to room temperature before continuing with the recipe.

MAKES 1 MEDIUM PIE
YOU WILL NEED: 1 X 1.25–1.5 LITRE PIE DISH

1 x 270g pack filo pastry (about 6 sheets)
50g unsalted butter, melted

For the filling
500g boneless braising venison, cubed
2 medium onions, roughly chopped
4 large garlic cloves, roughly chopped
1 x 4cm piece fresh root ginger,
   roughly chopped
3 tablespoons rapeseed oil

¼ teaspoon coarsely ground
   black pepper, or to taste
¼ teaspoon freshly grated nutmeg
1 cinnamon stick
seeds from 4 cardamom pods, crushed
3 tablespoons soy sauce, or to taste
3–4 teaspoons tamarind paste, to taste
1 tablespoon dark muscovado sugar
250ml vegetable or beef stock

1 If the pastry is frozen, thaw following the instructions on the pack. Meanwhile, start the filling as the meat needs long, slow cooking. Check the pieces of venison and cut if necessary so they are all roughly the same size. Put on one side until needed.

2 Put the onions, garlic and ginger in a food processor and chop very finely – almost to a purée (you can also do this with a large knife on a chopping board, but it takes time). Heat the oil in a deep, heavy-based flameproof casserole or saucepan over medium heat and stir-fry the onion mixture for 2–3 minutes until it is just starting to change colour (don't let the mixture burn).

3 Add the pieces of meat and stir-fry for 3–4 minutes until starting to colour. Stir in the ground pepper, nutmeg, cinnamon stick and crushed cardamom, followed a minute or so later by the soy sauce, tamarind paste, sugar and stock. Bring to the boil, then

stir well, cover the casserole or pan tightly and turn down the heat. Simmer very gently, stirring occasionally, for 1¼–1½ hours until the meat is very tender.

4 The sauce should be fairly thick, not a thin runny gravy, so if necessary remove the lid and simmer until the excess liquid has been cooked off. Taste the mixture – it should be spicy/hot with a balance of sweet and sour. Add more black pepper if the filling needs more 'heat', more tamarind paste if it is too bland, or more soy sauce if it lacks salt. When you are happy with the flavouring, tip the mixture into the pie dish and remove the cinnamon stick. Leave to cool.

5 Heat your oven to 180°C/350°F/gas 4. Brush the rim of the pie dish with water to dampen it. Unwrap the pastry and remove one sheet from the pack; keep the rest covered with a slightly damp tea towel (or sheet of clingfilm) to prevent it from drying out and

becoming hard to use. Lay the sheet of pastry flat on the worktop and brush it lightly with melted butter. Cover it with a second sheet of pastry and brush this lightly with butter. Lift both sheets over the filling in the pie dish and gently press the pastry on to the rim; leave any excess pastry hanging down.

6 Brush another pastry sheet lightly with butter, then tear into strips – they don't have to be neat or even of similar size. Drape the strips, slightly crumpled, on top of the pie. Repeat with the remaining 3 sheets of pastry to cover the top completely and evenly, taking care not to compress the strips (which would make the topping heavy and soggy). Now trim off the overhanging pastry with kitchen scissors.

7 Set the pie dish on a baking sheet (in case of drips) and place in the heated oven. Bake for 30–40 minutes until a good golden brown. Serve hot.

ROAST TOMATO TART

Unlike a quiche, this tart is made without a custard, and should be eaten warm from the oven. You can vary the filling very easily: try adding a few thin slices of prosciutto or cooked ham between the mustard and cheese layers, or use pesto and goats' cheese instead of mustard and Gruyère.

MAKES 1 MEDIUM TART
YOU WILL NEED: 1 X 23CM LOOSE-BASED DEEP FLAN TIN

For the rosemary shortcrust pastry
200g plain flour
1 teaspoon finely chopped fresh rosemary
140g unsalted butter, chilled and diced
3–4 tablespoons ice-cold water

For the filling
800g ripe tomatoes (about 10 medium)
1½ tablespoons Dijon mustard

175g Gruyère cheese, coarsely grated
1½ tablespoons virgin olive oil
½ teaspoon fresh thyme leaves
  OR a couple of pinches of dried
  herbes de Provence
salt and freshly ground black pepper

1 Put the flour, ¼ teaspoon salt and the rosemary into the bowl of a food processor and 'pulse' a couple of times to mix. Add the pieces of butter and run the machine just until the mixture looks like fine crumbs. With the machine running, add the water through the feed tube. Stop as soon as the mixture comes together in a ball of soft but not sticky dough. If the dough feels dry and hard, or won't come together, or there are dry crumbs in the bottom of the bowl, add more water a teaspoon at a time. (Alternatively, make the pastry dough by hand; see page 204.) Flatten the pastry into a disc about 3cm thick, wrap in clingfilm and chill for 15 minutes.

2 Lightly dust the worktop and your rolling pin with flour, then roll out the pastry to a circle about 32cm across. Use to line the flan tin (see page 12). Prick the base of the pastry case well, then chill for 15–20 minutes.

3 Heat your oven to 190°C/375°F/gas 5. Bake the pastry case 'blind' (see page 12). Remove from the oven and set on a wire rack to cool. Turn up the temperature to 200°C/400°F/gas 6, and put a baking sheet in the oven to heat up.

4 While the pastry case is baking and cooling, prepare the tomatoes for the filling. Cut into slices about 5mm thick, discarding the stalk ends. Put the slices in a colander and leave to drain for 30 minutes. Give the colander a gentle shake from time to time to dislodge as much excess liquid as possible.

5 Spread the mustard over the base of the cooled pastry case (still in the tin). Scatter the grated cheese evenly over the mustard. Arrange the well-drained tomato slices on top of the cheese, slightly overlapping and at an angle propped up against each other. Sprinkle the oil over the tomatoes and season to taste with salt and pepper. Finish with the herbs.

6 Set the flan tin on the heated baking sheet in the oven and bake for 20–25 minutes until the edges of the tomatoes are turning colour. Remove from the oven and leave to cool for 5 minutes before carefully unmoulding. Serve warm.

CRANBERRY-TOPPED TURKEY PIE

Everything for this large, open-topped pie – the filling of turkey strips and tiny stuffing balls, the hot water crust pastry and the cranberry chutney topping – can be made in stages. The pie really tastes best made a day or so before cutting.

MAKES 1 LARGE PIE
YOU WILL NEED: 1 X 20.5CM SPRINGCLIP TIN, LIGHTLY GREASED WITH BUTTER

For the filling
1kg skinless, boneless turkey or
   chicken breast
2 tablespoons brandy
250g good pork (or chicken
   or turkey sausages
1 tablespoon rapeseed oil
1 medium shallot, finely chopped
2 tablespoons finely chopped fresh herbs
   (parsley plus a sage leaf and a sprig each
   of rosemary and thyme if possible)
50g fresh breadcrumbs
80g cranberries (fresh or frozen)

For the pastry
300g strong white flour (not extra strong
   Canadian flour for breadmakers)

70g white fat
30g unsalted butter
150ml water

For the topping
2 tablespoons rapeseed oil
1 medium shallot, finely chopped
1 garlic clove, finely chopped
220g cranberries (fresh or frozen)
2 tablespoons caster sugar
1 tablespoon red wine vinegar
salt and freshly ground black pepper
1 tablespoon chopped fresh herbs
   (a mixture of parsley, sage, rosemary and
   thyme if possible)

1 To make the filling, cut the turkey or chicken into strips roughly 2 x 7cm. Put them in a large mixing bowl with the brandy, ¾ teaspoon salt and ¼ teaspoon black pepper. Mix thoroughly, then cover the bowl and chill for several hours if possible, or while preparing the other ingredients.

2 Next, make the stuffing balls. Squeeze the sausage meat out of the skins into a mixing bowl. Heat the oil in a small pan, add the chopped shallot and cook gently for about 3 minutes until softened. Cool, then add to the sausagemeat with the herbs and breadcrumbs. Season with a little salt and pepper.

Mix everything together thoroughly. Roll the mixture into about 35 tiny balls, no bigger than 2.5cm. Put on a plate, cover and chill. If using frozen cranberries, remove them from the freezer (those for the topping too).

3 To make the pastry, sift the flour and ¾ teaspoon salt into a heatproof bowl and make a well in the centre. Put the white fat and butter into a pan with the water and heat gently until the fat melts; don't let the mixture boil. Pour into the centre of the flour and mix vigorously with a wooden spoon to make a soft, paste-like dough – don't worry that it looks

and mix vigorously with a wooden spoon to make a soft, paste-like dough – don't worry that it looks a mess to begin with; it will come together as you beat. When the dough is cool enough to handle turn it out of the bowl on to a worktop lightly dusted with flour.

4 Heat your oven to 200°C/400°F/gas 6. Dust your rolling pin with flour and roll out the dough to a circle large enough to line the tin – about 34cm. Lightly flour the pastry circle with flour, then fold it in four and lift it into the tin. Unfold the pastry and press it on to the base and up the sides of the tin so it reaches the rim. Make sure there are no cracks or holes (the soft pastry is easy to mould and press together).

5 Add the stuffing balls and cranberries to the turkey strips and gently mix together until everything is evenly distributed. Pack the filling into the pastry case, making sure there are no pockets of air. Fold the pastry that extends above the filling over it to make a 1cm rim (trim off any excess with kitchen scissors).

6 Cover the tin tightly with foil to seal, then set it on a baking sheet. Place in the heated oven and bake for 15 minutes. Turn down the oven temperature to 180°C/350°F/gas 4 and bake for a further 2 hours.

7 While the pie is baking make the topping. Heat the oil in a medium pan, add the chopped shallot and garlic and cook gently for about 3 minutes until softened, stirring frequently. Add the cranberries, sugar, vinegar, ¼ teaspoon salt and the herbs. Cook gently, stirring occasionally, until the juices start to run, then simmer until the cranberries are soft and starting to break up, and the mixture is thick and jammy. Taste and add more salt, sugar or vinegar as needed to make a sweet/sour chutney-like mixture. Remove from the heat and set aside until needed.

8 Remove the pie from the oven and set it, on its baking sheet, on a wire rack. Remove the foil. Carefully run a round-bladed knife inside the tin to loosen the pastry (it will still be soft); do not unclip

the tin yet. Stir the cranberry mixture, then spoon on top of the pie to completely cover the turkey filling. Leave until cool, then carefully unmould. Serve at room temperature. Store tightly wrapped or in an airtight container in the fridge and eat within 5 days.

TANGY BLUE CHEESE BUNS WITH PECAN DIP

Adding a well-flavoured blue cheese, like a piquant Stilton, turns a basic choux dough into a crisp savoury treat. The simple dip is made from three cheeses plus crunchy pecans. If, when making the choux pastry, you don't need the last tablespoon or so of egg, mix it with a teaspoon of water and use instead of a fresh egg for glazing.

MAKES ABOUT 30
YOU WILL NEED: 1–2 BAKING SHEETS, LINED WITH BAKING PAPER

1 x quantity Choux Pastry
  (see page 200) - sift ¼ teaspoon
  cayenne pepper, or to taste, with
  the flour
75g tangy blue cheese, crumbled
1 medium free-range egg, lightly
  beaten with a pinch of salt

For the dip
50g pecan halves
50g tangy blue cheese
good pinch of cayenne pepper,
  or to taste
5 tablespoons fromage frais
75g mascarpone
1 tablespoon milk (optional)

1 Heat your oven to 200°C/400°F/gas 6. When you have finished beating the eggs into the choux pastry, mix in the crumbled cheese using a wooden spoon or plastic spatula. Spoon the choux pastry on to the lined baking sheets to make about 30 small mounds, each 3.5cm wide and 2.5cm high (the easiest way to do this is to take a heaped teaspoonful of the dough and use another teaspoon to push it off).

2 Lightly brush the mounds with the beaten egg to glaze, taking great care you don't accidentally 'glue' the pastry to the paper. Place in the heated oven and bake for about 20 minutes until the puffs are golden. Reduce the oven temperature to 180°C/350°F/gas 4, and quickly open and close the oven door to let out the steam. Bake for a further 5 minutes until the puffs feel crisp and firm.

3 Remove from the oven. Make a small hole at one side of each puff using a cocktail stick or skewer, to let out the steam. Return to the oven and bake for

4 minutes to make sure the centres are dry. Transfer to a wire rack and leave to cool until warm; leave the oven on. (The puffs can be stored in an airtight container for up to 24 hours.)

4 To make the dip, put the pecans in an ovenproof dish or tin and toast in the oven for 5 minutes. Leave to cool, then chop finely. Mash the blue cheese in a mixing bowl with a fork, then stir in the cayenne, fromage frais and mascarpone. If the mixture is a bit stiff for dipping, work in a little milk. When thoroughly combined stir in the pecans. Taste and add more cayenne if needed. Cover and chill until ready to serve (up to 24 hours).

5 If you've made the puffs ahead of time, gently reheat in the oven at 180°C/350°F/gas 4 for 5 minutes. Spoon the dip into a serving bowl, set on a large platter and surround with the warm puffs.

SWEET POTATO PASTIES

Roasting turns sweet potatoes into a rich, moist filling for pasties made with a Cheddar shortcrust. These are best eaten the same or next day (store in an airtight container in a cool place, but not the fridge).

MAKES 6
YOU WILL NEED: I BAKING SHEET, LINED WITH BAKING PAPER

For the filling
I large sweet potato, about 375g,
  cut into 4–5cm chunks
2 tablespoons rapeseed or olive oil
I large garlic clove, or to taste,
  finely chopped
I small sprig fresh rosemary,
  finely chopped
few grinds black pepper OR good pinch
  of dried chilli flakes
salt
2 tablespoons pine nuts or chopped
  roasted hazelnuts (optional)

I x 120g log goats' cheese
I medium free-range egg, for glazing

For the cheese shortcrust
200g plain flour
¼ teaspoon salt
cayenne pepper
100g unsalted butter, chilled and diced
100g mature Cheddar cheese, grated
about 3 tablespoons ice-cold water

I Heat your oven to 200°C/400°F/gas 6. Put the sweet potato into a roasting tin or ovenproof dish, add the oil and toss with your hands so the chunks are coated in oil. Place in the heated oven and roast for 30 minutes until the chunks are tender and the edges are turning brown.

2 Make the pastry while the sweet potatoes are roasting. Put the flour, salt and a couple of good pinches of cayenne into a food processor and 'pulse' a couple of times until combined. Add the pieces of cold butter and process for about a minute – just until the mixture looks like fine crumbs. Add the cheese and 'pulse' until mixed in. With the machine running, pour in the water through the feed tube.

The crumbs should come together in a ball of dough within a minute. If this doesn't happen, and there are dry crumbs in the bottom of the processor bowl, add more water a teaspoon at a time. (Alternatively, you can make the pastry by hand – see page 204.) Shape into a ball and flatten into a disc about 3cm thick, then wrap in clingfilm and chill for about 15 minutes.

3 Remove the tin of sweet potatoes from the oven, set it on a heatproof surface and stir in the garlic, rosemary, pepper or chilli flakes, and a couple of pinches of salt. Return the pan to the oven to roast for a further 3 minutes. Leave to cool for about 15 minutes. Turn down the oven to 180°C/350°F/gas 4.

4 Roughly mash the sweet potatoes with a fork – there should be some lumpy bits. Add the nuts and mix everything together so the nuts and herbs are evenly distributed. Cut the goats' cheese log into 6 even slices.

5 Lightly sprinkle the worktop and your rolling pin with flour, then roll out the dough to a rectangle about 26 x 39cm. With a large, sharp knife cut the rectangle lengthways in half, to make 2 strips 13 x 39cm. Cut each strip across in 3, to make six 13cm squares.

6 The squares are going to be folded in half diagonally to make triangles, so the filling should be placed on one side of a diagonal line: spoon a sixth of the potato mixture on to each square, leaving a 1cm border clear around the two outer edges. Set a slice of goats' cheese on top of each mound of potato filling.

7 Beat the egg in a small bowl with a fork, just to mix. Using a pastry brush, lightly brush the edges of each square with beaten egg. Fold the pastry over the filling to make triangular pasties. Press the seams firmly together to seal, then press all the way round with the back of a fork to give a striped pattern.

8 Arrange the pasties, slightly apart, on the lined baking sheet. Brush them with beaten egg, then place in the oven and bake for 25–30 minutes until a good golden brown. Leave the pasties to cool on the baking sheet for 4–5 minutes, then transfer to a serving plate and eat warm, or leave to cool on a wire rack and eat at room temperature.

WEEKEND BAKING

MARY'S WOBBLY APRICOT TART

Two layers of perfectly crisp, rich sweet pastry with a very simple, but glorious, filling of marzipan and tinned fruit.

SERVES 8
YOU WILL NEED: I X 23CM DEEP LOOSE-BASED FLAN TIN

For the pastry
225g plain flour
100g icing sugar
100g unsalted butter, chilled and diced
I medium free-range egg

For the filling
375g marzipan or almond paste
2 x 400g tins apricot halves in natural juice

To finish
sifted icing sugar, for dusting
crème fraîche or single cream,
 well chilled, to serve

I Put the flour, icing sugar and butter into a food processor. Run the machine until the mixture looks like crumbs or a crumble topping. Add the egg and process just until the mixture holds together in a loose dough. Lightly dust the worktop with flour, then turn out the dough and quickly gather it together into a ball. Wrap in clingfilm and chill for about 15 minutes.

2 While the pastry dough is chilling heat your oven to 200°C/400°F/gas 6. Put a baking sheet in the centre of the oven to heat up.

3 Take the pastry out of the fridge. Cut off a third (for the lid); wrap this and return it to the fridge. Roll out the rest of the pastry on the lightly floured worktop and use to line the flan tin.

4 Coarsely grate, or finely chop, the marzipan and scatter evenly over the base of the pastry case. Thoroughly drain the apricots (you won't need the juice) and pat dry with kitchen paper. Arrange the apricots, cut side down, on top of the marzipan.

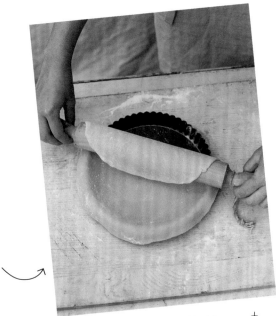

Line the flan tin with the pastry

5 Add any pastry trimmings to the pastry reserved for the lid, then roll out on the lightly floured worktop to a circle large enough to cover the top of the tin. Slightly dampen the edge of the pastry in the flan tin by brushing with water. Carefully lift the pastry lid on the rolling pin and lay over the top of the fruit filling. Press the 2 layers of pastry together where they meet at the edges to seal well.

6 Set the flan tin on the hot baking sheet in the oven and bake for 30–35 minutes until the pastry is a pale golden brown. Carefully remove from the tin and leave to cool for 10 minutes, then dust with icing sugar and serve immediately with crème fraîche or cream.

Cover the pie with the pastry lid

PECAN, CARAMEL AND ROSEMARY APPLE PIE

Two kinds of apples – Bramley cookers and Cox's dessert – are layered with roasted nuts and rich rosemary-scented caramel. Make rosemary sugar by sticking a fresh sprig in a jar of caster sugar and leaving it to infuse for a few days.

MAKES 1 PIE
YOU WILL NEED: 1 X 23CM DEEP LOOSE-BASED FLAN TIN

For the pastry
450g plain flour
50g ground almonds
250g unsalted butter, chilled and diced
100g rosemary sugar (see above)
2 large free-range eggs
beaten egg, to glaze

For the filling
150g pecans
700g Bramley apples (about 4 medium)
300g Cox's apples (2–3 medium)
4½ tablespoons cornflour

For the caramel sauce
200g rosemary sugar (see above)
100ml water
100ml double cream, at room temperature
40g unsalted butter, at room temperature
1 tablespoon very finely chopped
   rosemary leaves

1 To make the pastry put the flour and ground almonds into the bowl of a food processor and 'pulse' a few times to combine. Add the pieces of cold butter and run the machine until the mixture looks like breadcrumbs. Add the sugar and pulse again, just to combine. Lightly beat the eggs in a bowl with a fork, just to mix, then add to the processor and pulse until the mixture just comes together to make a soft but not sticky dough.

2 Carefully turn out the dough on to a lightly floured worktop and knead it very gently for a few seconds until smooth and even-textured. Shape into a flat disc about 3cm thick. Wrap in clingfilm and chill for about 30 minutes until firm but not hard. At the same time put your rolling pin into the freezer to chill.

3 Meanwhile, make the filling. Heat your oven to 180°C/350°F/gas 4. Put the nuts into a small ovenproof dish or tin, place in the heated oven and toast for about 5 minutes until lightly coloured. Cool, then chop roughly and set aside (leave the oven on). Peel, quarter and core all the apples. Cut them into medium thick slices, directly into a large mixing bowl. Sprinkle with the cornflour and gently toss with your hands until the slices are completely coated. Set aside.

4 Now make the caramel sauce. Put the sugar and water into a medium-sized pan, set over low heat and stir frequently until the sugar has completely dissolved. Turn up the heat and boil rapidly, without stirring, until the syrup turns a deep caramel colour. Remove the pan from the heat and quickly add the cream and butter (take care as the mixture is likely to splutter). Return the pan to low heat and stir gently until the caramel has melted and the sauce is smooth. Remove from the heat and stir in the rosemary. Leave to cool until needed, stirring occasionally.

5 Weigh the chilled pastry and divide by three – you need two-thirds for the base and one-third for the lid. Cut off the third for the lid, rewrap and return to the fridge. Set the larger portion of dough on a large sheet of baking paper lightly dusted with flour. Lay another sheet on top. Roll out the dough with the chilled rolling pin to a large circle about 32cm across. Remove the top sheet of paper. Lightly sprinkle the top of the dough and the rolling pin with flour, then loosely wrap the pastry around the pin and drape it into the flan tin. Flour your fingers and gently press the pastry into the tin (see page 12 for more details), leaving the excess pastry hanging over the rim for now. Prick the base with a fork.

6 Arrange a third of the apples in a neat, compact layer in the pastry case. Scatter over a third of the nuts, then spoon over a third of the caramel sauce. Repeat the layers twice, making sure the apple slices are tightly arranged and slightly domed in the centre of the pie. Brush the pastry rim with beaten egg.

7 Roll out the pastry for the lid of the pie between 2 sheets of baking paper, as before, to a circle large enough to cover the pie – about 26cm. Remove the top sheet of paper and cut a circle or apple shape out of the centre using a 6.5cm cutter. With a smaller cutter (about 1.5cm) or a piping tube, cut out 4 or 5 smaller shapes or holes halfway between the centre and the outside edge.

8 Carefully flip or invert the pastry lid on to the pie, lift off the remaining sheet of paper and gently press the edge of the lid on to the pastry rim to seal firmly. Lightly flour the heel of your hand and gently push down on the rim of the flan tin to trim off the excess pastry. Re-roll all the pastry trimmings and cut out small decorations with shaped cutters. Lightly brush the top of the pie with beaten egg, then attach the pastry shapes. Brush these with beaten egg.

9 Set the pie on a baking sheet and place in the heated oven. Bake for 55–60 minutes until the pastry is a good golden brown and crisp – check after 45 minutes and if the pastry looks pale but the apples feel tender (when poked through the

centre hole with the tip of a small knife) turn up the oven temperature to 190°C/375°F/gas 5 for the final 10 minutes or so of baking. Transfer the pie to a heatproof surface and leave to cool for 15–20 minutes, then carefully turn out. Serve warm or at room temperature.

MARY'S SUSSEX POND PUDDING WITH APPLES

I love the traditional steamed Sussex Pond Pudding, but the whole thing always collapses when served, so I thought it would be a good idea to pack the filling with apples too. The result is even more delicious! Don't be tempted to use Bramley cooking apples – not only will they collapse as they cook, but also they will taste too sharp.

SERVES 6–8
YOU WILL NEED: 1 X 1.5 LITRE PUDDING BASIN, THICKLY BUTTERED

For the suet crust
225g self-raising flour
100g shredded suet (beef or vegetable)
75ml milk
75ml cold water

For the filling
3 medium Cox's apples
150g unsalted butter, chilled
    and cut into cubes
175g light brown muscovado sugar
1 large unwaxed lemon, rinsed

1 First make the suet crust pastry. Put the flour and suet into a mixing bowl and mix well together. Add the milk and water to the flour mixture and mix to a soft dough using a round-bladed knife or spatula.

2 Turn out the dough on to a lightly floured worktop. Roll out to a circle 30cm across. Cut a quarter section out of the circle and set this aside for the lid. Lift the rest of the pastry circle into the prepared pudding basin and press it on to the sides and base. Be sure to press and seal the join together so the bowl is neatly lined.

3 For the filling, peel, quarter and core the apples, then dice them. Put the pieces of apple into a mixing bowl with the butter and sugar and mix together gently. Spoon a little of the mixture into the lined pudding basin. Using a cocktail stick, prick the lemon all over, then set it in amongst the apple mixture so that it is sitting upright. Pack the remaining apple mixture around the lemon.

Set the lemon in the apple mixture

4 Roll out the reserved suet pastry dough to a circle to fit the top of the pudding basin. Dampen the edge of the pastry lining the basin, then place the pastry lid on top and pinch the edges together to seal thoroughly.

5 Cut a square of foil and a square of greaseproof paper. Put them together and make a pleat in the centre. Use to cover the top of the pudding basin, paper side down, and tie the foil and paper cover securely in place around the basin rim with a long piece of string. Loop the end of the string over the top of the basin and then under the string running round the basin a couple of times, to make a handle. Tie securely. (Instead of making a string handle, you can also use a long strip of foil, folded lengthways in half and in half again, as a support for lifting the pudding in and out of the pan: set the basin in the centre of the foil strip and wrap it up the sides of the basin.)

6 Put the lid of a jam jar into a large saucepan (the lid will prevent the basin from touching the bottom of the pan) and set the pudding basin in the pan. Pour boiling water from the kettle around the basin so the water comes three-quarters of the way up the sides. Cover the pan with a tightly fitting lid and simmer for 3½ hours. Remember to check the pan occasionally and top it up with more boiling water as necessary.

7 To serve the pudding, remove the foil and paper on top and invert the basin on to a deep plate, then lift off the basin. Serve the pudding hot with cream or custard.

Make a string handle for the basin

PAUL'S SPANAKOPITA

Crunchy, flaky home-made filo pastry with a filling of fresh spinach and feta is a classic Greek recipe, and here Paul shows you how it's achieved.

SERVES 6
YOU WILL NEED: A PASTA MACHINE, 1 LARGE BAKING SHEET, GREASED WITH BUTTER,

For the pastry
200g strong white bread flour
pinch of salt
100–120ml warm water
1 tablespoon olive oil

For the filling
900g fresh spinach, thoroughly washed
salt and freshly ground pepper, to taste
freshly grated nutmeg, to taste
finely grated zest of 1 unwaxed lemon

1 large egg, at room temperature,
   beaten to mix
200g feta

To finish
cornflour, for dusting
100g butter, melted, for brushing
1 egg yolk, for glazing
1 tablespoon sesame seeds

1 Make the pastry first. Sift the flour and salt into a bowl and make a well in the middle. Mix 100ml of the warm water with the oil and slowly pour into the well, mixing in the flour as you go. You're aiming for a soft but not sticky dough, so if the mixture is too wet add a sprinkling of flour; if it's too dry add more warm water. Once the dough has come together tip it out on to the worktop (you shouldn't need any extra flour on the worktop if the dough is the right consistency). Knead the dough for 10–15 minutes until it is very smooth and elastic. Wrap the dough in clingfilm and leave it to rest in the fridge for at least an hour (or overnight).

2 While the dough is relaxing, make the filling. Heat a large, wide pan (one with a lid) over medium heat, then add the drained spinach to the pan, squashing it down. Season with salt and pepper and cover with the lid. Cook, stirring occasionally, for about 5 minutes until the spinach has collapsed right down in the pan and is completely cooked.

3 Tip the spinach into a colander in the sink to drain, then press down on the spinach with the back of a large spoon to remove as much moisture as you can. Finally, press with a wad of kitchen paper so

the spinach is squeezed as dry as possible. Return the spinach to the pan and dry out over low heat, stirring in the nutmeg and lemon zest. Remove from the heat and leave until completely cold. Once cold, stir in the beaten egg. Crumble the feta into the mixture and mix thoroughly. Taste and add more seasoning if necessary.

4 Before you start to work on the pastry it's important to have everything ready: lay a large sheet of baking paper on one side of the worktop and dust it generously with cornflour; melt the butter for brushing; have the buttered baking sheet at hand; and heat your oven to 180°C/350°F/gas 4.

5 Divide the pastry dough into 5 equal portions and shape each into a ball. Cover with a damp tea towel to prevent the pastry dough from drying out. Take one ball of dough and flatten it on the worktop to a rough rectangle, sprinkling your hands and the pastry with cornflour. Set the pasta machine roller to the widest setting and pass the rectangle of dough through the rollers. Keep passing the pastry strip through the machine until it has gone through to setting number 7 (of 9) – you don't want to take it through the thinnest settings as you will use your hands for the final stretching. The strip of pastry will be about 1 metre in length.

6 Slip your hands, palms down, under the strip of pastry and gently stretch it widthways until it is 20–25cm wide and as thin all over as you can manage. Don't worry about the odd tear or hole as the layers will cover it all up. Lay the rectangle of pastry on the cornflour-dusted baking paper. Brush the pastry sheet lightly with melted butter, then cover it with a damp tea towel. Continue rolling and stretching the rest of the pastry, laying each sheet on top of the previous sheet, brushing with butter and covering again.

7 When all 5 sheets of pastry are in the stack, spoon the spinach filling evenly along one long edge. Using the baking paper underneath to help you, roll up the spinach inside the pastry, folding in the sides before each roll to prevent the filling escaping. You'll now have a long, even sausage shape. Starting at one end, curl the sausage around into a spiral shape. Gently slide it off the paper and on to the prepared baking sheet.

8 Mix the egg yolk with the remaining melted butter and brush evenly over the whole thing. Sprinkle with the sesame seeds and sea salt. Place in the heated oven and bake for 30–35 minutes until golden brown. Serve warm.

PAUL'S EGG CUSTARD TARTS

One of the tests of a good baker, custard tarts sound plain and simple to make but require care and skill to achieve superb pastry cases – no holes or tears or soggy bottoms – and smooth creamy custard.

MAKES 12
YOU WILL NEED: 1 X 12-HOLE NON-STICK MUFFIN TRAY

For the sweet pastry
165g plain flour
25g ground almonds
120g unsalted butter, chilled and diced
55g caster sugar
1 medium egg

For the custard filling
700ml full-fat milk
7 medium egg yolks, at room temperature
90g caster sugar
freshly grated nutmeg

1 To make the pastry mix the flour and ground almonds together in a large bowl. Add the butter and rub in until the mixture looks like fine crumbs. Stir in the sugar. Break the egg into the bowl and work into the mixture with your fingers, then bring it all together to form a soft dough. Tip the dough out on to a lightly floured worktop and shape it into a ball. Flatten with your fingers to a disc, then wrap in clingfilm and chill for 30 minutes.

2 Roll out the pastry on a lightly floured worktop to about 5mm thickness. Using an 11cm fluted round cutter stamp out discs; reroll the pastry and stamp more discs until you have 12. Gently press into the muffin moulds to line evenly; the pastry should come slightly over the top of each mould so you can crimp the edges to give a pretty, neat finish. Chill the pastry cases while you make the custard.

3 Heat your oven to 200°C/400°F/gas 6. To make the custard filling, gently warm the milk in a medium pan until just below boiling. Whisk the egg yolks with the sugar in a heatproof bowl until pale and creamy. Pour the warm milk on to the yolk mixture in a thin, steady stream, stirring constantly to make a smooth liquid with tiny bubbles. Pour the mixture into a jug with a good pouring lip.

4 Carefully pour the custard filling into the pastry cases. Sprinkle the centre of each tart with a good pinch of nutmeg. Place in the oven and bake for about 15 minutes, then turn down the oven to 180°C/350°F/gas 4 and bake for a further 10 minutes. The tarts are done when the custard filling is slightly domed and still has a slight wobble. If the custard has too much of a dome then it's over-cooked – boiled – and will sink down as it cools, leaving a big dip. If this does happen, don't panic! You can help rescue the tarts by quickly removing the muffin tray from the oven and setting it in a sink or oven tray of cold water (don't let the water seep into the pastry though).

5 Leave the tarts to cool in the muffin tray for 30 minutes before carefully removing them.

STEAMED CHICKEN BUNS

Dim-sum at home! Try these steamed fluffy yeast buns filled with a rich savoury chicken mixture.

MAKES 16
YOU WILL NEED: A BAMBOO OR ELECTRIC STEAMER

For the dough
450g plain flour
good pinch of salt
1 x 7g sachet fast-action dried yeast
3 tablespoons caster sugar
1½ teaspoons baking powder
2 tablespoons black sesame seeds
pinch of saffron powder
about 275ml lukewarm water

For the filling
200g skinless boneless chicken breasts,
   free of sinews

1 tablespoon honey
1 tablespoon Shaoxing rice wine
2 teaspoons soy sauce
3 tablespoons hoisin sauce
1 tablespoon yellow bean sauce
1 star anise
1 x 227g tin water chestnuts
   (140g drained weight)

To serve
lotus root pickle or sweet
   chilli dipping sauce

1 To make the dough, put the flour, salt, yeast, sugar, baking powder, sesame seeds and saffron into a large bowl and mix well together. Add 275ml water and mix in with your hand, adding more water if necessary, to make a slightly soft dough. Cover the bowl with clingfilm and leave for about 1 hour until doubled in size.

2 Meanwhile, make the filling. Very finely chop or mince the chicken. Put it into a medium pan and add the honey, rice wine, soy sauce, hoisin sauce, yellow bean sauce and star anise. Simmer gently, stirring frequently, for about 12 minutes until the chicken is white and thoroughly cooked.

3 Drain the water chestnuts. Finely shred them if they are sliced; grate whole ones in a food processor. Add to the chicken and mix in. Remove the star anise. Taste and adjust the flavourings – you may need to add more soy sauce or rice wine. Leave to cool.

4 When ready to assemble, get your steamer ready and heating up. Divide the dough into 16 even-sized pieces. Shape each piece into a ball, then roll out to a thin circle about 9cm across. Divide the filling evenly among the circles. To shape each bun, gather up the edge of each circle over the filling – like a moneybag – and pinch together to seal firmly. If there is a large lump of dough at the top of the bun, carefully trim it (don't puncture the dough).

5 Place the buns seam-side up in the steamer, cover and steam for 10–12 minutes until the dough is thoroughly cooked and the filling piping hot. Serve hot with the pickle or dipping sauce.

PEA PURÉE AND HAM TARTLETS

Very thin, melt-in-the-mouth cheese pastry with a simple filling, these mini tartlets have an eye-catching decoration – crisp sails made from Parmesan and Parma ham.

MAKES 12
YOU WILL NEED: 1 X 12-HOLE BUN TRAY OR MINCE PIE TRAY; A BAKING SHEET, LINED WITH BAKING PAPER

For the cheese pastry
200g plain flour
120g salted butter, chilled and diced
15g Parmesan, freshly grated
leaves from 1 small fresh thyme sprig
1 large egg yolk
about 2 tablespoons cold water
1 egg, lightly beaten, to glaze

For the filling
25g unsalted butter
1 small white onion, finely chopped

250g frozen petits pois
100ml chicken stock
3 fresh mint leaves
pepper

To finish
50g Parmesan, freshly grated
30g Parma ham

1 Make the cheese pastry in a food processor. Put the flour and butter into the bowl of the processor and run the machine until the mixture looks like fine crumbs. Add the Parmesan and the thyme leaves and 'pulse' a few times until combined. Add the egg yolk and 2 tablespoons water and process just until the dough comes together in a ball – only add more water if needed to bring the dough together. Turn out the dough and shape it into a disc, then wrap in clingfilm and chill for 15 minutes.

2 Roll out the dough on a lightly floured worktop (or between 2 sheets of baking parchment) until quite thin – about 2–3mm – then cut out 12 circles using a 7cm plain round cutter. Re-roll the trimmings and cut out more rounds. Press the pastry circles into the bun tray to neatly line the cups. Prick the base of each pastry case with a fork, then chill for 15 minutes.

3 Meanwhile, heat your oven to 180°C/350°F/gas 4. Line each pastry case with a small square of baking parchment and fill with baking beans. Place in the heated oven and bake blind for 10 minutes. Remove the paper and beans, then lightly brush the pastry cases with beaten egg. Return them to the oven and bake for a further 7–10 minutes until crisp and golden brown. Leave to cool for 10 minutes before carefully removing the tartlet cases from the tray. Set them on a wire rack to cool completely. Leave the oven on.

4 To make the filling, melt the butter in a small pan, add the onion and cook gently for about 15 minutes until very soft and golden. Add the peas and stock and simmer for about 5 minutes until the peas are tender. Remove from the heat. Tear up the mint leaves and add to the pan. Cool for a minute, then

blend to a smooth, thick purée with a hand blender or in a food processor. Season to taste with pepper. Leave to cool.

5 Spoon the grated Parmesan on to the lined baking sheet in 4 piles about 2cm high, spacing them well apart. Place in the heated oven and bake for 10–12 minutes until a good golden colour and bubbling. Remove from the oven and leave on the baking sheet until completely cold and firm.

6 Using kitchen scissors, snip the Parma ham slices across into strips about 5cm wide. Put them in a cold non-stick frying pan and set over medium heat. Fry briefly – about 2 minutes – until crisp, stirring frequently. Transfer to a plate lined with kitchen paper and leave to cool.

7 To assemble, spoon the pea purée into the tartlet cases. Break each Parmesan crisp into 3 shards and stick into the purée. Finish with shards of Parma ham. Serve at room temperature.

NOTE: The vibrant green colour will fade, so these are best made and served straight away.

MARY'S RELIGIEUSES

A French favourite – choux pastry buns filled with a smooth vanilla crème pâtissière (pastry cream) and coated with dark chocolate ganache. Each bun is decorated with a frilly white collar of whipped cream to make it resemble a miniature nun.

MAKES 8
YOU WILL NEED: I LARGE BAKING SHEET, OR 2 MEDIUM ONES, LINED WITH BAKING PAPER

For the choux pastry
60g unsalted butter, cubed
150ml water
75g plain flour
2 medium eggs, at room temperature, lightly beaten

For the crème pâtissière filling
500ml full-fat milk
I vanilla pod, split lengthways
6 medium egg yolks, at room temperature
75g caster sugar
20g cornflour
25g plain flour

For the chocolate ganache
150ml double cream
200g dark chocolate (about 36% cocoa solids), broken into pieces

For the collar
150ml double cream, well chilled

I Start by making the choux pastry. Heat your oven to 220°C/425°F/gas 7. Draw eight 5cm circles and eight 2.5cm circles on the paper lining the baking sheet.

2 Put the butter and water into a heavy pan and heat over a medium heat until the butter has completely melted, then bring the mixture to the boil, taking care not to burn the butter. Remove from the heat and tip in the flour. Stir vigorously with a wooden spoon until the mixture forms a soft ball. Set the pan back on low heat and cook for 3–5 minutes, stirring constantly, to dry out the dough. Remove from the heat and leave to cool slightly. Gradually add the eggs, beating well after each addition, to make a smooth, shiny paste.

Stir well to form a soft ball

3 Spoon the choux dough into a piping bag fitted with a 1.5cm plain tube. Pipe discs inside the drawn circles on the baking sheet. Dip your finger in water and gently smooth the top of each disc. Place in the heated oven and bake for 10 minutes, then reduce the oven temperature to 190°C/375°F/gas 5 and bake for a further 10–15 minutes until a good golden brown.

4 Remove the baking sheet from the oven and pierce each bun with a skewer to allow the steam to escape. Return the choux buns to the oven and bake for 4–5 minutes so they dry out. Transfer the buns to a wire rack and leave to cool.

5 Meanwhile, make the crème pâtissière. Pour the milk into a heavy-based medium pan. Using the tip of a small knife, scrape out the vanilla seeds from the split pod and add to the milk. Slowly bring to the boil, then remove the pan from the heat and set aside. Put the egg yolks and sugar into a heatproof mixing bowl and whisk together until pale, then add the cornflour and flour and whisk in. Continue to whisk as you pour on the hot milk in a thin steady stream. Pour the mixture back into the pan. Set over medium heat and bring to the boil, whisking constantly. Cook for 1 minute until smooth and thick. Pour into a bowl and cover the surface of the crème pâtissière with clingfilm (this prevents a skin from forming). Leave to cool, then chill.

6 For the chocolate ganache, bring the cream to the boil in a small pan, then remove from the heat. Add the pieces of chocolate and stir until melted and the mixture is smooth and shiny. Transfer to a bowl and leave to cool, then cover and chill until the ganache has a thick coating consistency.

Pipe discs inside the drawn circles on the baking sheet

Gently smooth the top of each disc

7 To assemble the religieuses, spoon the crème pâtissière into a piping bag fitted with a long thin tube (or use a jam or icing syringe) and fill the choux buns through the 'steam hole' made earlier. Dip the tops of the filled buns into the chocolate ganache to coat them halfway up the sides. Set a small bun on top of each large bun.

8 Whip the cream until it will stand in peaks. Spoon into the clean piping bag fitted with a star tube. Pipe a line of cream around the join where the two buns meet to form a white collar. Serve as soon as possible after assembling.

Large
mixing bowl

Piping bag
and plain tube

Square brownie tin

Loaf tin

Spatula

Sieve

Measuring spoons

Small
saucepan

Balloon
whisk

Wooden
spoon

Ramekins

Food
processor

Springclip tin

Ovenproof
pudding basin

Rolling pin

Measuring jug

PUDDINGS

Puddings and desserts are the highlight of a meal for many and much anticipated. Chocolate gives flavour and colour, but it can also affect the texture of a pudding. Watch carefully during baking: a chocolate mix will carry on cooking after the pudding comes out of the oven, so can end up rather dry. Slightly underbake a chocolate pudding if in doubt.

When making creamy egg custards always add the heated milk and cream to the beaten eggs, pouring in a thin steady stream, and not the other way round. If you find your meringues sometimes 'weep' during baking, check your oven temperature. If it's too low, the meringues will be under-cooked and will collapse instead of solidifying. Beading – small drops of caramelised sugar on the top edge of the meringue – means the oven is probably a bit too high, making the exterior harden too quickly. Invest in a digital sugar thermometer – it's so helpful when you are melting and tempering chocolate or making sugar syrups and caramel.

ROASTED APPLES WITH BUTTERSCOTCH SAUCE

Home-made crisp, buttery biscuits plus hot apples and a warm butterscotch and hazelnut sauce – a delicious combination.

SERVES 4
YOU WILL NEED: 1 BAKING DISH LARGE ENOUGH TO HOLD THE APPLES UPRIGHT, GREASED WITH BUTTER

4 large, crisp eating apples
40g unsalted butter
4 tablespoons caster sugar
4 Vanilla Sablés (see page 78)

For the sauce
150g light brown muscovado sugar
75g unsalted butter, diced
100ml double cream
1 vanilla pod, split open
2 tablespoons chopped roasted hazelnuts

1 Heat your oven to 200°C/400°F/gas 6. Peel the apples. Using an apple corer or small sharp knife cut out the cores, leaving the fruit whole.

2 Melt the butter in a small pan, or in a shallow heatproof dish in the microwave. Put the sugar on to a small plate. One at a time, roll the apples first in the melted butter and then in the sugar so they are thickly coated. Set the apples upright, not touching, in the baking dish. Place in the heated oven and bake for 25–30 minutes until the fruit is tender and lightly coloured (the exact time depends on the apple variety).

3 While the apples are in the oven, make the sauce. Put the sugar, butter, cream and vanilla pod into a small pan. Heat gently, stirring frequently, until the butter has melted, then simmer for about 5 minutes until the sauce is thicker and sticky. Stir in the nuts. Keep warm until needed.

4 When the apples are ready, set a sablé on each of 4 heatproof plates. Carefully place an apple upright in the centre of each sablé. Gently reheat the sauce, if necessary, then remove the vanilla pod. Spoon a little sauce into the centre of each apple. Serve immediately, with the rest of the sauce in a jug.

STICKY TOFFEE APPLE PUDDING

This very simple all-in-one sponge mix is a good way to use slightly tart windfall apples. After baking, some of the sauce is spooned over the pudding so it seeps in and makes it sticky.

SERVES 6
YOU WILL NEED: 1 X 1.25–1.5 LITRE DEEP BAKING DISH, GREASED WITH BUTTER

For the sponge
4 medium tart eating apples (about 500g in total)
100g walnut pieces
2 medium free-range eggs, at room temperature
125g unsalted butter, softened

125g light brown muscovado sugar
150g self-raising flour

For the toffee sauce
200g dark muscovado sugar
100g unsalted butter, diced
150ml whipping or single cream

1 Heat your oven to 180°C/350°F/gas 4. Peel and quarter the apples. Cut out the cores, then chop the apples into pieces about 1cm – they don't need to be neat. Put into a bowl with the nuts and mix well. Set aside.

2 Put the eggs in a large bowl and beat with a fork, just to mix. Add the soft butter, sugar and flour and beat well with a wooden spoon or electric mixer until the mixture is smooth and even in colour. Tip the apples and nuts on to the sponge mixture and thoroughly fold in with a large metal spoon or plastic spatula.

3 Scrape the mixture into the greased dish and spread evenly. Place in the heated oven and bake for about 40 minutes until a skewer inserted into the centre of the sponge comes out clean.

4 While the sponge is baking make the sauce. Put the sugar, butter and cream into a small pan and melt gently over low heat, stirring now and then. Bring to the boil, then simmer gently for 5 minutes until the sauce is slightly thickened. Remove from the heat.

5 Remove the dish from the oven and set it on a heatproof surface. Reheat the sauce, if necessary. Using a table knife, cut several deep slits in the sponge, then spoon over about a third of the sauce. When the sauce has seeped in, return the pudding to the oven and bake for a further 3 minutes. Serve hot with the remaining sauce.

FRESH EGG CUSTARD

If you have spent time making a wonderful pie or pud, it's worth serving a proper custard too. You need rich, high-fat milk and a vanilla pod for the best flavour.

MAKES ABOUT 475ML

425ml creamy milk (eg Jersey or Guernsey)
1 vanilla pod
4 medium, free-range egg yolks, at room
    temperature

1 Put the milk into a medium pan (preferably non-stick). With the tip of a small, sharp knife, split the vanilla pod open along its length without cutting all the way through. Scrape some of the tiny specks – the seeds – into the milk, then add the pod. Bring to the boil, stirring frequently with a wooden spoon, then remove from the heat, cover the pan and leave to infuse for about 20 minutes.

2 Meanwhile, put the egg yolks and sugar into a heatproof mixing bowl set on a damp cloth (to stop it wobbling) and beat thoroughly with a wooden spoon until very smooth and much paler – this will take about a minute.

3 Remove the vanilla pod from the milk (the pod can be thoroughly rinsed and dried, then used to make vanilla sugar by adding it to a large screw-top jar filled with caster sugar), then slowly pour the warm milk on to the egg yolks in a thin steady stream, stirring constantly with the wooden spoon.

4 Tip the mixture back into the pan and stir constantly over medium heat until the custard thickens enough to coat the back of the spoon. Don't let the custard come to the boil or the eggs will scramble!

5 As soon as the custard has thickened pour it into a serving jug and serve immediately. Or, to serve the custard cold or chilled, sprinkle the surface with a thin layer of caster sugar to prevent a skin from forming, then cover the top of the jug with

clingfilm. Leave to cool and then chill, if wished. Stir the custard gently before serving. The custard can be kept, tightly covered, in the fridge for up to 2 days.

ICE-CREAM SHORTBREADS

Ice-cream sandwiches are not just for the kids, or for summer days. Try this recipe, putting maple pecan ice cream between layers of butter-rich, nutty shortbread.

MAKES 12
YOU WILL NEED: 1 SWISS ROLL TIN 20 X 30CM, GREASED WITH BUTTER AND BASE-LINED

For the shortbread
200g unsalted butter, softened
½ teaspoon vanilla extract
85g light brown muscovado sugar
1 medium free-range egg, at room
  temperature
80g self-raising flour
pinch of salt

100g pecan halves
1 tablespoon maple syrup

To serve
1 x 500g tub maple pecan ice cream
maple syrup, for pouring

1 To make the shortbread put the soft butter into a mixing bowl with the vanilla and sugar. Beat with an electric mixer or a wooden spoon until light and creamy. Put the egg into a small bowl and beat with a fork, just to mix. Add the egg, a tablespoon at a time, beating the mixture well after each addition and scraping down the sides of the bowl from time to time. Sift the flour and salt into the bowl and mix in (if using an electric mixer, use the lowest speed).

2 Scrape the mixture into the prepared tin and spread carefully, taking it right into the corners, to make a thin but even layer. Scatter the pecans over the top – don't press them on to the surface or they will disappear as the mixture rises while baking. Chill for 15 minutes.

3 Meanwhile, heat your oven to 190°C/375°F/gas 5. Place the tin in the heated oven and bake for 10 minutes until the shortbread is a light golden colour. Remove from the oven. Quickly drizzle the maple syrup over the shortbread, then return to the oven and bake for a further 2 minutes. Set the tin on a wire rack and leave until cold.

4 Invert the tin on to a chopping board, then lift off the tin and then the lining paper from the shortbread. With a large sharp knife, carefully cut the shortbread in half lengthways to make 2 long rectangles. Remove the ice cream from the freezer and leave until soft enough to scoop easily.

5 Set one rectangle nut-side down on a large sheet of clingfilm. Quickly spoon the ice cream on top to make an even layer. Cover with the second shortbread rectangle, nut side up, to make a large ice-cream sandwich. Wrap in clingfilm and freeze for about 2 hours until firm (it can be kept in the freezer for up to a week).

6 To serve, unwrap the sandwich and place it on a chopping board. Cut across into bars using a large sharp knife. Serve with extra maple syrup.

PASSIONFRUIT CHEESECAKE

Passionfruit works well in a fresh-tasting lemony cheesecake that's quick to put together. Baking the biscuit crust before adding the filling ensures the base will be crisp.

CUTS INTO 10
YOU WILL NEED: 1 X 20.5CM SPRINGCLIP TIN, GREASED WITH BUTTER, A BAKING SHEET

1 Heat your oven to 180°C/350°F/gas 4. Crush the biscuits, either in a food processor or by putting them into a closed plastic bag and bashing with a rolling pin. Tip them into a large mixing bowl.

2 Gently melt the butter in a small pan (or in a bowl in the microwave), then mix into the crumbs. Tip them into the greased tin set on a baking sheet. Make a case for the filling using about a third of the crumbs for the side and the rest for the base: push the crumbs for the side towards the edge of the tin, then spread out the crumbs remaining on the base and press them down firmly with the back of a spoon to make an even layer. With the back of the spoon ease the crumbs around the edge halfway up the side of the tin, gently pressing them to firm. Once the side looks fairly even in height and thickness, go all around again pressing the crumbs firmly with the back of the spoon and making sure that the angle between the base and the sides is 90 degrees.

3 Place the biscuit crust in the heated oven and bake for 5 minutes. Remove from the oven and set the tin, still on the baking sheet, on a heatproof surface. Leave to cool until needed. Don't turn off the oven.

4 To make the filling, put the cream cheese, soured cream, eggs, sugar, and lemon zest and juice into a large mixing bowl (set the bowl on a damp cloth so it won't wobble). Beat together with an electric mixer. Start on low speed at first to soften the cream cheese and break up the eggs, then scrape down the bowl and whisk on medium speed until the mixture is very smooth and creamy.

5 Pour and scrape the mixture into the biscuit crust in the tin and spread evenly – the filling will come slightly above the rim of the biscuit crust.

6 Halve the 4 passionfruits and scoop out the pulp and seeds into a small bowl. Stir well, then spoon on to the middle of the cheesecake filling. Using the handle of a teaspoon, gently swirl the passionfruit through the mixture to give a marbled effect.

7 Set the tin, still on the baking sheet, in the heated oven and bake for 40–45 minutes until the filling looks set and no longer damp – the filling will have a slight wobble when you gently shake the sheet. Turn off the oven and leave the cheesecake to cool inside with the door slightly ajar for 10 minutes.

8 Remove from the oven and set on a heatproof surface. Slip a round-bladed knife (or palette knife) down between the side of the tin and the cheesecake and gently run the knife around the cheesecake to loosen it from the tin (this helps to prevent it from cracking as it cools and contracts). Leave until cold, then cover the tin with clingfilm and chill for 6 hours (or overnight if possible).

9 When you're ready to serve the cheesecake unclip the tin side and set the cheesecake on a serving platter. Halve the 2 passionfruits, scoop out the pulp and seeds, and spoon on to the cheesecake. Store in a covered container in the fridge for up to 5 days.

For the biscuit crust
150g digestive biscuits
50g unsalted butter
For the filling
600g full-fat cream cheese,
    room temperature

150ml soured cream, at
    room temperature
3 medium free-range eggs,
    at room temperature
150g caster sugar

finely grated zest of
    1 unwaxed lemon
1 tablespoon lemon juice
4 passionfruits
2 passionfruits, to serve
    (optional)

MOCHA ROULADE

A moist and deeply flavoured coffee sponge, this is made with ground almonds rather than flour, and filled with chocolate mousse and whipped cream.

CUTS INTO 8
YOU WILL NEED: I SWISS ROLL TIN 20 X 30CM, GREASED WITH BUTTER AND BASE-LINED

For the sponge
4 medium free-range eggs, at
    room temperature, separated
150g caster sugar
2 tablespoons instant coffee granules
    dissolved in 1 tablespoon boiling water
50g ground almonds

For the filling
150g dark chocolate (about
    70% cocoa solids)

1 tablespoon water or brandy
3 medium free-range eggs, at
    room temperature, separated
1 tablespoon caster sugar
200ml whipping cream
2 tablespoons icing sugar, plus extra
    for dusting
2 teaspoons coffee liqueur or
    brandy (optional)
chocolate coffee beans, to decorate

1 Heat your oven to 180°C/350°F/gas 4. Make the sponge first. Put the egg whites in a large bowl and whisk with an electric mixer until stiff peaks will form when the whisk is lifted. Set aside until needed.

2 Put the sugar, coffee and egg yolks into another bowl and whisk (no need to wash the beaters) until the mixture is very thick and mousse-like and will make a ribbon trail on itself. Sprinkle the ground almonds over the mixture and gently fold in with a large metal spoon or plastic spatula.

3 Add a third of the whisked egg whites and gently fold into the yolk mixture. Fold in the rest of the whites in 2 batches. Spoon the sponge mixture into the prepared tin and spread evenly. Place in the heated oven and bake for 15–18 minutes until the sponge springs back when gently pressed in the centre. Remove the tin from the oven and set it on a wire rack. Cover lightly with a damp tea towel and leave until completely cold.

4 While the sponge is cooling, make the filling. Break or chop up the chocolate into even-sized pieces and put into a large heatproof bowl with the water or brandy. Set the bowl over a pan of hot water and

melt gently, stirring occasionally. Remove the bowl from the pan and gently stir in the egg yolks.

5 Put the egg whites into a large bowl and whisk until soft peaks will form when the whisk is lifted. Sprinkle the caster sugar over and whisk again until stiff. Fold the whites into the chocolate mixture in 3 batches using a large metal spoon or plastic spatula. Cover the mousse and chill until firm enough to spread.

6 Pour the cream into a large bowl, add the icing sugar and liqueur or brandy, and whip until stiff.

7 Lay a sheet of baking paper on the worktop and dust with icing sugar. Turn out the sponge on to the paper. Spread the chocolate mousse over the sponge, then top with the whipped cream. Roll up the sponge from one long side, using the paper to lift and guide the sponge (don't worry if it cracks). Wrap the baking paper tightly round the roulade to hold it in place, then chill for about 2 hours (and up to 24 hours) until firm.

8 When ready to serve unwrap the roulade and trim off the ends. Set on a serving platter. Dust with icing sugar and decorate with chocolate coffee beans. Serve in thick slices.

CRÈME BRÛLÉE

For the ideal smooth, creamy texture, the egg custard mixture must be cooked gently. Setting the ramekins in a bain-marie, or roasting tin of water, prevents the custard from overheating in the oven. Then when you melt and caramelise the sugar layer under the grill, keep checking — if this takes too long there's a chance the custard might start to heat up and bubble through.

MAKES 4
YOU WILL NEED: 4 X 9CM/175ML RAMEKIN DISHES

500ml double cream
1 vanilla pod, split lengthways
4 medium free-range egg yolks, at room
    temperature

1 tablespoon caster sugar
4 tablespoons demerara sugar, to finish

1 Pour the cream into a medium pan and add the vanilla pod. Heat gently until you see tiny bubbles appearing around the edge of the pan — don't let the cream start to boil. Stir the cream gently, then set the pan on a heatproof surface, cover and leave to infuse for 15 minutes. Meanwhile, heat your oven to 180°C/350°F/gas 4.

2 Put the egg yolks in a large heatproof bowl and add the caster sugar. Set the bowl on a damp cloth so it doesn't wobble, then whisk with a balloon whisk for 2 minutes until the yolks become paler in colour and thicker.

3 Remove the vanilla pod from the cream (it can be rinsed and thoroughly dried, then used to make vanilla sugar). Slowly pour the hot cream into the egg yolks, while whisking gently. Once all the cream has been incorporated, pour the mixture into a measuring jug. Divide equally among the ramekin dishes.

4 Set the ramekin dishes in a roasting tin. Pour cold water into the tin so it comes halfway up the sides of the ramekins. Carefully place the roasting tin in the oven and bake for 25–30 minutes until you can see that a skin has formed over the surface of the custard — it will still be wobbly underneath.

5 Remove the roasting tin from the oven and set it on a heatproof surface. Leave to cool, then lift the ramekins out of the water and cover them with clingfilm. Chill for at least 6 hours — overnight if possible — so the custard firms up.

6 Turn on the grill to its hottest possible setting, and wait for it to get properly hot. Uncover the custards and sprinkle a tablespoon of demerara sugar evenly over the top of each one — a thin even layer will give the best results, so don't add a bit of extra sugar for luck! Set the ramekins on the rack of the grill pan and slide it under the grill, as close to the heat as possible. Grill for a couple of minutes until the sugar has melted and turned to a golden caramel.

7 Leave the ramekins to cool for 10 minutes, then cover them lightly and return to the fridge to chill for about 1 hour. (Alternatively, melt and caramelise the sugar using a kitchen blowtorch; leave to cool and set for 10 minutes before serving.) Best eaten the same day before the caramel starts to soften.

Variation: Chocolate Brûlée
Finely chop 200g dark chocolate (about 70% cocoa solids). After removing the vanilla pod from the cream, gently reheat the cream until steaming hot (but not boiling). Add the chocolate. Leave for a minute, then stir until smooth. Continue with the recipe above.

ORANGE BRÛLÉE

A fresh summery version of crème brûlée, this is flavoured with fragrant orange flower water and served with caramel oranges.

SERVES 4
YOU WILL NEED: 4 X 9CM/175ML RAMEKIN DISHES

500ml double cream
finely grated zest of 1 unwaxed orange
4 medium free-range egg yolks, at room temperature
1 tablespoon caster sugar
2 teaspoons orange flower water

4 tablespoons demerara sugar, to finish

For the caramel oranges
5 medium oranges (seedless if possible)
175g caster sugar
125ml water

1 Pour the cream into a medium pan and add the orange zest. Heat gently until you see tiny bubbles appearing around the edge of the pan – don't let the cream start to boil. Stir the cream gently, then set the pan on a heatproof surface, cover and leave to infuse for 15 minutes. Meanwhile, heat your oven to 180°C/350°F/gas 4.

2 Put the egg yolks in a large heatproof bowl and add the sugar and orange flower water. Set the bowl on a damp cloth so it doesn't wobble, then whisk with a balloon whisk for 2 minutes until the yolks become paler in colour and thicker.

3 Slowly pour the hot cream into the egg yolks while whisking gently. Once all the cream has been incorporated, pour the mixture into a measuring jug. Divide equally among the ramekin dishes.

4 Set the ramekin dishes in a roasting tin. Pour cold water into the tin so it comes halfway up the sides of the ramekins. Carefully place the roasting tin in the oven and bake for 25–30 minutes until you can see that a skin has formed over the surface of the custard – it will still be wobbly underneath.

5 Remove the roasting tin from the oven and set it on a heatproof surface. Leave to cool, then lift the ramekins out of the water and cover them with clingfilm. Chill for at least 6 hours – overnight if possible – so the custard firms up.

6 Peel the oranges and cut into very thin slices with a serrated knife. Put the slices, and any juice, in a heatproof bowl.

7 To make the caramel combine the sugar and half the water in a small, heavy-based pan. Set over low heat and stir frequently until the sugar has completely dissolved. Turn up the heat and boil rapidly (without stirring) until the syrup turns a deep chestnut caramel colour. Remove the pan from the heat. Cover your hand, then quickly pour the rest of the water into the caramel (it will splutter alarmingly). Return the pan to low heat and stir until smooth and melted. Pour the caramel over the oranges. Stir well, then cover and keep in the fridge.

8 Turn on the grill to its hottest possible setting, and wait for it to get properly hot. Uncover the custards and sprinkle a tablespoon of demerara sugar evenly over the top of each one – a thin even layer will give the best results, so don't add a bit of extra sugar for luck! Set the ramekins on the rack of the grill pan and slide it under the grill, as close to the heat as possible. Grill for a couple of minutes until the sugar has melted and turned to a golden caramel.

9 Leave the ramekins to cool for 10 minutes, then cover and return to the fridge to chill for about 1 hour. (Alternatively, caramelise the sugar using a kitchen blowtorch; leave to cool for 10 minutes before serving.) Serve with the caramel oranges.

BROWNIE ICE-CREAM SANDWICHES

The brownies here are slightly firmer and less sweet than usual, to make it easier to sandwich them with ice cream. If you have only one baking sheet, scoop the second batch on to a sheet of baking paper cut to fit the sheet. When the first batch of brownies has been baked, slide them, on the lining paper, on to a wire rack to cool. Quickly cool the baking sheet under running cold water and dry it, then slide the paper with the second batch on to it and bake as before.

MAKES 12
YOU WILL NEED: 1–2 BAKING SHEETS, LINED WITH BAKING PAPER

200g dark chocolate (about 70% cocoa solids), chopped or broken up
50g unsalted butter, diced
150g light brown muscovado sugar
2 medium free-range eggs, at room temperature
½ teaspoon vanilla extract
40g self-raising flour
good pinch of salt
50g good milk chocolate, chopped into small chunks
50g pecan or walnut pieces
1 x 500g tub vanilla or coffee ice cream
icing sugar, for dusting

1 Put the dark chocolate in a large heatproof bowl and add the butter. Set the bowl over a pan of hot water and melt gently, stirring occasionally. Remove the bowl from the pan and set on a damp cloth on a heatproof surface (the cloth will stop the bowl wobbling). Stir in the sugar. Leave to cool for a couple of minutes.

2 Using a fork, beat the eggs with the vanilla in a small bowl until frothy. Check that the chocolate mixture is barely warm, then add the eggs and beat with a wooden spoon to incorporate thoroughly.

3 Sift the flour and salt into the bowl and gently stir in. Add the milk chocolate and nuts and stir in. Cover the bowl and chill for 30 minutes to firm up the mixture. Meanwhile, heat your oven to 180°C/350°F/gas 4.

4 Scoop out the mixture in tablespoon-sized portions on to the lined baking sheets; set the scoops well apart to allow for spreading. Gently flatten the mounds of dough with your fingers to make even-sized rounds about 1cm high – they will look a bit lumpy rather than neat.

5 Place in the heated oven and bake for 10 minutes until the surface of the brownies is lightly cracked and they feel just firm (the centres will still be soft – the brownies will continue cooking for a few minutes after they come out of the oven, and will firm up as they cool). Remove from the oven and place the baking sheets on a wire rack. Leave the brownies to cool before peeling them off the baking paper. Once cold, the brownies can be stored in an airtight container for up to 5 days.

6 Remove the ice cream from the freezer about 10 minutes or so before serving, to make it easier to scoop. Sandwich the brownies in pairs with a scoop of ice cream. Dust with icing sugar and eat immediately.

LEMON SYRUP SPONGE PUDDING

Old-fashioned but still a real treat! The sponge is a quick all-in-one flavoured with fresh lemon zest and syrup, and there's more syrup in the basin to give the turned-out pudding a sticky sweet coating. Measuring the syrup is easier if you warm the spoon first. Serve with home-made vanilla custard (see the recipe on page 255).

SERVES 4–6
YOU WILL NEED: 1 X 500ML OVENPROOF PUDDING BASIN, WELL GREASED WITH BUTTER

5 tablespoons golden syrup

For the sponge
120g unsalted butter, at room temperature
100g caster sugar
1 tablespoon golden syrup

2 medium free-range eggs, at room
temperature
finely grated zest of 1 medium lemon
1 tablespoon lemon juice
130g self-raising flour

1 Heat your oven to 180°C/350°F/gas 4. Spoon the 5 tablespoons syrup into the bottom of the buttered basin.

2 Put all the ingredients for the sponge into a large mixing bowl and beat well with a wooden spoon or an electric mixer until very smooth and light. Spoon the mixture into the basin.

3 Cut a sheet of foil big enough to cover the basin generously. Butter the foil, then fold a pleat in the centre (to allow for the expansion of the pudding during baking). Lay the foil, butter side down, over the top of the basin and seal tightly under the rim.

4 Place in the heated oven and bake for 45–50 minutes until a skewer inserted in the centre comes out clean. Remove the basin from the oven and set it on a heatproof surface. Take off the foil. Run a round-bladed knife around the pudding to loosen it from the basin, then set an upturned warmed serving plate on top. Holding the plate and basin firmly together, turn them over so the pudding is unmoulded on to the plate. Serve immediately.

MERINGUE BERRY SORBET CAKE

Three layers of crunchy meringue sandwiched with berry sorbets and finished with fresh fruit for a gluten-free dairy-free dessert. You can replace one of the sorbets with ice cream, such as a rich fruity berry ice cream or vanilla ice cream for a creamy flavour.

CUTS INTO 10
YOU WILL NEED: 1 X 20.5CM SPRINGCLIP TIN, LINED WITH CLINGFILM, 3 BAKING SHEETS

For the meringue layers
4 medium free-range egg whites, at
  room temperature
2 good pinches of cream of tartar
225g caster sugar

To assemble
1 x 500g tub raspberry sorbet
1 x 500g tub strawberry or mango sorbet

To decorate
fresh raspberries, blueberries, tiny
  strawberries, redcurrants and/or
  sliced mango
Fresh Raspberry Sauce (see page 275),
  to serve

1 Heat your oven to 120°C/250°F/gas ½. Using the base of the springclip tin as a guide, draw three 20.5cm circles on 3 sheets of baking paper. Lay the baking paper, drawn-circle side down, on 3 baking sheets (or upturned roasting tins).

2 Put the egg whites into a large mixing bowl and whisk with an electric mixer for about 30 seconds until foamy. Add the cream of tartar and whisk until the whites will form a soft peak when the whisk is lifted.

3 Whisk in 4 tablespoons of the sugar, one at a time, and keep on whisking for about a minute to make a thick, glossy meringue that will form a stiff peak when the whisk is lifted. Sprinkle the rest of the sugar over the meringue and very lightly fold in with a large metal spoon.

4 Spoon a third of the meringue into the centre of each circle drawn on the paper. Gently spread out to make an even disc slightly smaller than the circle (to allow for spreading). Place in the heated oven and bake for 1½–1¾ hours until crisp and dry. Turn off the oven and leave the meringues inside to cool.

5 About 10 minutes before assembling the cake, remove the sorbets from the freezer so they can become soft enough to scoop. Clear a space in the freezer.

6 Set one meringue disc in the base of the lined springclip tin. Spoon the raspberry sorbet on top to make an even layer. Cover with a second meringue disc and gently press down with both hands to slightly compress the layers – don't worry if the meringue starts to crack or crumble. Cover with the second sorbet, again spooned on in an even layer. Then top with the last meringue disc and press down gently again to mould it all together. Cover tightly with clingfilm and freeze for at least 2 hours (the cake can be kept in the freezer for up to a week).

7 When ready to serve, unwrap the cake and unclip the tin. Set the cake on a serving plate. Decorate the top with berries and/or slices of mango, and serve cut into wedges with the raspberry sauce.

CINNAMON, BLUEBERRY AND APPLE COBBLER

Quicker than a fruit pie, and better-looking than a crumble, a cobbler topping has a crunchy surface and soft, tender crumb. Using a good wild blueberry conserve instead of sugar deepens the flavours of the fruit filling and thickens the juices.

SERVES 4–6
YOU WILL NEED: 1 X 1.25–1.5 LITRE BAKING DISH OR PIE DISH

1 large Bramley apple
450g blueberries
finely grated zest of 1 unwaxed lemon
1 tablespoon lemon juice
6 tablespoons blueberry conserve

For the topping
200g self-raising flour
¼ teaspoon ground cinnamon
good pinch of salt
3 tablespoons caster sugar, plus extra
   for sprinkling
50g unsalted butter, chilled and diced
about 140ml single cream

1 Heat your oven to 180°C/350°F/gas 4. Peel, quarter and core the apple, then cut into slices the thickness of a pound coin. Put into a mixing bowl and add the blueberries, lemon zest and juice, and blueberry conserve. Mix everything together well. Transfer to the baking dish and spread evenly. Put on one side while you make the topping.

2 Sift the flour, cinnamon, salt and sugar into a bowl. Add the pieces of butter and rub into the flour until the mixture looks like fine crumbs. Make a well in the centre and pour in the cream. Mix into the crumbs using a round-bladed knife to make a soft but not sticky dough. Work in more cream if the mixture feels dry and stiff or there are dry crumbs in the bowl.

3 Divide the dough into 14 or 15 walnut-sized balls. One at a time, slightly flatten the balls so they are about 1cm thick but slightly irregularly shaped and knobbly – like cobblestones. Arrange on top of the fruit, higgledy-piggledy rather than in a neat pattern. Sprinkle the cobbles with sugar.

4 Place in the heated oven and bake for 30–35 minutes until the cobbles are golden brown and the fruit is tender and bubbling. Serve warm with ice cream.

LEMON CURD BRIOCHE PUDDING

A sliced brioche loaf makes the lightest of bread and butter puds, and good lemon curd adds great flavour to the creamy custard. A really easy but special pudding.

SERVES 6
YOU WILL NEED: 1 X 1.5 LITRE BAKING DISH OR PIE DISH, GREASED WITH BUTTER, A ROASTING TIN

8 slices brioche (about 220g in total)
50g unsalted butter, softened
100g Lemon Curd (see page 38)
30g dried apricots, roughly chopped
300ml single cream

300ml milk (whole or semi-skimmed)
35g caster sugar
4 medium free-range eggs, at room
   temperature
icing sugar, for dusting

1 Make sandwiches with the brioche, butter and lemon curd (there's no need to cut off the soft crusts). Cut each sandwich diagonally into 4 triangles. Fit into the dish, placing them crust edge down, almost vertical; scatter in the apricots as you go.

2 Pour the cream and milk into a pan and add the caster sugar, then heat gently, stirring frequently, just until the sugar has dissolved (or do this in a heatproof jug in the microwave). Don't let the mixture come to the boil. Remove from the heat and leave to cool for a couple of minutes.

3 While it's cooling beat the eggs in a heatproof jug, or bowl with a lip, using a wire whisk or wooden spoon, just to mix. Slowly pour in the warm sweetened cream, stirring to mix.

4 Pour the custard mixture evenly over the lemon curd sandwiches in the baking dish, making sure that each one is moistened. Leave to stand for about an hour so the sandwiches can soak up the custard. Towards the end of this time, heat your oven to 160°C/325°F/gas 3.

5 Set the dish in a roasting tin and pour enough water into the tin to come halfway up the sides of the dish. Carefully place the roasting tin in the heated oven and bake for about 40 minutes until just set. Lift the dish out of the roasting tin, dust the top of the pudding with icing sugar and serve warm.

CHESTNUT MERINGUE ROULADE

This classic combination of meringue and a bitter chocolate and chestnut filling is perfect for a celebration. You can find tins of French crème de marrons (sweetened chestnut purée) in supermarkets.

MAKES 1 LARGE ROULADE
YOU WILL NEED: 1 SWISS ROLL TIN 20 X 30CM, BRUSHED WITH VEGETABLE OIL AND LINED WITH BAKING PAPER (NOT GREASEPROOF)

1 Heat your oven to 150°C/300°F/gas 2. Put the egg whites into a large bowl and whisk with an electric mixer until frothy. Add the cream of tartar and whisk until the egg whites will stand in stiff peaks when you lift out the whisk. Mix the sugar with the cornflour. Quickly whisk into the whites, a heaped tablespoon at a time, to make a glossy meringue that will form a stiff peak when the whisk is lifted.

2 Transfer the meringue to the prepared tin and spread evenly, taking care to fill the corners. Sift the cocoa powder over the top of the meringue so it is dusted with an even layer.

3 Place in the heated oven and bake for about 45 minutes until puffed, very slightly coloured and crisp to touch – the centre layer of the meringue will still be a bit soft. While the meringue is baking, cover a wire rack with a sheet of baking paper. As soon as the meringue is ready flip it over on to the paper. Lift off the tin, but allow the meringue to cool for 5 minutes before carefully peeling off the lining paper. Leave until cold.

4 To make the mousse, break or chop up the chocolate into even-sized pieces and put into a large heatproof bowl with 100ml of the cream. Set the bowl over a pan of hot water and melt gently, stirring occasionally. When the mixture is smooth, remove the bowl from the pan and leave to cool to room temperature.

5 Whip the remaining cream until thick enough to stand in soft peaks when the whisk is lifted. Leave on the worktop to come up to room temperature. Spoon the crème de marrons into a small bowl, add the rum or brandy and stir gently until well mixed. Set aside until needed.

6 When the cream and the chocolate mixture are roughly the same temperature, stir the crème de marrons into the chocolate. When thoroughly combined, fold in the whipped cream with a large metal spoon. Cover the bowl and chill for about 15 minutes until the mousse is almost on the point of setting but still soft enough to spread easily.

7 Spread the mousse evenly over the cold meringue. Roll up from one long side, using one hand to guide the meringue into shape and your other hand to lift the paper under the meringue to support the roll and pull it into shape as it rolls up – be bold and don't worry if it cracks. Once you have a roulade use the paper around it to hold it in shape, wrapping it firmly – again, don't worry if the filling starts to ooze out as it will soon firm up.

8 Set the wrapped roulade on a board or platter and chill for at least an hour (and up to 8 hours) before serving. When ready to serve remove the wrapping paper and decorate with marrons glacés and chocolate curls or grated chocolate, and a dusting of cocoa powder.

For the meringue

4 medium free-range egg
  whites, at room temperature
large pinch of cream of tartar
225g caster sugar
1 teaspoon cornflour
1–2 teaspoons cocoa powder,
  for dusting

For the mousse

100g dark chocolate
  (about 70% cocoa solids)
200ml whipping cream
1 x 250g tin crème de marrons
  (sweetened chestnut purée)
1 teaspoon dark rum or brandy

To decorate
marrons glacés (optional)
grated chocolate OR chocolate curls
  (see page 68)

PEACH TIRAMISU

When peaches are at their very best (and cheapest) towards the end of summer, try this fruity combination – a Peach Melba cream that is half trifle, half tiramisu.

SERVES 8–10
YOU WILL NEED: I X 1.25–1.5 LITRE TRIFLE BOWL OR SERVING DISH

I Arrange a layer of sponge fingers in the base of the dish – trim them, if necessary, so they fit snugly. Combine the orange juice and brandy or liqueur in a shallow dish. One at a time, remove the sponge fingers from the dish and dip them in the liquid to moisten, then replace them in the dish. Save the rest of the sponge fingers and orange liquid for the second layer.

2 Whip the cream until it will stand in stiff peaks when the whisk is lifted. Cover the bowl and keep in the fridge until needed.

3 Put the egg yolks and sugar into another bowl and whisk with an electric mixer until very pale, thick and mousse-like, and the mixture will make a ribbon trail on itself.

4 Gently stir the mascarpone in its tub, just to soften it, then fold it into the yolk mixture using a large metal spoon or plastic spatula. Gently fold in the whipped cream. When thoroughly combined, spoon half the mixture into the bowl on top of the sponge fingers. Spread evenly.

5 Make a small slit in the skin of each peach near the stem. Put them in a heatproof bowl or a saucepan and pour over enough boiling water to cover. Leave for 15 seconds, then drain the peaches and slip off the skins. Cut the peaches in half and remove the stones. Cut into very thin slices with a serrated knife.

6 Arrange half the peach slices over the cream mixture in the dish. Cover the cream mixture with another layer of sponge fingers, dipped in the orange liquid to moisten as before. They don't have

to look neat but try to avoid any gaps. Spread the rest of the cream mixture on top. Finally, add the rest of the peach slices.

7 Cover the bowl and chill for 2–4 hours. Serve with fresh raspberries or a jug of raspberry sauce.

18–20 Sponge Fingers
  (see page 274) or bought sponge
  fingers
100ml fresh orange juice
3 tablespoons Grand Marnier or brandy
200ml whipping cream, well chilled
4 medium free-range egg yolks,
  at room temperature

50g caster sugar
500g mascarpone
3 large peaches
fresh raspberries and/or Fresh
  Raspberry Sauce (see page 275), to serve

SPONGE FINGERS

Crisp on the outside, soft in the middle, home-made sponge fingers are quick to make and taste much nicer than the commercial types. They form the basis for many favourite desserts, including trifle and tiramisu.

MAKES 20
YOU WILL NEED: 1–2 BAKING SHEETS, LINED WITH BAKING PAPER

3 medium free-range eggs, at room
   temperature, separated
75g caster sugar
½ teaspoon vanilla extract

75g plain flour
good pinch of salt
icing sugar, for dusting

1 Heat your oven to 180°C/350°F/gas 4. Put the egg whites in a large mixing bowl and whisk with an electric mixer until they will stand in stiff peaks when the whisk is lifted. Sprinkle half the caster sugar over the whites and whisk for a few more seconds until stiff and glossy. Set aside.

2 Put the egg yolks in another bowl and add the rest of the caster sugar and the vanilla. Whisk with the electric mixer (there's no need to wash the beaters) until the mixture is very thick and mousse-like and will make a ribbon trail on itself. Sift the flour and salt on to the yolk mixture and fold in gently with a large metal spoon.

3 Add half of the whisked whites to the yolks and fold in quickly but gently, using as few movements as you can. Fold in the rest of the whites in the same way. You want the mixture to be fairly stiff so resist the urge to overmix as it will quickly turn runny.

4 Spoon the mixture into a large disposable piping bag, or a piping bag fitted with a 2cm plain tube. Fold over and twist the top of the bag so the mix cannot escape. If using a disposable bag snip off the end to make a 2cm wide opening. Holding the bag with one hand, and squeezing from the top with your other hand, pipe 10cm fingers on to the lined baking sheets, spacing the fingers slightly apart to allow for spreading.

5 Dust the fingers with icing sugar, then place in the heated oven and bake for 11–14 minutes until just firm and a light golden brown. (Rotate the baking sheets half way through the time, if the fingers are baking unevenly.) Remove the baking sheets from the oven and set on a heatproof surface. Leave to cool and firm up for a couple of minutes, then transfer the fingers to a wire rack and leave to cool. Once cold, the sponge fingers can be stored in an airtight container for up to a week.

FRESH RASPBERRY SAUCE

A very quick, vibrant sauce you can make from fresh or frozen fruit. Serve chilled with ice cream and frozen desserts, or warm with waffles or pancakes or instead of custard.

MAKES ABOUT 300ML

250g raspberries (fresh or frozen)
1 teaspoon lemon juice
4 tablespoons icing sugar, or to taste

1 If using frozen raspberries, remove them from the freezer 15–20 minutes in advance.

2 Put all the ingredients into a food processor and run the machine to make a very thick purée. Taste and add a little more sugar if you think it's needed. For a smoother, seedless sauce, push the purée through a fine sieve into a bowl.

3 Cover and chill until needed – the sauce can be kept in the fridge for 4 days.

CHOCOLATE AND BRANDY PARFAIT

You don't need an ice-cream maker or masses of time to make this glamorous iced dessert. Home-made sponge fingers dipped in brandy and coffee encase a light but very rich chocolate mocha mousse. You could serve it with the Mocha Sauce on page 201.

CUTS INTO 12
YOU WILL NEED: 1 X 900G LOAF TIN (ABOUT 26 X 12.5 X 7.5CM), LINED WITH CLINGFILM

For the chocolate mousse
200g dark chocolate (about
   70% cocoa solids)
200ml whipping cream, chilled
2 medium free-range eggs plus 2 yolks,
   at room temperature
100g caster sugar
1 teaspoon instant coffee granules
   dissolved in 1 tablespoon boiling water
1 tablespoon brandy

To assemble
2 tablespoons brandy
1 teaspoon instant coffee granules
   dissolved in 2 tablespoons
   boiling water
about 20 Sponge Fingers (see page 274)
cocoa powder, for dusting

1 Clear shelf space in the freezer, then break or chop up the chocolate into even-sized pieces. Put into a heatproof bowl, set over a pan of hot water and melt gently, stirring occasionally. Remove the bowl from the pan and leave to cool.

2 Whip the cream until it will stand in soft peaks when the whisk is lifted. Set the bowl aside on the worktop.

3 Put the whole eggs and the yolks into a large mixing bowl. Add the sugar and whisk with an electric mixer until the mixture is very pale, thick and mousse-like, and will make a ribbon trail on itself.

4 When the coffee has cooled to lukewarm add it to the egg mixture with the brandy and whisk for a few seconds until combined. Gently stir the melted chocolate, then add to the mixture and whisk until thoroughly combined. Using a large metal spoon or plastic spatula, gently fold in the whipped cream.

5 Now assemble the parfait. Mix the brandy and coffee in a shallow dish. One at a time dip the flat underside of about half of the sponge fingers into the mixture, just to moisten, then arrange rounded side down on the base of the lined tin (it looks best if the fingers run longways down the length of the tin). Trim the ends of the fingers, if necessary, so they fit snugly and cover the base completely.

6 Spoon the chocolate mousse on top and spread it evenly. Gently tap the tin on the worktop to dislodge any bubbles. Cover the mousse with sponge fingers, dipping them in the brandy/coffee mixture as before and arranging them rounded side up. Gently bang the tin again to settle the mixture, then cover the tin with clingfilm. Freeze for at least 2 hours (the parfait can be left in the freezer for up to a week).

7 When ready to serve unwrap the clingfilm and invert the parfait on to a serving platter. Lift off the tin and clingfilm lining. Dust with cocoa powder, then cut into slices with a large knife.

EASY PETITS FOURS

Home-made chocolates are always popular as petits fours. For these, a rich, dark brownie mixture is layered with either after-dinner mint thins or their ginger equivalent and then, after baking, the tiny cubes are dipped in melted dark chocolate. They look great served in tiny foil or paper petits fours cases. You can also cut larger brownies to serve for dessert.

MAKES 80 PETITS FOURS
YOU WILL NEED: I BROWNIE TIN OR CAKE TIN 20.5 X 25.5CM, WELL GREASED WITH BUTTER AND BASE-LINED

For the brownies
100g dark chocolate (about
   70% cocoa solids), chopped
100g unsalted butter, diced
3 medium free-range eggs
200g caster sugar
100g plain flour
¼ teaspoon salt
3 tablespoons cocoa powder
20 after-dinner mint thins or ginger thins
   (about 200g)

To finish
500g dark chocolate
   (about 70% cocoa solids)
3 tablespoons syrup from the ginger jar
   (optional)
1–2 lumps stem ginger, drained and very
   finely chopped (optional)

1 Heat your oven to 180°C/350°F/gas 4. Put the chocolate into a heatproof bowl with the butter. Set over a pan of hot water and melt gently, stirring occasionally. Remove the bowl from the pan and cool.

2 Put the eggs and sugar into a large mixing bowl and whisk with an electric mixer for 3–4 minutes until very thick and foamy. Add the chocolate mixture and whisk again for a minute or so until thoroughly combined. Sift the flour, salt and cocoa into the bowl and fold in with a large metal spoon or plastic spatula.

3 Spoon half of the mixture into the prepared tin and spread evenly, right into the corners. Cover with a layer of the mint or ginger thins. Carefully cover with the rest of the brownie mixture, spreading it in an even layer, into the corners too.

4 Place in the heated oven and bake for 25 minutes until the top is firm to a light touch – the centre will still be sticky. Remove the tin from the oven and set it on a damp tea towel laid on a heatproof surface. Cover with a dry tea towel and leave to cool.

5 Once the brownie cake is cold, carefully cut it into 80 tiny cubes. Don't worry if the crust crumbles, just press it back together.

6 To finish the petits fours, break up the chocolate and melt as before, adding the ginger syrup if you used ginger thins. Remove the bowl from the heat and set it on a towel on the worktop. Lay a large sheet of baking paper next to the bowl.

7 One at a time, briefly dip the brownie cubes in the melted chocolate (the easiest way to do this is to hold the brownie cube between 2 forks), then place on the paper. If the chocolate starts to thicken and set, set the bowl over the steaming water for a couple of minutes to gently re-melt it. Just before the chocolate has completely set, you can decorate ginger-flavoured brownies with a few pieces of stem ginger. Once the chocolate has set completely store in an airtight container and eat within 4 days.

RASPBERRY AND CHOCOLATE PAVLOVA

A pretty centrepiece for a special meal or party – the meringue base, made with melted bitter chocolate, is filled with whipped cream and covered with dark red berries.

SERVES 8
YOU WILL NEED: 1 BAKING SHEET, LINED WITH BAKING PAPER

100g dark chocolate (about
   70% cocoa solids), chopped
3 medium free-range egg whites,
   at room temperature
½ teaspoon cream of tartar
pinch of salt
175g caster sugar

1 ½ teaspoons cornflour

For the topping
300ml double cream, well chilled
300–400g fresh raspberries, tayberries
   or dessert blackberries
icing sugar, for dusting

1 Heat your oven to 140°C/275°F/gas 1. Put the chocolate into a heatproof bowl. Set the bowl over a pan of hot water and melt gently, stirring occasionally. Remove the bowl from the pan and leave to cool.

2 Put the egg whites into a large mixing bowl and whisk with an electric mixer on low speed for about 20 seconds until the whites are slightly frothy. Add the cream of tartar and salt. Whisk on full speed until the whites will form a soft peak when the whisk is lifted.

3 Whisk in half the caster sugar, a heaped tablespoon at a time, and continue whisking until the meringue is very glossy and will form a stiff peak when the whisk is lifted. Mix the cornflour into the rest of the sugar, then sprinkle over the meringue and gently but thoroughly fold in with a large metal spoon.

4 Drizzle the melted chocolate over the meringue and quickly fold through using just 2 or 3 strokes or movements to give a nice streaky effect.

5 Spoon the meringue on to the lined baking sheet and gently spread out to a disc about 23cm across and 3cm high. Use the back of the spoon to make a slight hollow in the centre. The disc shouldn't look neat and even, so make sure there are some swirls.

6 Place in the heated oven and bake for 1¼ hours until firm to the touch – the centre will still be slightly soft. Turn off the oven and leave the pavlova inside to cool down. (Once cold the pavlova can be stored in an airtight container for up to 2 days before finishing.)

7 To assemble, set the pavlova on a serving platter. Whip the cream until stiff, then spoon into the hollow in the pavlova. Scatter the berries over the top and dust with icing sugar. Keep in the fridge until needed – best eaten as soon as possible.

WEEKEND BAKING

Recipes from Mary, Paul and the bakers

- Mary's Tipsy Trifle

- Mary's Charlotte Royale

- Mary's Floating Islands

- Ninety-niners with a Twist

- Chocolate and Cherry Amaretto Parcels

- Mary's Hazelnut Dacquoise

MARY'S TIPSY TRIFLE

A trifle for any time of the year, this is created from a home-made sponge swiss roll, real egg custard and tinned pears plus plenty of sherry! Ratafia biscuits – tiny macaroon-like almond biscuits – have a bittersweet flavour, rather like amaretti.

SERVES 10
YOU WILL NEED: 1 SWISS ROLL TIN 23 X 33CM, GREASED AND LINED; 1 X 20CM STRAIGHT-SIDED GLASS BOWL

For the swiss roll
4 large eggs, at room temperature
100g caster sugar, plus extra for sprinkling
100g self-raising flour
170g strawberry jam or conserve

For the filling
20 ratafia biscuits
1 x 800g tin pear halves in natural juice
250ml medium-dry sherry

For the custard
3 large egg yolks, at room temperature

50g caster sugar
50g cornflour
1 teaspoon vanilla extract
600ml full-fat milk
300ml single cream

To decorate
250ml whipping cream, well chilled
25g flaked almonds, toasted
10 fresh cherries with stalks

1 Start by making the swiss roll. Heat your oven to 220°C/425°F/gas 7. Using an electric mixer, whisk the eggs with the sugar in a large mixing bowl until the mixture is very light and frothy, and it will make a ribbon trail on itself. Sift the flour on to the mixture and carefully fold it in using a large metal spoon or plastic spatula.

2 Transfer the mixture to the prepared tin and give the tin a gentle shake so the mixture settles and finds its own level (if necessary, gently push the mixture into the corners so they are evenly filled). Place in the heated oven and bake for 10–12 minutes until the sponge is golden and starting to shrink away from the sides of the tin.

3 While the sponge is baking lay a sheet of baking paper (cut slightly larger than the tin) on the worktop and sprinkle it with caster sugar. As soon as the sponge is ready, turn it out on to the sugared paper and carefully peel off the lining paper. Trim the edges of the sponge with a sharp knife, then score

Whisk until you can make a ribbon

a line across the sponge 2cm in from one short edge (take care not to cut right through the cake). Leave to cool slightly. Spread the jam evenly over the sponge, then gently roll it up from the scored end, using the paper to help you. Leave until cold before slicing.

4 Cut the swiss roll across into 14 slices. Arrange 8 of the slices, cut face outwards, closely together around the sides of the glass bowl. Arrange the 6 remaining slices over the base of the bowl. Crumble the ratafia biscuits over the top.

5 Drain the pears, saving the juice; set the pears aside. Measure 150ml of the juice (you won't need the rest) and mix it with the sherry. Sprinkle the sherry/pear liquid over the sponge and biscuits in the bowl. With the back of a spoon gently press the sponge layer on the base to make it as level as possible. Leave to soak while you make the custard.

6 Put the egg yolks, sugar, cornflour and vanilla extract into a large heatproof bowl and whisk together until smooth. Heat the milk and cream in a large heavy-based pan until hot but not boiling. Pour the hot liquid on to the yolk mixture in a thin, steady stream, whisking constantly, then pour the mixture back into the pan. Stir constantly over medium heat until the custard just comes to the boil and thickens. Remove from the heat and set aside.

7 Quickly cut each pear half lengthways into 3 slices and arrange on the sponge/biscuit layer in the bowl. Pour the warm custard over the pears. Cover the bowl and leave until cold, then transfer to the fridge to chill for at least 2 hours until set.

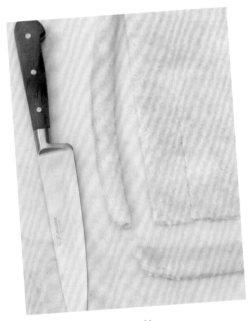

Trim the edges of the sponge

8 Whip the whipping cream until it will make a ribbon trail on itself. Set aside 3 tablespoons of cream for the final decoration, and gently spread the rest over the set custard. Scatter the flaked almonds over the surface. Whip the reserved cream until it will stand in soft peaks, then spoon in 10 'blobs' around the top of the trifle – one for each portion. Decorate each 'blob' with a cherry. If not serving immediately, cover the bowl (without damaging the decoration) and keep in the fridge until ready to serve.

MARY'S CHARLOTTE ROYALE

One of best summer desserts, a charlotte royale is a combination of light sponge, fresh raspberry mousse studded with tiny strawberries, and whipped cream – exquisitely decorated of course!

SERVES 10–12

YOU WILL NEED: 2 SWISS ROLL TINS 23 X 33CM, GREASED WITH BUTTER AND LINED WITH BAKING PAPER; 1 X 2 LITRE ROUND BOWL, LINED WITH CLINGFILM; A SUGAR THERMOMETER

For the jam
400g strawberries, hulled and chopped
500g jam sugar (sugar with added pectin)
small knob of butter

For the sponge rolls
6 large eggs, at room temperature
150g caster sugar, plus extra for sprinkling
150g self-raising flour

For the bavarois
9 gelatine leaves
550g raspberries
2 tablespoons framboise (raspberry liqueur)

600ml full-fat milk
8 egg yolks, at room temperature
100g caster sugar
300ml double cream, chilled
100g small strawberries, hulled

To decorate
75g caster sugar
125ml water
1 tablespoon arrowroot
150ml double cream, chilled
25g icing sugar, sifted
10 medium strawberries

1 Start by making the jam for the swiss rolls. Put the prepared strawberries into a medium-sized pan with the sugar and cook gently over low heat, stirring occasionally, until the sugar has melted. Bring the mixture to the boil and boil vigorously for about 4 minutes until the temperature reaches 104°C on a sugar thermometer, or setting point (see page 89). Remove from the heat and whisk in the butter. Transfer to a heatproof bowl and leave to cool and set.

2 To make the sponges, heat your oven to 220°C/425°F/gas 7. Put the eggs and sugar into a large bowl and whisk with an electric mixer until the mixture is light and frothy and it will make a ribbon trail on itself. Sift the flour over the mixture and carefully fold it in using a large metal spoon or plastic spatula.

3 Divide the mixture evenly between the 2 prepared tins. Give them a gentle shake so the mixture finds its own level; gently push the mixture into the corners if necessary. Place in the heated oven and bake for 10–12 minutes until the sponges are golden and starting to shrink away from the sides of the tin.

4 While the cakes are baking, lay 2 sheets of baking paper (cut a little larger than the tins) on the worktop and sprinkle them with caster sugar. As soon as the sponges are ready, turn them out on to the sugared paper and carefully peel off the lining paper. Trim the edges of the sponges with a sharp knife (this makes them easier to roll neatly) and score a line across each sponge 2cm in from one of the short edges (be careful not to cut right through). Leave the sponges to cool slightly before

spreading the jam evenly over them. Roll up each sponge firmly from the scored end and set aside until needed.

5 To make the bavarois, soak the leaves of gelatine in a bowl of cold water for about 10 minutes until softened. Meanwhile, tip 450g of the raspberries into the bowl of a food processor and blitz to a purée. Pour into a sieve set over a mixing bowl and press the purée through the sieve to remove the seeds. Stir the framboise into the purée. Set aside until needed.

6 Pour the milk into a pan and heat to just under boiling point. While the milk is heating, whisk the egg yolks with the sugar in a heatproof bowl until pale and creamy. Pour the hot milk on to the yolk mixture in a slow steady stream, whisking constantly. Drain the gelatine and squeeze out all the excess water, then add to the bowl and whisk until melted. Pour the mixture back into the pan and cook gently, stirring constantly, until thickened enough to coat the back of the spoon and you can draw a line through with your finger (don't let the custard come to the boil or it will split). Pour the custard into a clean heatproof bowl and allow to cool slightly before folding in the raspberry purée. Leave to cool for at least 1 hour or until the custard has thickened to the consistency of thick, whipped cream.

7 Cut the swiss rolls across into 1.5cm slices and use to line the base and sides of the clingfilm-lined bowl; pack the slices close together so that very little of the filling will be able to seep through. Reserve enough slices to cover the top (which will become the base of the charlotte).

8 Whip the 300ml cream for the bavarois until it will form soft peaks. Gently fold into the raspberry bavarois mixture. Fold in the remaining 100g raspberries and the small strawberries, then spoon into the lined bowl. Cover with the reserved slices of swiss roll. Cover with clingfilm and chill overnight until set and firm.

Stir the custard until it is the right consistency

9 To finish, turn out the charlotte on to a serving plate and peel off all the clingfilm. Put the caster sugar into a small pan, add the cold water and bring to the boil, stirring to make a light syrup. Mix the arrowroot with 2 tablespoons cold water until smooth, then stir into the sugar syrup (it will thicken). Bring back to the boil, stirring, then immediately remove from the heat. Leave to cool slightly before spooning the sugar syrup over the charlotte to give an even, shiny glaze. Leave to set for about 5 minutes, then clean up the serving plate to remove any glaze.

10 Whip the cream with the icing sugar to soft peak stage. Spoon it into a piping bag fitted with a star tube and pipe a continuous design of scallops around the base of the charlotte. Decorate with strawberries cut in fans.

MARY'S FLOATING ISLANDS

A classic homely French dessert that is also served in the best restaurants; rich, creamy vanilla egg custard topped with the lightest of poached meringues embellished with crowns of spun sugar. When poaching the meringues, make sure the liquid doesn't boil or the meringues will puff up and then collapse instead of setting.

SERVES 6

For the crème anglaise
300ml full-fat milk
300ml double cream
1 teaspoon vanilla bean paste
6 medium egg yolks, at room temperature
100g caster sugar

For the meringues
6 medium egg whites, at room temperature
150g caster sugar

For the spun sugar
100g caster sugar

1 Start by pouring the milk and cream for the crème anglaise into a large sauté pan or deep-sided frying pan that has a lid. Stir in the vanilla bean paste and bring to a simmer (a very gentle boil with tiny bubbles).

2 While the milk is heating put the egg whites for the meringues into a large, spotlessly clean bowl and whisk with an electric mixer on high speed until the whites will form stiff peaks. Add the 150g caster sugar, a tablespoon at a time, whisking continuously to make a thick, glossy meringue.

3 Turn down the heat under the poaching milk so it is barely simmering. Dip 2 large serving spoons in cold water (the spoons need to be really wet to make a perfect quenelle), then scoop out about a sixth of the meringue mixture on one of the spoons. Use the other spoon to neatly form the meringue into an oval quenelle shape. Slip the meringue off the spoon into the hot milk, then quickly repeat to make a total of 6 large quenelles. Cover the pan and poach the meringues gently over very low heat for 9–10 minutes until puffed up and just firm to touch. Carefully remove the quenelles from the poaching liquid with a slotted spoon on to a wire rack and leave to drain.

Use another spoon to neatly form the quenelle

4 Now make the crème anglaise. Strain the poaching liquid through a sieve into a large heatproof jug. Put the egg yolks and 100g caster sugar in a large mixing bowl and whisk until pale and fluffy. Pour on the warm poaching milk in a thin steady stream, whisking constantly. Pour the mixture into a heavy-based saucepan and cook over very low heat, stirring constantly, for 3–4 minutes until the custard is very smooth and thick enough to coat the back of the spoon. Remove the pan from the heat and set aside for now.

5 To make the spun sugar you'll need an oiled rolling pin or knife steel. Melt the sugar in a small stainless steel pan over medium heat, then let it boil, without stirring, until it turns to a dark golden caramel. Remove from the heat and leave to cool slightly, then dip the back of a fork or a dessertspoon in the caramel and quickly flick the caramel back and forth over the rolling pin or knife steel to create a mass of very fine strands. Gather the strands into a rough ball shape and set on a sheet of baking paper. Repeat to make 6 balls of spun sugar.

6 To serve, decorate each quenelle with a ball of spun sugar. Spoon the cold crème anglaise into 6 bowls, or into one large, shallow bowl, then set the quenelles floating on top of the custard 'sea'. Serve immediately.

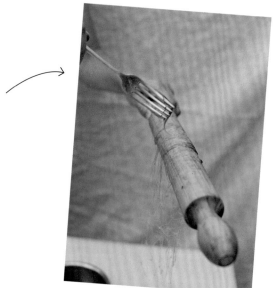

Quickly flick the caramel back and forth to make fine strands

NINETY-NINERS WITH A TWIST

Pretty, delicate brandy snap cones filled with a lemony mousse and finished with a raspberry, nut sprinkles and a tiny chocolate bar – a childhood treat re-invented!

MAKES 20
YOU WILL NEED: 1–2 BAKING SHEETS, LINED WITH BAKING PAPER

For the brandy snap cones
50g unsalted butter
50g golden syrup
50g light brown muscovado sugar
50g plain flour
1 teaspoon ground ginger
finely grated zest of 1 medium
   unwaxed lemon
1 tablespoon lemon juice
1 teaspoon brandy (optional)

For the filling
125g mascarpone

1½ tablespoons caster sugar
finely grated zest of 1 medium
   unwaxed lemon
1½ tablespoons lemon juice
2 tablespoons double cream

To finish
30g dark chocolate, finely chopped
150ml double cream
20 fresh raspberries, halved
50g pistachios, finely chopped

1 Heat your oven to 160°C/325°F/gas 3. To make the brandy snap mixture, put the butter, syrup and sugar in a medium pan and stir over medium/low heat until melted and smooth. Remove from the heat and sift the flour and ground ginger into the pan. Add the lemon zest and juice and the brandy if using, and mix thoroughly with a wooden spoon – make sure there are no lumps. Leave to cool until firm enough to scoop.

2 Use a heaped teaspoonful of mixture for each brandy snap (to make about 10), and bake in small batches: drop 2 or 3 spoonfuls on to the lined baking sheet, spacing them well apart to allow for spreading. Place in the heated oven and bake for 8–9 minutes until a deep golden brown. While the brandy snaps are baking, set out non-stick cream horn moulds or cone-shaped wooden moulds on your worktop plus a pizza wheel-cutter.

3 Remove the sheet from the oven and set it on a heatproof surface. Working quickly, cut one snap in half with the pizza wheel, then wrap a half, curved edge uppermost, around a mould and gently pinch the seams together. Repeat to shape the other half of the brandy snap, and then the remaining snaps. Once the brandy snap cones have set, you can slide them off the moulds on to a wire rack, then re-use the moulds. If the snaps cool and firm up before you can shape them, return them to the oven for 20–30 seconds to soften.

4 Continue baking and shaping the cones in small batches as before (you can re-use the baking sheet and lining paper). Leave to cool completely and set firm on the wire rack.

5 Next make up the filling. Put the mascarpone in a bowl and mix in the sugar and lemon zest and juice. When thoroughly combined stir in the double cream. Cover and keep in the fridge until ready to assemble.

6 Put the chocolate for the sticks into a heatproof bowl, set over a pan of hot water and melt gently. Remove the bowl from the pan and stir the chocolate gently until smooth. Leave to cool for a couple of minutes, then spoon the melted chocolate into a disposable piping bag. Snip off the tip to make a narrow opening – about 3mm – then pipe sticks 3cm long on a sheet of baking paper. Leave to set.

7 Once the cones are assembled they should be eaten as soon as possible, so make sure everything is at hand, including a serving platter or stand, before you begin. Whip the cream until stiff and spoon it into a piping bag fitted with a star tube. Drop a half raspberry into the bottom of each cone (tweezers help!), then fill the cone with the lemon mousse using a teaspoon. Decorate with the other raspberry half and a sprinkling of chopped nuts. Add a tiny swirl of cream and gently press in a chocolate stick. Finish with another sprinkle of nuts and serve.

CHOCOLATE AND CHERRY AMARETTO PARCELS

Cubes of ultra-rich chocolate cake with a dark cherry centre and covered in a dark chocolate ganache – a pretty treat!

MAKES 16

YOU WILL NEED: 1 X 20.5CM DEEP SQUARE CAKE TIN, GREASED WITH BUTTER AND BASE-LINED

For the cake mixture

- 1 x 425g tin pitted black cherries in light syrup
- 1 tablespoon Amaretto liqueur
- 150g dark chocolate (about 70% cocoa solids), finely chopped
- 150g unsalted butter, softened
- 120g caster sugar
- 5 large free-range eggs, at room temperature, separated
- 60g ground almonds
- 90g plain flour

To finish

- 60g unsalted butter, softened
- 120g icing sugar, sifted
- pink food colouring
- 1–2 tablespoons Amaretto liqueur
- 1 x quantity Ganache (see page 299), made with dark chocolate
- gold leaf (optional)

1 Heat your oven to 180°C/350°F/gas 4. Drain the cherries, saving the syrup. Put 16 cherries into a small bowl with the liqueur and 1 tablespoon of the syrup (you won't need the rest of the cherries and syrup for this recipe). Stir, then leave to soak until needed.

2 Put the chopped chocolate into a heatproof bowl. Set over a pan of hot water and melt gently. Remove the bowl from the pan and stir the chocolate until smooth, then leave to cool until needed.

3 Put the soft butter and sugar into a mixing bowl and beat with an electric mixer or wooden spoon until light and creamy. Add the egg yolks one at a time, beating well after each addition and scraping down the sides of the bowl from time to time. Beat

in the cooled chocolate. Sift the almonds and flour into the bowl and fold in with a large metal spoon or plastic spatula. Put the egg whites into a very clean, large bowl and whisk just until stiff peaks form. Fold into the cake mixture in 2 batches.

4 Spoon the mixture into the prepared tin and spread evenly. Place in the heated oven and bake for about 30 minutes until a skewer inserted into the centre of the cake comes out clean. Remove from the oven and set the tin on a wire rack. Run a round-bladed knife around the sponge to loosen it from the tin. Firm up in the tin for 5 minutes, then carefully turn out the sponge on to the rack and leave until cold.

5 When ready to finish, make up the icing by beating the soft butter with the icing sugar until smooth and evenly blended. Spoon half of the icing into another bowl and tint with a little pink colouring – this icing will be used for piping the decoration, so if it seems a bit stiff add a few drops of the cherry soaking liquid. Set aside at room temperature. Add 1 tablespoon of liqueur and 1 tablespoon of the cherry soaking liquid to the icing in the first bowl – this will be used as part of the filling.

6 Cut the sponge into 16 squares, then trim each one so the sides are exactly 4cm. Turn the squares upside down and remove a plug of cake from the centre of each with an apple corer (or the tip of a small sharp knife). Make sure the hole is large enough to fit a cherry, and keep the sponge 'plugs'. Lightly brush the inside of each hole with the remaining liqueur, then carefully fit a cherry into the hole. Add a dab of the liqueur-flavoured icing and press a small slice of the cake 'plug' on top. Turn the square right way up (so the plug is underneath) and set back on the wire rack.

7 Carefully spoon the ganache over the sponge squares, helping it down the sides with a small palette knife. Leave to set in a cool spot.

8 When ready to decorate, spoon the pink icing into a small disposable piping bag and snip off the tip so the opening is about 2mm wide. Pipe the icing over each square to resemble ribbon on a parcel, then pipe a small bow on top of each. Add gold leaf, if using.

Remove a plug of cake from the centre of each square

Spoon the ganache over the sponge squares to cover them

GANACHE

This rich, smooth chocolate and cream mixture is used for making truffles as well as fillings and coverings for cakes and pastries. Top-quality chocolate is essential – dark chocolate with around 70% cocoa solids, or well-made white chocolate (not children's bars). Take care not to overheat or overbeat the mixture or it may 'seize up' and become hard and unusable. White chocolate ganache doesn't firm up as well as dark chocolate; if you need something that sets well replace a small quantity of the cream with butter.

MAKES 200G

100g dark or white chocolate (see above), finely chopped

100ml whipping cream (or, for a firmer set if using white chocolate, 80ml whipping cream plus 20g unsalted butter)

1 Put the chocolate into a heatproof bowl. Heat the cream (or cream and butter) in a small pan until hot but not boiling, then pour in a slow, steady stream over the chopped chocolate. Leave to stand for a couple of minutes, then stir gently until smooth and glossy.

2 Leave to cool and thicken slightly, then stir gently again – don't overbeat or the mixture will separate. The ganache is now ready to use to pour over a cake to cover.

3 For a ganache that can be spread as a filling or piped, leave it to thicken until firm enough to hold its shape. You can add powdered praline at this point (see recipe for praline on page 303). If the ganache gets too firm to spread it can be gently warmed in a bowl set over a pan of warm water; do not overheat or the mixture will seize up.

MARY'S HAZELNUT DACQUOISE

A truly impressive, gluten-free cake, this is fit for the most glamorous celebration: nutty meringue layers, sandwiched with a rich and creamy coffee crème pâtissière and decorated with swirls of ganache and hazelnut praline. You can make the dacquoise in advance – it will still be delicious served the next day.

SERVES 12

YOU WILL NEED: 3 BAKING SHEETS, LINED WITH BAKING PAPER; A ROASTING TIN; PIPING BAG AND 1.5CM PLAIN TUBE; A SUGAR THERMOMETER

For the dacquoise
250g blanched (skinned) whole hazelnuts
300g caster sugar
25g cornflour
6 large egg whites, at room temperature
pinch of salt

For the chocolate ganache
150g dark chocolate (about 36% cocoa solids)
110ml double cream

For the coffee filling
600ml full-fat milk
3 large egg yolks, at room temperature
125g caster sugar
2 tablespoons chicory and coffee essence
50g cornflour
300ml whipping cream, chilled

For the praline
50g caster sugar
36 blanched (skinned) whole hazelnuts
½ teaspoon lemon juice
100g toasted hazelnuts, chopped, to finish

1 Arrange your oven racks in the upper, middle and lower thirds of the oven (you can use the grill tray on the bottom of the oven if you don't have a third rack). Heat the oven to 180°C/350°F/gas 4. Using a 21cm dinner plate or cake tin as a guide, draw a circle on the paper lining each of the baking sheets. Set aside for now.

2 To make the dacquoise, put the hazelnuts into the bowl of a food processor and 'pulse' just until coarsely ground. Spread the nuts in an even layer in a roasting tin and toast in the oven for 10–12 minutes until golden, stirring every 3 minutes. Remove the tin from the oven. Tip the nuts into a large heatproof bowl and leave to cool. Reduce the oven temperature to 150°C/300°F/gas 2.

3 When the nuts are cold, stir in 100g of the caster sugar and the cornflour. Pour the egg whites into the bowl of an electric mixer fitted with the whisk attachment. Add the salt. Whisk at medium speed for about 2 minutes until the whites are frothy. Increase the speed and continue to whisk while adding the remaining 200g sugar, a tablespoon at a time, to make a stiff glossy meringue that stands in peaks when the whisk is lifted out. Gently fold the toasted hazelnut mixture through the meringue using a large metal spoon or plastic spatula.

4 Transfer the meringue to a piping bag fitted with a 1.5cm plain tube. Starting in the centre of each drawn circle, pipe a spiral of meringue on to each prepared baking sheet. Place in the heated oven and bake for 1 hour, swapping the top and bottom baking sheets halfway through so the meringue discs cook evenly. Turn off the oven and open the oven door so it is just ajar, then leave the discs inside until completely cold.

5 Meanwhile, make the chocolate ganache. Break up the chocolate into even-sized pieces and put into a heatproof bowl. Pour the cream into a pan and heat until simmering. Pour the hot cream over the chocolate and stir gently until smooth. Leave to cool, then cover the bowl and chill until really thick and with a piping consistency (like whipped cream). Once the ganache is thick, spoon it into the clean and dry piping bag fitted with a star tube. Set aside at room temperature until needed.

6 For the coffee filling, pour the milk into a heavy-based pan and slowly bring to the boil over low heat. Meanwhile, put the yolks, sugar and coffee and chicory essence into a medium-sized heatproof bowl and whisk to combine. Whisk in the cornflour a tablespoon at a time to make a smooth, thick paste. Pour on the hot milk in a thin steady stream, whisking constantly. Pour the mixture into the pan and whisk until it comes to the boil, then lower the heat so the mixture just simmers. Whisk for 2–3 minutes until thickened and very smooth. Remove the pan from the heat and leave to cool for at least an hour.

7 Whip the cream until it will stand in soft peaks. Whisk half of the whipped cream into the cold coffee mixture, then gently fold in the rest. Cover and chill until needed.

Pipe a spiralled disc of meringue

8 To make the praline, put the caster sugar into a small frying pan and melt it, without stirring. Continue cooking until it turns to a golden caramel or it reaches 300°C on a sugar thermometer. Add the whole hazelnuts and lemon juice and stir well with a wooden spoon, then tip on to a baking sheet lined with baking paper or silicone paper. Working quickly before the caramel sets, use 2 teaspoons (don't touch the caramel as it will be very hot!) to form 12 equal clusters of hazelnut praline for the decoration. Leave to cool and set.

9 To assemble the dacquoise, set one of the meringue layers on a large flat serving plate and spread with a third of the coffee cream. Place another meringue layer on this and spread with half the remaining coffee cream. Top with the last meringue layer. Spread the remaining coffee cream over the sides of the cake, leaving the top bare. Press the chopped toasted nuts on to the sides of the dacquoise. Pipe 12 swirls of chocolate ganache on the top of the cake and decorate with the praline clusters.

BRILLIANT BAKERS

Series 4

Christine

'I am a classic everyday baker. I love well-tried recipes that use old-fashioned methods, especially the ones that my grandmothers used to make, and then putting a modern twist on them. These are my family's favourites and always go down well.'

Toby

'My style of baking is to master a particular technique or recipe and then make my own version, generally laying waste to the kitchen in the process. I love to use my knowledge to adapt or combine ideas in an experimental and excited burst of precision chaos!'

Frances

'I'm a quirky, creative baker who loves to bake not just cakes but also memories and experiences. I like to surprise and inspire people when I bake. If my baking can make someone curious enough to experiment with food, then even better.'

Ali

'Baking is not a chore, it's not a mother's work; it's a skill and a talent. If you enjoy baking, then bake away! I come from a community that sometimes tells me a man shouldn't bake cakes, but I tell you that if you have a talent, then listen to no one! It's a gift, not something to hide.'

Howard

'Baking is a fantastic creative outlet for me - using unusual ingredients, trying out new techniques, thinking up flavour combinations and how I can present my bakes in a way that will make people smile. After a hard day at work it's my bake escape!'

Glenn

'For me, baking is about giving yourself and others permissible indulgence. I love the tactile, satisfying processes involved in making such a lovely end result. I bake in generous portions and like nothing better than people enjoying what I have made.'

Beca

'Baking formed part of my upbringing and is an integral part of who I am. I approach baking like I would any extreme sport... nothing is too much of a challenge! Baking is messy and doesn't always go to plan. If it goes wrong, then who cares?! I can guarantee it will be better next time!!'

Ruby

'I am a messy baker - I love baking too much to be cold and clinical about it. What great love affair doesn't go through turmoil and tears and thrown kitchen utensils before the happily ever after?'

Deborah

'I am a working mum who has a passion for baking, both to feed my family and for fun. I hope to have the opportunity to share with others the idea that good food is simple to make with your family, for your family.'

Mark

'Baking is the perfect way to relax and unwind, it's so stressful that it makes everything else seem so much better! I love to bake because it's an escape, it's good to block everything out for a few hours and just focus on something that's going to taste awesome and make people smile.'

Kimberly

'I love the generosity of baking. Baking is for sharing, it's a show of love and the most delicious and satisfying way of bringing people together. When it comes to baking, I am experimental, flavour-focused and up for a challenge!'

Robert

'The expression of joy on someone's face as they are presented with a simple handmade loaf is priceless – and that's why I love baking. How would I describe myself as a baker? Hungry? Fascinated? Obsessive? Bordering on insane? Yep, all of those.'

Lucy

'Growing and baking are at the heart of life. Even a tiny garden can produce the most special ingredients to be baked into the best possible things to eat. Baking unites luxury with nature.'

INDEX

BAKER'S NOTES

FAN ASSISTED OVENS For fan assisted ovens, set the temperature 20C lower than stated in the recipes.

MEASUREMENTS All teaspoons and tablespoons are level unless otherwise stated.

RAW INGREDIENTS Some recipes contain raw or partially cooked eggs. Pregnant women, the elderly, babies and toddlers, and people who are unwell should avoid these recipes.

ACCURACY is essential when baking. Weigh all ingredients, use accurate scales and a kitchen timer and the correct equipment.

OVEN THERMOMETER Oven temperatures can vary (even from the front to the back of the oven, as well as between the top and bottom shelves) so practice makes perfect. An oven thermometer is useful.

ACKNOWLEDGEMENTS

BBC BOOKS AND LOVE PRODUCTIONS WOULD LIKE TO THANK THE FOLLOWING PEOPLE FOR THEIR INVALUABLE CONTRIBUTION TO THIS BOOK …

Linda Collister, Norma Macmillan, Susanna Cook, Maeve Bargman and Allies Design, Kristin Perers (and Ben, Emma and Martin), Jane Hornby (and Amanda and Katy), Cynthia Inions, Stephanie Evans and Lisa Footit, Sam Beddoes, Adriana Caligiuri, Tom Bowman and Tallulah Radula-Scott.

Thank you to Mary Berry and Paul Hollywood for contributing their recipes and also to the amateur bakers: Ali, Beca, Christine, Deborah, Frances, Glenn, Howard, Kimberly, Lucy, Mark, Robert, Ruby and Toby.

THIS BOOK IS PUBLISHED TO ACCOMPANY THE
TELEVISION SERIES ENTITLED *THE GREAT BRITISH
BAKE OFF*, FIRST BROADCAST ON BBC TWO IN 2013.

Executive producer: Anna Beattie
Series editor: Amanda Westwood
Series producer: Samantha Beddoes
Series director: Scott Tankard
Producers: Tallulah Radula-Scott, Adriana Caligiuri
Unit manager: Nina Richards
BBC commissioning executive: Emma Willis
Head of production: Letty Kavanagh
Series home economists: Rebecca Watson, Georgia May
and Faenia Moore

10 9 8 7 6 5 4 3 2 1

Published in 2013 by BBC Books, an imprint of Ebury
Publishing. A Random House Group Company.

Text © Love Productions
Photography and design © Woodlands Books Ltd

The Random House Group Limited Reg. No. 954009

Addresses for companies within the Random House
Group can be found at www.randomhouse.co.uk

A CIP catalogue record for this book is available from the
British Library.

ISBN: 978 1 849 90608 1

The Random House Group Limited supports The Forest
Stewardship Council (FSC®), the leading international
forest certification organisation. Our books carrying the
FSC label are printed on FSC® certified paper. FSC is the
only forest certification scheme endorsed by the leading
environmental organisations, including Greenpeace. Our
paper procurement policy can be found at
www.randomhouse.co.uk/environment

Commissioning editor: Muna Reyal
Project editor: Laura Higginson
Copyeditor: Norma Macmillan
Design: Allies Design
Photography: Kristin Perers
Food styling: Jane Hornby
Prop styling: Cynthia Inions
Production: Helen Everson and Beccy Jones

Colour origination by Altaimage, London.
Printed and bound in the UK by Butler Tanner and Dennis Ltd

To buy books by your favourite authors and register for
offers visit www.randomhouse.co.uk